THE BOOK
OF BROADWAY

THE BOOK OF BROADW

THE 150 DEFINITIVE PLAYS AND MUSICALS

ERIC GRODE

Voyageur
Press

Quarto is the authority on a wide range of topics.

Quarto educates, entertains and enriches the lives of our readers—enthusiasts and lovers of hands-on living.

www.quartoknows.com

First published in 2015 by Voyageur Press, an imprint of Quarto Publishing Group USA Inc., 400 First Avenue North, Suite 400, Minneapolis, MN 55401 USA. This edition published 2016. Telephone: (612) 344-8100 Fax: (612) 344-8692

QuartoKnows.com
Visit our blogs at QuartoKnows.com

Voyageur Press titles are also available at discounts in bulk quantity for industrial or sales-promotional use. For details contact the Special Sales Manager at Quarto Publishing Group USA Inc., 400 First Avenue North, Suite 400, Minneapolis, MN 55401 USA.

ISBN: 978-0-7603-4562-7

The Library of Congress has cataloged the hardcover edition of this book as follows:

Grode, Eric.
  The book of Broadway : the 150 definitive plays and musicals / Eric Grode.
     pages cm
  Includes bibliographical references and index.
  ISBN 978-0-7603-4562-7 (hc)
  1. Theater--New York (State)--New York--History--20th century. 2. American drama--20th century--History and criticism. 3. Musicals--New York (State)--New York--History and criticism. I. Title.
  PN2277.N5G75 2015
  792.09747'10904--dc23
                                          2015001991

Editor: Grace Labatt
Project Manager: Caitlin Fultz
Art Director: James Kegley
Layout: Diana Boger

Cover image: *Broadway at Night* by Larry Nicosia

Title page: Sandra Church as Louise in *Gypsy*, which debuted in 1959.

Dedication: The marquee for the original production of *South Pacific*, which ran on Broadway from 1949 to 1954.

Printed in China

10 9 8 7 6 5 4 3

TO B, J, AND E,
WITH ALL MY LOVE.

CONTENTS

INTRODUCTION

The use of the word *definitive* in selecting the 150 plays and musicals in this book allows for a certain amount of solipsism. Why are these particular works definitive? Because I defined them as definitive.

Choosing these shows in earnest couldn't really begin until the parameters had been set. A list of the 150 greatest Broadway shows would look very different from a list of the 150 biggest Broadway shows. A quick cut-and-paste from Wikipedia would determine the 150 most popular shows, although that list would be egregiously skewed toward contemporary theater (and egregious on several other levels). But the smash hits both past and present have played an enormous role in defining Broadway for the creators who operated in their shadow, as well as for paying customers. Long runs certainly played a role in my logic, but so did inherent quality, which is as subjective a notion as any show's number of performances is objective.

The changing economy of Broadway also played a role. Bear in mind that live theater had essentially no competition from radio or film for the first fifty years covered here, which affected the intersection of commerce and art in any number of ways. The idea of a nonprofit theater would have been ludicrous in 1905. (These days, plenty of jaded theater professionals would be no less dumbfounded at the idea of a *for*-profit theater.) The concept of art for art's sake didn't surface on the Broadway stage until about the 1960s, and I tried to consider this switch as I assessed works from before then.

The biggest hurdle was off-Broadway. A trend has surfaced in recent years of what I think of as semi-canonical plays reaching Broadway after having debuted years earlier off-Broadway, and I grappled with what to do with these late entries. It took twenty-six and sixteen years, respectively, before *Top Girls* and *Hedwig and the Angry Inch* made it uptown, and Sam Shepard's Broadway credentials consist mostly of decades-old transfers. Caryl Churchill's *Top Girls* might be my favorite play from the twentieth century, but if it qualifies, then why not Shakespeare's *Timon of Athens*, which didn't grace a Broadway stage until 1993? So I decided, with a heavy heart, to confine the candidates to those that made the transfer more or less directly from their off-Broadway incarnations.

This criterion also pertained to plays traveling from around the world—in order to be considered, a show's Broadway debut had to have come in fairly close proximity to its premiere. That is why the likes of Shakespeare and Chekhov (whose first Broadway production didn't occur until more than a decade after his death) are absent. If any of the great pre–Broadway era works were fair game, Shakespeare alone would gobble up more than 20 percent of the book! Shaw, Ibsen, and Wilde happened to be in the right place at the right time, at least for the purposes of this book. (Given Wilde's unconscionable legal troubles, being born a century later might have been a blessing. Also, can you imagine what his Twitter feed would be like?)

As I debated these shows ad nauseum with a group of peers, the question of "children" frequently came up. How different did Broadway pre–*Show X* look from Broadway post–*Show X*? This worked to the advantage of nearly all of the smash hits, as I mentioned above, but also to that of many of the playwrights featured in these pages. Though several of their works ran for just a few weeks, their words and ideas reverberate a century later in the plays of many others.

And then there are the ones that made the list for the reason that every child vows they will never give as a parent, and that every parent eventually gives: because I said so.

The result was a fairly grueling winnowing process. I originally scribbled down some 350 contenders, then hacked my way—with a minimum of teeth-gnashing—to just under 200. That's when it got tough. Two or three titles were demoted near the end in the course of writing the book, as I'd pore over the texts and realize that they just didn't hold up the way I had remembered them. (And no, I'm not saying which entries crept in as a result, let alone which ones slipped out.)

All of this is to say that your list of 150 might look very different from mine. Let the arguments begin.

ABIE'S IRISH ROSE

BY ANNE NICHOLS

DATES:
May 23, 1922–October 1, 1927 at the Fulton Theater and Theater Republic (2,327 performances)

SYNOPSIS:
Abraham Levy brings his new bride, Rosemary Murphy, home to meet his parents. Neither the Levys nor, later on, the Murphys are pleased.

AWARDS:
None

NOTED REVIVALS AND ADAPTATIONS:
Broadway revivals in 1937 and 1954; movie versions in 1928 and 1946; radio series in 1942

ORIGINAL STARS:
Robert B. Williams, Marie Carroll, Mathilde Cottrelly

Abie's Irish Rose is perhaps the ultimate labor of love, a reminder of an era when one person could more or less singlehandedly bring a show to Broadway. Anne Nichols sunk $5,000 of her own money into producing it, and much of her subsequent career was devoted to Abie's maintenance: directing a pair of Broadway revivals, roaming the country to make sure the road companies stuck to the script, even suing the producer of a movie called The Cohens and Kellys for copyright infringement. (More on that shortly.) It's hard to imagine a show titled Marriage in Triplicate, her original name for the show, requiring quite so much of her time—or earning her a reported $6 million for her trouble.

Along the way, Nichols assembled around her the kind of characters that could make 1920s Broadway seem like a living Damon Runyon short story. (*See also entry on* Guys and Dolls.) *Abie's* weathered its lean early months after Nichols secured a $30,000 loan from the famous gangster Arnold Rothstein. (When Rothstein had married a Catholic in 1909, his father covered the mirrors in his home and said Kaddish.) Mathilde Cottrelly, an onstage force in the 1880s who never came close to shedding her thick German accent, capped off her career by playing the hypochondriac Mrs. Cohen. Leblang's Ticket Office, a precursor to TKTS that operated out of the basement of a Broadway drugstore, sold tons of cut-rate tickets for the show.

Arrayed against Nichols was a formidable army of theater critics, including Heywood Broun, George Jean Nathan, and, especially, Robert Benchley, whose forked tongue had earned him the respect of even the hard-to-please Algonquin Round Table circuit. Benchley turned attacks on *Abie's* into a weekly feature in his *Life* magazine capsule reviews. ("Will the Marines never come?" is a personal favorite, followed close behind by "The comic spirit of 1876," a line that must have pleased Mathilde Cottrelly.) Lorenz Hart and Harpo Marx were among others who took shots at the show.

Perhaps the most important opinion about *Abie's Irish Rose*, however, was written not by a journalist but by a court stenographer. Nichols' lawsuit against the producer of *The Cohens and Kellys* made its way to the United States Court of Appeals for the Second Circuit, where the esteemed judge Billings Learned Hand basically pointed out that when it came to appropriation, the barn door had been open for quite some time. "The defendant has not taken from

her more than their prototypes have contained for many decades," Hand wrote in his opinion; in other words, we have seen the likes of Abie and Rose before and cannot be surprised to see them again. Stock characters have been part of theater tradition since ancient Greece, and *Abie's Irish Rose* serves as a reminder of why these tropes pop up again and again. People really like to see them.

OPPOSITE PAGE: Anne Nichols, born in Dales Mill, Georgia, in 1891, began her career as an actress, appearing in two silent films by the time she was twenty.

RIGHT: From left, Mathilde Cottrelly, Alfred White, and Bernard Gorcey in the original production of *Abie's Irish Rose*.

THE ADDING MACHINE

BY ELMER RICE

Dudley Digges (Mr. Zero) and Margaret Wycherly (Daisy Diana Dorothea Devore) in *The Adding Machine*, 1923. Both later appeared in separate revivals of the play *Liliom*, which also shifts between Earth and heaven (*see entry on* Carousel).

Expressionism has aged less gracefully in theater than it has in a lot of other art forms. You're a lot more likely to see a reference to painters and poets—Munch, say, or Rilke—than to dramatists like Georg Kaiser or Lajos Egri. Eugene O'Neill dabbled in this famously amorphous style, with its visual dislocations and unreal emotional timbre, but works like *The Hairy Ape* and *The Emperor Jones* are far more obscure than his later plays. So it was a bit of a shock when a musical adaptation of *The Adding Machine*, perhaps America's quintessential Expressionist theater piece, became a cult off-Broadway hit in 2008. But it shouldn't have been: Elmer Rice's Molotov cocktail of a play packs no less of a punch now than it did almost a century ago.

Rice, a curious fellow who straddled the worlds of capitalism (he owned New York's Belasco Theater for a time) and socialism (he was the first New York director of the WPA's Federal Theater Project), tended to swing for the fences in his work. His first play, *On Trial*, introduced the idea of flashbacks to

DATES:

March 19–May 19, 1923 at the Garrick Theater and the Comedy Theater (72 performances)

SYNOPSIS:

When Mr. Zero finds out that his job of twenty-five years is about to be rendered obsolete by an adding machine, he murders his boss. After his trial and execution, he finds himself in heaven, only to learn that he still has several more go-arounds on Earth to endure.

AWARDS:

None

NOTED REVIVALS AND ADAPTATIONS:

None

ORIGINAL STARS:

Dudley Digges, Helen Westley, Margaret Wycherly

the stage, while 1925's *Sidewalks of New York* had no words, consisting entirely of what he called "a series of situations in which there was no need for speech." True to course, *The Adding Machine*—which he wrote in just seventeen days—made little attempt to ingratiate itself to Broadway audiences more accustomed to anodyne fare like *Barnum Was Right* and *The Love Habit*, both of which opened the same week as Rice's play.

With its fantastically, almost mockingly bleak view of humanity (encapsulated in the aptly named Mr. Zero), the play juggles virtuosic monologues with staccato interjections and stagy repetitions. Rice was fortunate to have fallen in with the pioneering Theater Guild, which had its hand in such daring works as *Strange Interlude* and *Porgy and Bess*. (Not even it could get on board with *Sidewalks of New York* two years later, however.) The Guild had among its creative team the gifted designer Lee Simonson, who delivered a visual analogue to Rice's surreal tale. Numbers hurtled across the stage, the courtroom for Mr. Zero's murder trial was distorted and elongated, and the enormous adding machine awaiting him in heaven had keys as big as barstools.

Audiences at the time were used to eye-popping visuals. After all, in the latest iteration of *The Ziegfeld Follies*, Gilda Gray had introduced the scandalous dance

Wycherly in *The Adding Machine*.

known as the shimmy. She also sang a cautionary song called "It's Getting Dark on Old Broadway," a reference to the preponderance of black entertainment at the time that could just as easily have referred to Elmer Rice's visionary experiment a few blocks south. And thank heaven for that.

AMADEUS

BY PETER SHAFFER

Veneration can come through odd channels. Sometimes all it takes is a hit play condemning you as a jealous, conniving murderer.

In 1979, Antonio Salieri was all but forgotten despite having written thirty-seven operas and taught the likes of Schubert, Beethoven, and Liszt. His work has since been recorded by the world's top sopranos and featured in films such as *Iron Man*, and he now has an annual opera festival named after him.

This rehabilitation has everything to do with Peter Shaffer's factually questionable but theatrically impeccable *Amadeus*, which accuses Salieri of poisoning Mozart in 1791. (These accusations have been all but debunked, but they were certainly around in Salieri's lifetime. Thirty years after Mozart's death, the older composer was still brooding over them.) Alexander Pushkin made the same accusation in the 1830s when he dabbled in playwriting, but it was Shaffer's version that rallied scholars to speak up on Salieri's behalf.

Shaffer was inspired to write the play by the disconnect between Mozart's transcendent music and the juvenile, vulgar letters he wrote. But as notable as this was, Shaffer got far

ABOVE: The original Broadway cast of *Amadeus*.

OPPOSITE PAGE: Ian McKellen (Antonio Salieri), Jane Seymour
(Constanze, Mozart's wife), and Tim Curry (Mozart) in the original
Broadway production, directed by Sir Peter Hall. The play
premiered in London in 1979, with Paul Scofield as Salieri and
Simon Callow as Mozart.

greater mileage out of the contrast between disciplined
craftsmanship (exemplified by Salieri) and inexplicable,
arguably undeserved genius (Mozart). "Spiteful, sniggering,
conceited, infantine Mozart," the heretofore pious Salieri
thunders at God. "*Him* You have chosen to be Your sole
conduct! And my only reward—my sublime privilege—is
to be the sole man alive in this time who shall clearly
recognize Your Incarnation!"

Shaffer had plenty of help conveying this rage. The most
obvious contributor was Ian McKellen, then virtually
unknown in the United States, who would win a Tony Award
for his performance as Salieri. Even less recognized was
the esteemed composer Harrison Birtwistle, at the time the
musical director at the Royal National Theater in London.
Shaffer has credited Birtwistle with manipulating Mozart's
music to make it suggest "the sublime work of a genius
being experienced by another musician's increasingly
agonized mind."

When the Milos Forman–directed film version came out
in 1984, the tagline trumpeted, "Everything you heard is
true." Actually, just about everything Shaffer said about
Salieri in *Amadeus* was false. (His subsequent revisions
to the play, while still implicating Salieri in Mozart's
death, at least have the old guy feel a lot worse about it.)
But as his anguished protagonist would be the first to
admit, just because something disobeys the rules doesn't
mean it isn't great.

ANGEL STREET

BY PATRICK HAMILTON

Vincent Price and Judith Evelyn as Mr. and Mrs. Manningham in *Angel Street*, 1941. José Ferrer and Uta Hagen played the Manninghams in the 1948 revival at City Center.

More than any other element, a good melodrama needs a great bad guy. The Victorians grasped this, churning out scores of lurid titles like *Spring-Heeled Jack, the Terror of London*, and *The Murder in the Red Barn* for the London stage. It was the 1839 melodrama *Jack Sheppard* that first prompted audiences to hiss at a villain.

Nearly a century later, a six-foot-four Midwesterner named Vincent Price gave Broadway one of its most hissable specimens when he played Jack Manningham in *Angel Street*. Better known as *Gaslight*, the name of the original 1938 London

DATES:

December 5, 1941–December 30, 1944 at the
John Golden Theater and the Bijou Theater
(1,295 performances)

SYNOPSIS:

The misplaced grocery bill, the unaccountably
missing picture on the wall: fragile, sleep-deprived
Bella Manningham fears she is losing her mind.
Her husband is doing what he can to keep her
calm—but what is he doing during his mysterious
nighttime outings?

AWARDS:

None

NOTED REVIVALS
AND ADAPTATIONS:

Broadway revivals in 1948 and 1975; movie versions
in 1940 and 1944

ORIGINAL STARS:

Vincent Price, Judith Evelyn, Leo G. Carroll

Evelyn and Leo G. Carroll, who played the police detective Rough.
Carroll, like his costars, was an exceptional fit for a psychological
drama: in addition to his stage work, he appeared in six Alfred
Hitchcock films.

production and the subsequent hit film, *Angel Street* offers
an unusually intimate concept of villainy. The audience
only gradually realizes that Mr. Manningham, whom
we see ministering to his mentally fragile wife, is in fact
methodically nudging her into insanity. (Patrick Hamilton,
who also wrote the unnerving thriller *Rope*, understood
the appeal of keeping villain and victim in unusually close
proximity, especially within the tight confines of the stage.)

During his brief tenure as an assistant stage manager
and actor early in his career, Hamilton absorbed the
conventions of melodrama and, according to his biographer
Sean French, "realized how successful such plays might
be if written and presented in a sophisticated way." By
setting his play in the Victorian era—in "a gloomy and
unfashionable quarter of London" in 1880—he could set
contemporary ideas of female hysteria within the Gothic
trappings of melodrama's heyday.

And in the silken-voiced Price, who was just thirty
at the time, Hamilton found a performer who could
instantly conjure the mustache-twirling baddies of the
past while grasping the play's modern psychological
underpinnings. (Things reportedly went downhill over
the course of Price's lengthy stay in the show. He began
playing Abraham Lincoln in an experimental production

during his days off in 1942, and at least one backer saw
bits of Honest Abe creeping into Jack Manningham.)

The *Angel Street* producers played it safe at first, printing
only three days' worth of tickets. Despite the fact that the
third day was December 7, 1941—the day which will live in
infamy, with the bombing of Pearl Harbor—they were still
printing tickets three *years* later.

ANGELS IN AMERICA

A GAY FANTASIA ON NATIONAL THEMES

BY TONY KUSHNER

Turning tragedy into art takes time: after almost fifteen years, the great 9/11 play has yet to be written, while the most affecting wartime narratives never seem to be about the most recent war.

So even as AIDS ravaged the New York theater community as irreparably as it did any individual group in the 1980s, the central theater works from that time—

William M. Hoffman's *As Is*, Larry Kramer's *The Normal Heart*—focused on a ripped-from-the-headlines approach. Playwrights began to sidle up to the material later in the decade through more indirect methods, as when Craig Lucas wrestled with the physical decline of a loved one in *Prelude to a Kiss* or Paula Vogel eulogized her deceased brother by coining the new Acquired Toilet Disease (ATD) in *The Baltimore Waltz*.

Then came *Angels*.

As the subtitle made clear, Tony Kushner was neither ripping from any headlines nor being coy about anything. No, this was seven hours of poetic, graphic, fanciful, cerebral, mind-blowing theater over two evenings—a panoramic synthesis of Walt Whitman, Walter Benjamin, Charles Ludlam, and especially Bertolt Brecht. First in *Millennium Approaches* and then in its continuation, *Perestroika*, Kushner pinwheeled from the ghost of Ethel Rosenberg saying Kaddish over the detestable Roy Cohn to a pitiably gaunt, lesion-covered Prior Walter cracking wise over the arrival of an angel to Prior's tormented ex-lover spilling forth page upon page of defensive/self-scouring/obfuscating text after leaving him.

The results commandeered national attention in a way that a nonmusical play had not done in decades. Thirty-six-year-old Kushner instantly became an American George Bernard Shaw—Shaw's *Heartbreak House* was subtitled "A Fantasia in the Russian Manner on English Themes," something Kushner claims not to have known

DATES:
May 4, 1993–December 4, 1994 at the Walter Kerr Theater (584 combined performances of its two plays, *Millennium Approaches* and *Perestroika*)

SYNOPSIS:
Where to begin? Mormons, former drag queens, Valium-addicted wives, closeted McCarthyists, and a long-dead Ethel Rosenberg converge in 1980s New York City, all imperiled in different ways by the AIDS virus.

AWARDS:
7 Tony Awards combined; Pulitzer Prize

NOTED REVIVALS AND ADAPTATIONS:
TV miniseries in 2003

ORIGINAL STARS:
Stephen Spinella, Ron Leibman, Joe Mantello, Jeffrey Wright

when he named his play—and an entire generation of theater performers began their ascent under the wings of *Angels*. Jeffrey Wright, Kathleen Chalfant, and replacement performer Cherry Jones all became New York acting royalty, while costars David Marshall Grant and Ellen McLaughlin would begin playwriting careers of their own. Joe Mantello, meanwhile, would soon make a name for himself as one of Broadway's most dependable directors.

Belize, the flamboyant hospital orderly, describes heaven to a dying Roy Cohn as a place where "race, taste, and history finally overcome." In his sublime gay fantasia, Kushner came astonishingly close to creating just such a place on stage.

LEFT: Ron Leibman played Roy Cohn, a ruthless lawyer who, after contracting HIV, insists he is succumbing to liver cancer. The real-life Cohn was an aide to Senator Joseph McCarthy. © *Joan Marcus*

OPPOSITE PAGE: Stephen Spinella (Prior Walter) and Ellen McLaughlin (the Angel) in the original Broadway production. © *Joan Marcus*

ANNIE

BY CHARLES STROUSE, MARTIN CHARNIN, AND THOMAS MEEHAN

Except for the occasional *Sound of Music* or *Peter Pan*, Broadway was pretty close to a kid-free zone for a long time. For one thing, until the early 1970s the shows began at 8:30 p.m. (That's why the big solo near the end of a musical is still called the "eleven o'clock number," based on the time it usually took place. These days, most people are on the subway or stuck in the Lincoln Tunnel by 11:00.) And for decades, the prevailing image of Broadway was one of furs and cocktails: Cole Porter, not Walt Disney.

Cut to 2014, when fully half of the eight *Cinderella* performances a week are matinees and about a quarter of Broadway musicals cater to a young crowd. *Annie* can't take total credit for the shift, but

ABOVE: Reid Shelton and Andrea McArdle as Daddy Warbucks and Annie. Shelton played Warbucks for five years on Broadway and on tour. Sarah Jessica Parker was among the actresses who played Annie during the show's original run.

LEFT: Lily St. Regis (Barbara Erwin), Rooster (Robert Fitch), and Miss Hannigan (Dorothy Loudon) dream of "Easy Street," "where the rich folks play."

DATES:

April 21, 1977–January 2, 1983 at the Alvin Theater, ANTA Playhouse, Eugene O'Neill Theater, and Uris Theater (2,377 performances)

SYNOPSIS:

It's a hard-knock life for Little Orphan Annie, what with the Great Depression going on and the villainous Miss Hannigan running the orphanage. But chance encounters with the rich Oliver "Daddy" Warbucks, Franklin D. Roosevelt, and a dog named Sandy could mean a new deal for Annie.

AWARDS:

7 Tony Awards

NOTED REVIVALS AND ADAPTATIONS:

Broadway revivals in 1997 and 2012; two different attempts at a sequel, in 1989 and 1993; movie versions in 1982 and 2014; TV movie in 1999

ORIGINAL STARS:

Andrea McArdle, Reid Shelton, Dorothy Loudon, Sandy

The original orphans: Diana Barrows (Tessie), Robyn Finn (Pepper), Donna Graham (Duffy), Danielle Brisebois (Molly), Shelley Bruce (Kate), and Janine Ruane (July).

beachhead with *Beauty and the Beast* and *The Lion King*—and a general sprucing up of Times Square.

To be clear, the creators of *Annie* were less concerned with blazing a trail than they were with just getting the damn thing produced. Lyricist/director Martin Charnin spent years trying to get the beloved *Little Orphan Annie* comic strip to the stage. He ended up producing it at the Goodspeed Opera House in Connecticut, where a major storm on opening night resulted in Act II being performed with flashlights. Luckily, director Mike Nichols came to see the show later in the run; he called Charnin the next day offering to produce it on Broadway.

One of Nichols' ideas—to expand the role of Miss Hannigan as a vehicle for Dorothy Loudon—helped cut the cute quotient to a palatable degree for the grown-ups by the time *Annie* reached New York. (A good bit of cuteness remained courtesy of Sandy, a mutt who had been rescued from a Connecticut animal shelter just hours before being put to sleep.) Add to that the last full-fledged theater song to penetrate the consciousness, Annie's chin-up anthem "Tomorrow," and you get a smash hit bested in the 1970s only by the family-unfriendly *A Chorus Line*.

it did have plenty to do with introducing many young audience members (this one included) to the joys of Broadway. By the time it closed, *Cats* had arrived; by the time *that* show closed, Disney had established its

ANNIE GET YOUR GUN

BY IRVING BERLIN, DOROTHY FIELDS, AND HERBERT FIELDS

Ray Middleton (Frank Butler) and Ethel Merman (Annie Oakley) with the original cast of *Annie Get Your Gun*, including William O'Neal (Buffalo Bill) and George Lipton (Pawnee Bill), left and right "riding" horses.

The real-life Annie Oakley was apparently a demure, petite woman who preferred doing needlepoint when she wasn't showing off her marksmanship. So who better to play her in *Annie Get Your Gun* than Ethel Merman?

Mary Martin seemed like a far more natural fit for the role, and in fact, Martin played Annie both in a TV production and on tour, winning a special Tony Award for "Spreading Theatre to the Country While the Originals Perform in New York." But *Annie Get Your Gun* was one of those glorious flukes that went the unconventional route and hit paydirt each time.

The producers were a pair of songwriters, for one thing. But not just any pair of songwriters: Richard Rodgers and Oscar Hammerstein II, fresh off the success of *Oklahoma!*, had begun producing shows. *Annie Get Your Gun* was just their second, after the hit play *I Remember Mama*. They enlisted

DATES:

May 16, 1946–February 12, 1949 at the Imperial Theater (1,147 performances)

SYNOPSIS:

Anything the sharp-shooting Frank Butler can do, on or off the stage of Buffalo Bill Cody's Wild West show, a young spitfire named Annie Oakley can do better. But is it true that "You Can't Get a Man With a Gun"?

AWARDS:

None

NOTED REVIVALS AND ADAPTATIONS:

Broadway revivals in 1966 and 1999; movie version in 1950; TV movie in 1957

ORIGINAL STARS:

Ethel Merman, Ray Middleton

Hammerstein's *Show Boat* collaborator Jerome Kern to write the score, with Dorothy Fields as lyricist; Dorothy would also write the book with her brother, Herbert Fields. But Kern, who had moved to the East Coast to begin work, died of a stroke before having written a note of the score. Rodgers scrambled to bring Irving Berlin on board as both composer and lyricist. Merman followed shortly thereafter.

The fledgling producers, sibling librettists, fill-in composer, and miscast star, along with the more logical choice of Joshua Logan as director, combined to create a boisterous, heartfelt specimen of musical comedy. It didn't hurt that Berlin supplied, by a wide margin, his best top-to-bottom score, generating a half-dozen standards and providing Merman with a virtual theme song in "There's No Business Like Show Business." (He gave her yet another good one for the 1966 revival, "An Old-Fashioned Wedding," the last song he wrote for the stage.)

As with Merman's other signature roles—Reno in *Anything Goes*, Rose in *Gypsy*—Annie continues to reward the right performer handsomely. In what seemed like a bit of stunt casting, country singer Reba McEntire replaced Bernadette Peters in the 1999 revival—and got the kind of notices that most Juilliard-trained triple threats would kill for. "It was one of the best performances I've ever seen," said Broadway icon Barbara Cook, who has seen a few.

Along with Cole Porter's *Gypsy* and Adam Guettel's *The Princess Bride*, Jerome Kern's *Annie Get Your Gun* score remains one of the great what-might-have-beens. But what is instead is pretty great, too.

Reba McEntire with, from left, Peter Marx (Charlie Davenport), Brent Barrett (Frank), and Conrad John Schuck (Buffalo Bill). McEntire replaced Bernadette Peters in the 1999 revival at the Marquis Theater.

ANYTHING GOES

BY COLE PORTER, GUY BOLTON, P. G. WODEHOUSE, HOWARD LINDSAY, AND RUSSEL CROUSE

It's hard to know whom to congratulate when a musical does well. The director? The songwriter? The ingénue? The chandelier? On the other hand, the bookwriter is nearly always scapegoated when things go wrong. *Anything Goes* deserves mention for many reasons, not least of which is a Cole Porter score stuffed to the gills with classics: "You're the Top," "I Get a Kick Out of You," "Blow, Gabriel, Blow," and the still-scandalous title song. ("If love affairs you like / With young bears you like / Why nobody will oppose.") But let's not lose sight of the libretto, which was created in waves by four of the five men listed above.

Under usual circumstances, Guy Bolton and P. G. Wodehouse would have represented more than sufficient manpower to write a shipboard musical comedy, having collaborated on more than a dozen musicals by 1934. Here's where things get a little complicated. We know that producer Vinton Freedley wanted extensive revisions. We also know that on September 8, just before rehearsals began, 137 people died when a luxury liner named the *Morro Castle* caught fire and burned. The result, according to a nearly universally held anecdote, was that a panicked Freedley junked a shipwreck plot (along with the rest of the script) and—with Bolton laid up in a UK nursing home with a burst appendix, and Wodehouse in northern France—enlisted the show's director, Howard Lindsay, to write a new one with Lindsay's friend Russel Crouse.

The catch, according to the Bolton-Wodehouse historian Lee Davis, is that *Anything Goes* (or *Hard to Get*, as it was then called) never had a shipwreck plot in the first place. What was there, he says, was "confusion and convoluted plotting—a Chinese puzzle, complete with Chinamen."

In its place came a libretto scrounged together on a few weeks' notice, one that helped the show become one of the decade's most popular musicals. The writing team of Lindsay and Crouse would endure for another twenty-seven years, resulting in, among other titles, *Life With Father* and the libretto to *The Sound of Music*.

In *Anything Goes*, the two also found a way to accommodate the pretty much foolproof trick of shoehorning a roof-raising gospel number into Act II regardless of suitability, already a familiar gambit by 1934. (Subsequent versions have not been interwoven as deftly, including in one Pulitzer Prize–winning musical; *see entry on* How to Succeed . . . .) If an elaborate subplot involving a chanteuse and a gangster dressed up as an evangelist and a minister is what it takes to get Ethel Merman on a stage singing "Blow, Gabriel, Blow," so be it. The Lord and His librettists work in mysterious ways.

OPPOSITE PAGE: Ethel Merman and sailors in the original Broadway production.

BELOW: The 1987 revival starred, from left (following two showgirls), Bill McCutcheon, Linda Hart, Kathleen Mahony-Bennett, Howard McGillin, Patti LuPone, Anthony Heald, Anne Francine, and Rex Everhart. The production won the Tony Award for Best Revival of a Musical and ran for 784 performances.

DATES:
November 21, 1934–November 16, 1935 at the Alvin Theater and the 46th Street Theater (420 performances)

SYNOPSIS:
What do you get when you plunk a nightclub singer, an heiress, a stowaway, Public Enemy No. 13, and the stowaway's boss on an ocean liner? Among other things, a game of strip poker, a beard made out of the fur of a Pomeranian, and a dramaturgically unearned revival meeting.

AWARDS:
None

NOTED REVIVALS AND ADAPTATIONS:
Broadway revivals in 1987 and 2011; movie versions in 1936 and 1956; TV movie in 1954

ORIGINAL STARS:
Ethel Merman, William Gaxton, Bettina Hall, Victor Moore

ARCADIA

BY TOM STOPPARD

DATES:

March 31–August 27, 1995 at the Vivian Beaumont Theater (173 performances)

SYNOPSIS:

As the play's characters will be happy to explain and/or demonstrate, getting the narrative right can be tricky. But it involves an English country house and the cuckolds, mathematical geniuses, poseurs, Byronic tutors, hermits, biographers, and gardeners who inhabit it in the early 1800s and the modern day.

AWARDS:

None

NOTED REVIVALS AND ADAPTATIONS:

Broadway revival in 2011

ORIGINAL STARS:

Billy Crudup, Jennifer Dundas, Blair Brown, Robert Sean Leonard

Who needs a Tony Award when you can be the author of one of the four best science books ever written? Leaving such also-rans as Charles Darwin and James Watson in the dust, Tom Stoppard earned that distinction in 2006 from the Royal Institution of Great Britain on the strength of *Arcadia*, his towering riff on gardening, literary history, Newtonian physics, sex, determinism, and the men and women who (with one or two exceptions) get all of it wrong.

The science comes into play with the first two characters we meet, a thirteen-year-old prodigy named Thomasina and her hunky tutor Septimus. She's more interested in talking about the birds and the bees and barely seems to realize that she is discovering the second law of thermodynamics and chaos theory in 1809, a few decades before anyone else.

Lord Byron, that mythic Romantic (and the real father of a real mathematical savant, Ada Lovelace), brought a fair amount of chaos with him wherever he went, and Stoppard has fun with the idea of Byron seducing his way through a country house. The play frequently flash-forwards to modern-day academics as they try to make sense of what happened during Byron's 1809 visit, to determine whether

those events had anything to do with his fleeing to France. Was there a seduction? (Of course.) Was there a duel? (No, despite the insistences of one gloriously insufferable modern-day academic.)

Arcadia walks a tantalizing tightrope between comedy and tragedy. Stoppard had wanted to go with *Et in Arcadia Ego* for the title, alluding to death's presence even in the most idyllic of settings, but even Stoppardians have their limits. The amount of gray matter may have limited the play's commercial prospects—it lost that year's Tony Award to Terrence McNally's very fine *Love! Valour! Compassion!*—but *Arcadia* has emerged as one of the most piercing works of the twentieth century.

In Thomasina's exquisite preview of chaos theory, she points out that jam stirred into rice pudding cannot be unstirred out of it. Similarly, the ideas of *Arcadia*, once

ABOVE: From left, Bel Powley (Thomasina Coverly), Raúl Esparza (Valentine Coverly), Lia Williams (Hannah Jarvis), and Tom Riley (Septimus Hodge) in the 2011 Broadway revival, which also starred original Broadway cast member Billy Crudup as Bernard Nightingale. © Carol Rosegg

OPPOSITE PAGE: Crudup (Septimus Hodge) and Lisa Banes (Lady Croom), with David Manis (Captain Brice) in the background, in the original Broadway production. Lady Croom holds the book *The Couch of Eros*, written by a visitor to the Crooms' manor, the foolish poet Ezra Chater (Paul Giamatti).

slipped into the brain in the guise of drawing-room farce, never leave. "Comparing what we're looking for misses the point," explains Hannah, one of the modern academics and perhaps the play's most level-headed character. "It's wanting to know that makes us matter."

AS THOUSANDS CHEER

BY IRVING BERLIN AND MOSS HART

These days, when new musicals typically take five to seven years to put together, the idea of including topical material seems absurd. But in 1933, Irving Berlin and Moss Hart had no trouble looking to the headlines, just as they had the year before with *Face the Music*. That show made at least a rudimentary stab at surrounding gags about Tammany Hall and actress Helen Morgan with a plot.

DATES:

September 30, 1933–September 8, 1934 at the Music Box Theater (400 performances)

SYNOPSIS:

A series of newspaper headlines sets the stage for accompanying scenes and songs, finding room for matters major (Gandhi's latest hunger strike, a lynching) and minor (the Easter parade, a Noël Coward sighting).

AWARDS:

None

NOTED REVIVALS AND ADAPTATIONS:

None

ORIGINAL STARS:

Marilyn Miller, Clifton Webb, Ethel Waters, Helen Broderick

As Thousands Cheer is about . . . a newspaper. Not a newsroom. It features the contents of one day's paper, from the front page to the lonely-hearts column to the funnies.

Gags about socialite Barbara Hutton's relationship woes and John D. Rockefeller's ninety-fourth birthday sound about as fresh today as a *Forbidden Broadway* spoof of *Footloose* or *Bombay Dreams*. What makes *As Thousands Cheer* worth mentioning was the presence of Ethel Waters in the cast. Waters had three Broadway shows under her belt by 1933: *Africana*, *Rhapsody in Black*, and *Lew Leslie's Blackbirds*. Care to guess what those three had in common?

Ten years later, Irving Berlin would make history by insisting on a racially integrated cast for his World War II musical *This Is the Army*, with a cast made up of enlisted men. Here he took the even bolder step of casting Waters, whose national radio program and nightclub performances made her a familiar face and voice, to star in what was otherwise an all-white show. (Among her costars was Marilyn Miller, at one point the highest-paid performer on Broadway. She never appeared on the stage again and died three years later, at the age of thirty-seven.) Berlin even gave Waters easily the weightiest song he would ever write, "Supper Time," in which she prepared a dinner table for her children. They do not yet know that their father has been lynched.

Most of the show was nowhere near that serious; the highlight for many was "Easter Parade," in which Miller and Clifton Webb stepped right out of a sepia-tinted photo from the faux newspaper's rotogravure section. But "Supper Time" heralded a welcome new direction for Broadway, in terms of both content and casting. While she was in *As Thousands Cheer* (and juggling her other standing commitments), Waters supplanted Miller as Broadway's highest-paid performer. Now that's a headline worth setting to music.

OPPOSITE PAGE: Pioneering modern choreographer, dancer, and teacher Charles Weidman choreographed *As Thousands Cheer*. José Limón performed in the show, thirteen years before founding his own groundbreaking dance company.

LEFT: Ethel Waters in *As Thousands Cheer*. By age seventeen, Waters was singing professionally in Baltimore; within a few years, she was a star in Harlem. The same year she performed in *As Thousands Cheer*, she was also the first person to sing Harold Arlen and Ted Koehler's "Stormy Weather," which she debuted at the Cotton Club.

AWAKE AND SING!

BY CLIFFORD ODETS

From left, Morris Carnovsky, John Garfield, Art Smith, Stella Adler, and Phoebe Brand in *Awake and Sing!*

RALPH: Where's advancement down the place? Work like crazy! Think they see it? You'd drop dead first.

MYRON: Never mind, son, merit never goes unrewarded. Teddy Roosevelt used to say—

HENNIE: It rewarded you—thirty years a haberdashery clerk!

RALPH: All I want's a chance to get to first base!

These are the first four lines of *Awake and Sing!*, set just as the Berger family is finishing supper, and the fact that they don't seem that odd to modern readers shows just how influential Clifford Odets' play was. Not for Odets the helpful maid answering the phone or the unexpected houseguest inquiring after the family. This was drama *in media res*, without any audience-friendly exposition. In 1935, it was all but unheard of.

Odets had been tinkering with the play with fellow members of the Group Theatre collective for two years, even if that meant promising more than one actor the same part, and their tight-knit camaraderie resulted in a palpable sense of familiarity. Crammed into their snug Bronx apartment, the Bergers know each other all too well. So did the cast, a virtual who's who of early-twentieth-century acting. (Two of the original performers, Stella Adler and Sanford Meisner, belong on any Mount Rushmore of iconic acting teachers.) No wonder multiple actors wanted these parts: for better and for worse, Odets is the most quotable American playwright ever, throwing one juicy line after the next into a combustible mix. ("Cut your throat,

sweetheart. Save time." "She's so beautiful you look at her and cry! She's like French words!")

Awake and Sing! opened in the immediate wake of Odets' similarly crusading *Waiting for Lefty*, which had become a sensation during a series of benefit performances in Lower Manhattan. The Group quickly moved *Lefty* uptown to the Belasco, where it joined *Awake* in repertory with its own stellar cast: Odets himself was joined on stage by Lee J. Cobb and Elia Kazan.

Among all these heavy hitters, perhaps the brightest light was John Garfield, a Broadway bit player and Odets' acquaintance. He was a smash in the central role of Ralph Berger in *Awake and Sing!* and would soon amass thirty-five Hollywood credits in less than fifteen years—until his career screeched to a halt after his appearance in front of the House Un-American Activities Committee. Garfield had never been a member of the Communist Party, but he still refused to name names. The lessons of *Awake and Sing!* had left their mark.

From left, Garfield, Carnovsky, J. Edward Bromberg, Stella Adler (founder of the Stella Adler Studio of Acting), Luther Adler, Sanford Meisner (creator of the Meisner acting technique), and Smith. Harold Clurman, cofounder of the Group Theatre as well as an influential theater critic for *The New Republic* and *The Nation*, directed.

DATES:

February 19–July 27 and September 9–28, 1935 at the Belasco Theater (208 performances total)

SYNOPSIS:

The Berger family struggles to stay afloat in the Depression-era Bronx, with idealism and practicality duking it out over the future of young Ralph and his flinty sister, Hennie.

AWARDS:

None

NOTED REVIVALS AND ADAPTATIONS:

Broadway revivals in 1938, 1939, 1984, and 2006; TV version in 1972

ORIGINAL STARS:

Luther Adler, Stella Adler, Morris Carnovsky, John Garfield, Sanford Meisner

BABES IN ARMS

BY RICHARD RODGERS AND LORENZ HART

Imagine settling into your Broadway seat as the lights go down on a new show and hearing "Where or When" for the first time. Then imagine that song followed by "Babes in Arms" and *that* song followed by "I Wish I Were in Love Again." I'm not cherry-picking or skipping around; those are literally the first three songs in *Babes in Arms*. And before the evening is over, you'll also get "Johnny One-Note," "The Lady Is a Tramp," and "My Funny Valentine."

With that kind of score, sung by no fewer than fifty fresh-faced performers, who cares what happens between the songs? And as the synopsis makes clear, it's not like Richard Rodgers and Lorenz Hart were pioneering new narrative territory, right?

Well, actually, they were. This was the very first "Let's put on a show!" musical, and it hardly seems fair to blame Rodgers and Hart for subsequent generations of unoriginality. Their version had a lot more teeth than the completely rewritten 1939 film, starring

ABOVE: Richard Rodgers, left, with Lorenz Hart, 1936.
Library of Congress

OPPOSITE PAGE: The original cast of *Babes in Arms* included, from left, Mitzi Green, Alex Courtney, Alfred Drake, Aljan de Loville, Ray Heatherton, and Wynn Murray. The renowned tap-dancing duo the Nicholas Brothers (Harold and Fayard) were also in the cast.

DATES:
April 4–December 18, 1937 at the Shubert Theater and Majestic Theater (289 performances)

SYNOPSIS:
A plucky group of youngsters decides to put on a show.

AWARDS:
None

NOTED REVIVALS AND ADAPTATIONS:
Movie version in 1939

ORIGINAL STARS:
Alfred Drake, Mitzi Green, Ray Heatherton, Harold and Fayard Nicholas

Judy Garland, would indicate: there were a Communist and a white supremacist among the youngsters' ranks, and the whole gang was threatened with being hauled off to a work farm. Rodgers had a very different mindset in 1937 than he did in 1959, when he commissioned drama critic George Oppenheimer to write a far more sanitized script for regional productions. That version was the only one available for nearly forty years.

In writing the original book, Rodgers and Hart drew upon their cast's skills and personalities, from Mitzi Green's knack for impersonations to another performer's ability to dance on stilts. They also changed one character's name to Val, so that "My Funny Valentine" would make sense.

That script relied on a bizarre act of providence (a French aviator falling out of the sky), but the survival of *Babes in Arms* hinged on an even more curious turn of events. The show was floundering at the box office despite strong reviews, until it became—literally—*the* musical to see on Broadway. There were just three others playing when *Babes in Arms* opened; all three closed in the summer of 1937. With the field all to themselves, those fifty youngsters and their unprecedented stack of future standards soldiered on for another five months.

THE BAND WAGON

BY ARTHUR SCHWARTZ, HOWARD DIETZ, AND GEORGE S. KAUFMAN

DATES:
June 3, 1931–January 16, 1932 at the New Amsterdam Theater (260 performances)

SYNOPSIS:
Various revue sketches, including a lampoon of the Old South, a bit about a well-heeled woman buying bathroom fixtures, and a send-up of the conventions of New York theatergoers.

AWARDS:
None

NOTED REVIVALS AND ADAPTATIONS:
Two (very different) movie versions in 1949 and 1953

ORIGINAL STARS:
Fred and Adele Astaire, Helen Broderick, Frank Morgan, Tilly Losch

The original Broadway revues were more like television variety shows: novelty acts brought their bits with them, and a passel of writers threw in their contributions. Scenes and songs came and went, depending on what was in vogue.

One writer who stayed in vogue for a staggeringly long time was George S. Kaufman. On top of his day job as the *New York Times* drama editor and his contributions to the Algonquin Round Table (not to mention as many bridge games and paramours as he could fit in), Kaufman directed and/or wrote dozens of Broadway plays and musicals, including *Guys and Dolls*, *The Front Page*, and *Of Thee I Sing*. He was responsible for a particularly popular sketch involving a hotel fire in

ABOVE: Tilly Losch, Fred Astaire, Adele Astaire, Frank Morgan, and Helen Broderick perform "I Love Louisa" in *The Band Wagon*, 1931. The staging featured a merry-go-round, which made clever use of the production's rotating stage.

OPPOSITE PAGE: Fred and Adele Astaire in "White Heat." The siblings began performing together when he was five and she was eight; *The Band Wagon* was their final show together.

The Little Show, a 1929 revue that introduced the songwriting team of Arthur Schwartz and Howard Dietz to Broadway.

Two years and two lesser shows later, Schwartz and Dietz decided to deviate from the revue-by-committee format. Just as George White had turned heads by having a single composer work on each of his *Scandals* revues, *The Band Wagon* had just one bookwriter: Kaufman. (As it happens, the Dietz/Schwartz/Kaufman trio might be the greatest batch of multitaskers Broadway had—or has—ever seen. Schwartz worked as a lawyer until 1928, and Dietz had a day job as a publicist at MGM, where he invented the lion logo.)

With the help of director Hassard Short's then-unheard-of pair of rotating turntables, the creators were able to whisk on and off the stage a phenomenal cast, which included Frank Morgan, Helen Broderick, and the brother-sister dance team of Fred and Adele Astaire. Schwartz made a major contribution during rehearsals when he decided to add a slower, moodier tune; before the day was over, he had written "Dancing in the Dark" (for Tilly Losch, not the Astaires). Many historians hail the result as the pinnacle of the nearly 150 revues that flooded Broadway during the 1920s and 1930s.

While the ranks were profitably being thinned behind the scenes, a more worrisome streamlining was about to take place on stage. *The Band Wagon* was the final stage performance of Adele Astaire, who would marry Lord Charles Cavendish and move to his castle in Ireland. After twenty-seven years, the brother-sister act was over. Adele's balding younger brother was going to have to try to make it on his own.

THE BEAUTY QUEEN OF LEENANE

BY MARTIN McDONAGH

Written in just six days, *The Beauty Queen of Leenane* is a boisterous, altogether astonishing glimpse at the lonesome western stretches of Ireland, the ones that John Millington Synge anatomized almost a century earlier. It would be impossible to replicate for modern audiences the shock waves that convulsed Dublin in 1907 when Synge mentioned ladies' "shifts" (undergarments) in *The Playboy of the Western World*, though Lord knows McDonagh tried. *Leenane*, like so many of his other plays, uses

ABOVE: Anna Manahan and Marie Mullen performed the roles of Mag and Maureen Folan in the 1996 London production at the Royal Court Theater and continued to play them on Broadway. © Robbie Jack, Corbis

OPPOSITE PAGE: Manahan as Mag, the domineering matriarch, in the Broadway production of *The Beauty Queen of Leenane*. © Carol Rosegg

DATES:
April 23, 1998–March 14, 1999 at the Walter Kerr Theater (365 performances)

SYNOPSIS:
Middle-aged Maureen Folan and her controlling mother live in a far-too-small cottage in Connemara, Ireland. The arrival of two young men raises the possibility of a way out for Maureen—until it doesn't, with monstrous consequences.

AWARDS:
4 Tony Awards

NOTED REVIVALS AND ADAPTATIONS:
None

ORIGINAL STARS:
Marie Mullen, Anna Manahan, Tom Murphy, Brían F. O'Byrne

ambling rhythms and absurd syntax to lull audiences into a state of chortling relaxation—and then rips their throats out mid-chuckle.

The jolts are a central part of McDonagh's appeal. In another of his plays, when a cat everyone thought was dead reappeared at the end, the audience response was so tumultuous that the cat's handler had to retrain it to handle the gasps and shrieks. Clever as these reversals are, though, they mask McDonagh's gift for structure. He sets the stage for each one so cunningly—and usually within such an unremarkable environment—that the "surprises" are all the more shocking for having been in plain sight all along.

Actors flock to his works, in part because at least a few of them get Tony Award nominations each time. Brían F. O'Byrne, who at press time has starred in nine new Broadway plays and received Tony nominations for seven of them, was the only one of the four *Leenane* cast members *not* to win the actual prize.

In many ways, other McDonagh plays have packed a comparable punch: *The Pillowman* (2003) found ghastly resonances in the beloved Irish knack for storytelling, while 2001's *The Lieutenant of Inishmore* (the one with the prodigal cat) reached levels of onstage carnage that have yet to be equaled by McDonagh or anyone else. But *Leenane*, under the crystalline direction of Garry Hynes, set the template for the first unmistakable playwriting voice of the twenty-first century.

THE BLACK CROOK

BY GEORGE BICKWELL, THEODORE KENNICK, CHARLES M. BARRAS, AND VARIOUS OTHERS ALONG THE WAY

Dialogue like what you're about to read would not ordinarily be found in any list of significant Broadway shows—not even if it were being done in an ultra-arch, campy style:

WOLFENSTEIN: (Aside.) Tis he, the lover. He braves me, too. (Aloud.) Wulfgar! (WULFGAR advances. Speaks apart to him.) Track yonder knave, take Bruno with you. Seize him, but let no eye see you. Place him in the secret vault beneath the eastern wing. Once there—you know the rest.

And for the record, *The Black Crook* wasn't intended to be performed tongue in cheek. In fact, playwright Charles M. Barras reportedly bristled when he heard that some enterprising producers wanted to taint his

DATES:

September 12, 1866–January 4, 1868 at Niblo's Garden (475 performances)

SYNOPSIS:

Count Wolfenstein and a crook-backed black magician named Hertzog plot to have the unjustly jailed painter Rodolphe sent to hell. Their plan gets derailed when Rodolphe saves the life of a dove, who is actually Stalacta, Queen of the Golden Realm. As a result, Rodolphe gets to go to fairyland instead, while Hertzog is dragged to hell.

AWARDS:

None

NOTED REVIVALS AND ADAPTATIONS:

Broadway revivals in 1870 and 1871

ORIGINAL STARS:

A "Ballet Troupe of Seventy Ladies," plus Charles Morton and Annie Kemp Bowler

ABOVE: Some of the seventy ladies, who were an undeniable draw for *Black Crook* audiences. *Napoleon Sarony, Library of Congress*

OPPOSITE PAGE: A *Black Crook* poster, c. 1882, left no doubt about the show's extravagance. *Library of Congress*

text by interpolating musical numbers. It took a $1,500 bonus to change his mind.

This is just one of the many bizarre facts leading up to what is frequently (though not without vocal dissenters) described as the first Broadway musical. Unquestionably, it was America's first nationwide smash success. When the Academy of Music on Fourteenth Street in Manhattan caught fire, a Parisian ballet troupe had nowhere to perform. At the same time, the enterprising owner of the 3,200-seat Niblo's Garden was in rehearsals with a metaphysical melodrama that, as the earlier text illustrates, stood to be augmented a bit.

The commingled result, with an array of songs from various composers, ran a reported five and a half hours

and set Broadway on its ear. American railroads had improved greatly during the Civil War, resulting in the show's ability to go on tour. It did so profitably for decades.

Each step of the way, two aspects of *The Black Crook* got the bulk of the attention: the onstage transformation of a grotto into a fairyland throne room, and the aforementioned ballet troupe, which performed in skin-colored tights that were euphemistically described as pink. (A 1953 Broadway musical called *The Girl in Pink Tights* paid homage to the show, with new—and presumably improved—choreography by Agnes de Mille.) This last aspect earned the show what every producer dreams of: fulminating editorials and sermons galore.

THE BOOK OF MORMON

BY ROBERT LOPEZ, TREY PARKER, AND MATT STONE

The Mormons practice their pitch in the opening number, "Hello!" Josh Gad (top row, second from left) played truth-stretching Elder Cunningham; Andrew Rannells (bottom center) was self-admiring Elder Price. © Joan Marcus

What does it take to get a cast album onto the *Billboard* Top 10 chart, something that hadn't happened since *Hair* in 1969? Well, that album featured a number called "Sodomy"; how about a song that involves sodomizing frogs instead of babies?

On one level, it's hard to believe that the highest-charting cast album in more than forty years employs the phrase "I have maggots in my scrotum" on more than one occasion. But *The Book of Mormon* is a canny packaging of provocations, whose creators had spent the previous decade or more pushing the envelope just enough.

When Robert Lopez and Jeff Marx were writing the naughty-puppet musical *Avenue Q* (2003), they drew heavily upon *South Park: Bigger, Longer & Uncut*, Trey Parker and Matt Stone's uproariously filthy film version of their long-running TV series, *South Park*. (Stephen Sondheim is another fan of the film.) The four of them—not Sondheim, the other four—met after a performance of *Avenue Q* and quickly realized that they were all interested in writing something about Joseph Smith and the religion he founded/created, Mormonism.

Elder Price and the general (Brian Tyree Henry) as Price sings "I Believe." The general expresses his discontent soon after.
© Joan Marcus

Mormon took nearly seven years to complete. (Marx eventually departed from the team.) The result straddles irreverence and sincerity with consummate skill and, thanks to the ever-inventive director Casey Nicholaw, pizzazz.

Packed with tributes to *The Lion King*, *Oklahoma!*, and especially *The King and I* (another show about the West exporting its values), *Mormon* is a virtual crash course in Musical Theater 101, albeit one given by the stoners in the back row. With just a few tweaked lyrics, "Sal Tla Ka Siti"—a Ugandan girl's phonetic tribute to Salt Lake City, "where flies don't bite your eyeballs and human life has worth"—could fit comfortably into Act I of a Rodgers and Hammerstein show.

Do a few satiric punches get pulled by the end? Sure. They did in *Avenue Q*, too, and that tiny show nearly managed to crack the all-time list of Top 20 long runs in Broadway history. *The Book of Mormon* is poised to cross that threshold, and then some.

DATES:
Opened March 24, 2011 at the Eugene O'Neill Theater (1,614 performances as of February 1, 2015)

SYNOPSIS:
A mismatched pair of Mormon missionaries, hoping to be placed in Orlando, instead find themselves in famine- and AIDS-ravaged Uganda.

AWARDS:
9 Tony Awards

NOTED REVIVALS AND ADAPTATIONS:
None

ORIGINAL STARS:
Andrew Rannells, Josh Gad, Nikki M. James, Rory O'Malley

BORN YESTERDAY

BY GARSON KANIN

DATES:
February 4, 1946–December 31, 1949 at the Lyceum Theater and Henry Miller's Theater (1,642 performances)

SYNOPSIS:
Boorish junk dealer Harry Brock comes to Washington, D.C., in search of even more ill-gotten gains, but his brassy mistress, the former chorus girl Billie Dawn, proves to be a social liability. So he hires a left-leaning journalist to class her up a bit—and quickly regrets the decision.

AWARDS:
None

NOTED REVIVALS AND ADAPTATIONS:
Broadway revivals in 1989 and 2011; movie versions in 1950 and 1993

ORIGINAL STARS:
Judy Holliday, Paul Douglas, Gary Merrill

Poor Jean Arthur. William Goldman devoted a chunk of his irresistible book *The Season: A Candid Look at Broadway* to an ill-fated 1967 Broadway play that was to have been the triumphant return to the stage for the *Shane* and *Mr. Smith Goes to Washington* actress. It never got past previews, owing in part to Arthur's debilitating stage fright. Years later, because of the same condition, she was replaced by Jane Alexander in *First Monday in October*; Alexander got a Tony Award nomination for her performance.

And back in 1946, Arthur's stage fright lost her a much better role, one that her friend Garson Kanin had written for her.

During his time serving in the army during World War II, Kanin found time to write *Born Yesterday*, a particularly sanguine—some might say naïve—glimpse at how to fix Washington, D.C. (No wonder he wanted the costar of *Mr. Smith* in it.) All it takes, apparently, are a showgirl and a journalist.

Arthur Laurents (*Home of the Brave*) and Howard Lindsay and Russel Crouse (*State of the Union*) were among the other playwrights taking America's political temperature at this heady time. The fact that Kanin's play far outsold those and other plays suggests the appeal of

the "spoonful of sugar" school of moralizing. In telling the story of a not-so-dumb blonde who spoils her boyfriend's attempts to buy himself a US senator, Kanin essentially transplanted Damon Runyon's malaprop-prone hoodlums and chorines to the nation's capital.

In the central role of Billie Dawn, he created a formidable floozy rivaled only by Adelaide, the Runyon composite immortalized in *Guys and Dolls*. Judy Holliday, with her reported IQ of 172, took over the role in Philadelphia—three days after getting the script—and emerged as perhaps the era's preeminent stage comedienne. It took the machinations of George Cukor, Spencer Tracy, and Katharine Hepburn, along with Kanin, to convince the studio heads at Columbia Pictures to let Holliday repeat the role in the 1950 film version. The result was an Academy Award over the likes of Gloria Swanson and Bette Davis. Just like her often imitated but rarely equaled creation, Holliday was all too easy to underestimate.

OPPOSITE PAGE: Judy Holliday and Paul Douglas as Billie Dawn and Harry Brock.

BELOW: Madeline Kahn played Billie in the 1989 revival at the 46th Street Theater, opposite Ed Asner as Harry. From left, Franklin Cover, Kahn, Asner, and Daniel Hugh Kelly.

BRIGADOON

BY FREDERICK LOEWE AND ALAN JAY LERNER

By 1947, the shift from operetta to integrated musical was well under way; Rodgers and Hammerstein had already written two pioneering examples of the latter, *Oklahoma!* and *Carousel*, and composers like Leonard Bernstein (*On the Town*) and Irving Berlin (*Annie Get Your Gun*) had begun to follow suit. But not everyone was ready or willing to abandon the lush vistas and even lusher melodies that had kept audiences entertained for nearly a century.

Alan Jay Lerner and Frederick Loewe, whose three Broadway attempts had been unremarkable up to this point, essentially split the difference with *Brigadoon*, coupling R&H's basic template (a romantic main couple and a secondary comic couple) and their visionary choreographer, Agnes de Mille, with a phantasmagoric Scottish setting that operetta composers Victor Herbert and Franz Lehar would have embraced.

ABOVE: *Brigadoon*, 1947, with Virginia Bosler (Jean) center.

OPPOSITE PAGE: *Brigadoon* original production. Agnes de Mille choreographed the musical with a keen eye toward—and as a tribute to—traditional Scottish dance forms.

Though some critics have tried, it's hard to quibble too much with the corny ending or glut of folk dances in the face of songs like "Almost Like Being in Love," "There But for You Go I," "The Heather on the Hill," "Come to Me, Bend to Me," and the haunting title song. There's even a comedy number, "My Mother's Wedding Day," that's reasonably funny by Lerner and Loewe's rather mirthless standards, *My Fair Lady* excepted. (By contrast, 1947's other hit fantasy musical, *Finian's Rainbow*, packs more laughs into some *verses* than Lerner and Loewe mustered in their entire careers.)

Loewe, in particular, had a taste for novelty: before hitting it big on Broadway, the Berlin-born piano prodigy had done time as a boxer, gold miner, ranch hand, and mail carrier (in rural Montana, on horseback). But just like the two New Yorkers pulled hypnotically toward Brigadoon, Loewe and Lerner were hardly immune to the timeless, sumptuous qualities of the old. Neither were their audiences.

DATES:
March 13, 1947–July 31, 1948 at the Ziegfeld Theater (581 performances)

SYNOPSIS:
A pair of New Yorkers vacationing in the Scottish Highlands stumbles upon the magical village of Brigadoon, which materializes once every hundred years—and vanishes forever if anyone leaves it. After one of the men falls in love with a native, the village's disappearance becomes a real possibility.

AWARDS:
1 Tony Award

NOTED REVIVALS AND ADAPTATIONS:
Broadway revival in 1980; movie version in 1954; TV version in 1966

ORIGINAL STARS:
David Brooks, Marion Bell, George Keane, Pamela Britton, James Mitchell

BUS STOP

BY WILLIAM INGE

As nightclub singer Cherie, Kim Stanley (with Albert Salmi as cowboy Bo Decker) gave a "glowing performance that is full of amusing detail," wrote Brooks Atkinson, "cheap, ignorant, bewildered, but also radiant with personality."

"I never got tired of watching Kim Stanley," Elaine Stritch once said. "Never. Never." Theater history is stuffed with revered figures whose film and television credits offer little more than a peek at their gifts. Unlike such stage holdouts as Laurette Taylor and Uta Hagen, Kim Stanley at least managed to fit two Academy Award–nominated movie roles onto her résumé. (She might have snagged a third had she not turned down the

DATES:
March 2, 1955–April 21, 1956 at the Music Box Theater and Winter Garden Theater (478 performances)

SYNOPSIS:
A freak snowstorm forces a busload of passengers to cool their heels in a diner twenty-five miles outside of Kansas City, Missouri. Among them are a seen-it-all "chantoozie" named Cherie and a lovesick cowboy, Bo, who is hellbent on making an honest woman of Cherie after the fact.

AWARDS:
None

NOTED REVIVALS AND ADAPTATIONS:
Broadway revival in 1996; movie version in 1956; TV version in 1982

ORIGINAL STARS:
Kim Stanley, Albert Salmi, Elaine Stritch

Crahan Denton (cowboy Virgil Blessing), Salmi, and Stanley.

Kim Novak role in *Vertigo*.) But it was the stage where Stanley became her generation's premier dramatic actress. And the plays of William Inge, particularly *Bus Stop*, were where this "female Brando"—to crib from the title of her biography—earned her reputation.

Without the political fervor that animates Arthur Miller's plays or the hothouse poetry that invigorates Tennessee Williams', Inge's major works have been largely neglected and/or condescended to in the last several years. (The nickname "The Playwright of the Midwest" is not exactly a compliment to many.) But Inge's portrayals of conflicted, red-blooded men and women—especially women—chafing under a restrictive mid-twentieth-century morality are no less sympathetic today than when they debuted. Inge made the seemingly simple act of wanting as natural as a sunny Kansas day and as unpredictable as the snowstorm that interrupts it.

Yet normalcy isn't easy, at least not on stage, which is one reason why Stanley's work in *Bus Stop* invariably makes it onto a short list of indelible stage performances. An early habitué of the Actors Studio, Stanley rivals Marlon Brando as the definitive master of Method acting. She ultimately created ten Broadway roles in twelve years, including in new works by Eugene O'Neill and Horton Foote (to whom the condescending designation of "regional playwright" would soon be handed). Alcohol cut her career short, as it did for Inge himself. But when they were both on, they were hard to beat.

BYE BYE BIRDIE

CHARLES STROUSE, LEE ADAMS, AND MICHAEL STEWART

It's hard to imagine now, with Elton John, Carole King, Frankie Valli and the Four Seasons, ABBA, Sting, Bob Dylan, and Bon Jovi all having been represented in Times Square, but for a long time Broadway viewed rock and roll as a problem, not a cash cow. Prior to 1960, the sole musical nod to rock was a song in the 1957 edition of *The Ziegfeld Follies*, of all places. A character in that show named "The Juvenile Delinquent" (played by a fifty-year-old Billy De Wolfe) sang "I Don't Wanna Rock." Broadway agreed with him.

In December 1957, however, the perfect pretext for rock on Broadway presented itself when Elvis Presley received his draft notice. Though Presley had implored his manager, Colonel Tom Parker, to keep him out of the army, the cagy Parker saw this

ABOVE: Conrad Birdie (Dick Gautier) croons "Honestly Sincere" to a rapt audience.

OPPOSITE PAGE: "Did they really get pinned?" "What's the story, morning glory?" In "The Telephone Hour," the teenagers of Sweet Apple, Ohio, trade the latest news. Original Broadway production, 1960.

DATES:

April 14, 1960–October 7, 1961 at the Martin Beck Theater, the 54th Street Theater, and the Shubert Theater (607 performances)

SYNOPSIS:

With Conrad Birdie about to be shipped overseas, agent Albert Peterson comes up with a press stunt for his rock-star client. They descend on idyllic Sweet Apple, Ohio, to give a lucky fan "One Last Kiss" live on *The Ed Sullivan Show*. Things don't go as planned.

AWARDS:

4 Tony Awards

NOTED REVIVALS AND ADAPTATIONS:

Broadway revival in 2009; Broadway sequel in 1981; movie version in 1963; TV version in 1995

ORIGINAL STARS:

Chita Rivera, Dick Van Dyke, Dick Gautier, Susan Watson, Kay Medford, Paul Lynde

as a chance to modify Presley's image. The teachers and parents of America liked this rock music about as much as Broadway did, and a tour of duty was a great way to recalibrate Presley's appeal to reach a much wider (and, at the time, far more lucrative) audience.

What better setting for a musical about a rock singer than his final hours in America? How much damage to America's youth could possibly come from one last kiss to an adoring fan?

The story would almost seem to write itself, but *Bye Bye Birdie* went through all sorts of turmoil before coming together in 1960. Mike Nichols took a crack at the book, Fred Astaire was recommended as a choreographer, and the name of Conrad Birdie only surfaced after the suggested Conway Twitty (!) resulted in the threat of a lawsuit. By the time the dust settled, Gower Champion had definitively made the transition from performer to director/choreographer, putting the energetic youngsters and exasperated parents through their paces. Such huge hits as *Hello, Dolly!* and *42nd Street* lay ahead in Champion's future.

Songs like "Kids" and "Put on a Happy Face" would have fit perfectly comfortably in any number of 1940s musicals. Deep down, Broadway still didn't wanna rock in 1960; that would have to be put on hold until *Hair* forced the issue seven years later. *Bye Bye Birdie*, which has since been established as a fixture in American schools, jauntily dipped its toe into waters that would soon become a flood.

CABARET

BY JOHN KANDER, FRED EBB, AND JOE MASTEROFF

DATES:
November 20, 1966–September 6, 1969 at the Broadhurst Theater, Broadway Theater, and Imperial Theater (1,165 performances)

SYNOPSIS:
As Weimar Republic–era Germany burns and an American writer named Cliff Bradshaw bears horrified witness, the denizens of the decadent Kit Kat Klub fiddle, grope, and croon, led by a ghoulish Emcee and the star attraction, a nineteen-year-old British gamine named Sally Bowles.

AWARDS:
8 Tony Awards

NOTED REVIVALS AND ADAPTATIONS:
Broadway revivals in 1987, 1998, and 2014; movie version in 1972

ORIGINAL STARS:
Joel Grey, Jill Haworth, Bert Convy, Lotte Lenya, Jack Gilford

From its opening notes, a sinister drumroll and cymbal crash in lieu of an overture, *Cabaret* blew open the scope of what could be tackled in a Broadway musical. Director Harold Prince's stunning, Spartan gloss on Bertolt Brecht and Kurt Weill—complete with the casting of Weill's ex-wife, the inimitable Lotte Lenya—uncovered seemingly limitless amounts of malice in its toe-tapping score.

The juxtaposition of conventional book scenes with brassy nightclub material was a vexing one from the very beginning, and Bob Fosse's 1972 movie version junked the former entirely. (It did, however, keep Joel Grey's career-making performance as the Emcee.) Fosse's innovations were so pervasive—and so successful—that virtually every subsequent stage version has had to grapple with them. When and why do the characters burst into song? Who's gay and who isn't? Just how good of a performer is Sally

Jill Haworth (Sally Bowles) in *Cabaret*, 1966, with Bert Convy (Clifford Bradshaw) far left, seated.

Bowles, the Kit Kat Klub's headliner? And what about those Nazis, perpetually looming on the periphery?

Sam Mendes found provocative answers to many of these questions in a 2003 London production, in which Cliff kisses one of the Kit Kat boys and the Emcee (Alan Cumming) ends up in a concentration camp. The production eventually transferred to Broadway (codirected by Rob Marshall) and ran twice as long as the original, in part because a flurry of stars rotated in and out of the show: Brooke Shields, Deborah Gibson, Gina Gershon, and Molly Ringwald were among the more-than-a-dozen prominent Sallys. Michelle Williams and then Emma Stone took over when the Mendes-Marshall production came back to Broadway in 2014, again with Cumming running the show as the Emcee.

(Interesting sidenote: Joel Grey brought the original Prince staging back to Broadway in 1987, more than twenty years after creating the role. Unless I'm mistaken, that makes *Cabaret* the first show ever to have two completely different stagings each deemed worthy of a second production on Broadway.)

LEFT: Sam Mendes and Rob Marshall's revival of *Cabaret*, starring Alan Cumming, came to Broadway in 1998 and ran 2,377 performances. It returned in 2014 (shown). © *Joan Marcus*

RIGHT: Poster for the 1972 film, directed by Bob Fosse and starring Liza Minnelli and Joel Grey (all of whom won Oscars). © *Allied Artists Pictures, courtesy Photofest*

The strong responses to both the revival and the film have had the unfortunate effect of recasting the original as slightly damaged goods, as a promising but problematic show that just needed to be fixed. That is not the case. Many gifted people have found many perfectly marvelous ways to present *Cabaret*. Fosse, Mendes, and Marshall are three of them. But they all took their cues from Hal Prince.

CAPTAIN JINKS OF THE HORSE MARINES

BY CLYDE FITCH

DATES:

February–July and September–October 1901
at the Garrick Theater (192 performances)

SYNOPSIS:

Jersey girl Aurelia Johnson returns from
Europe as a celebrated prima donna,
inspiring Captain Jinks to wager $1,000 that
he can woo her. He wins, but what happens
when she learns of the bet—right before her
big US concert?

AWARDS:

None

NOTED REVIVALS
AND ADAPTATIONS:

Broadway revivals in 1907 and 1938;
movie version in 1916

ORIGINAL STARS:

Ethel Barrymore, H. Reeves-Smith,
Mrs. Thomas Whiffen

Clyde Fitch may well be the forgotten giant of the American theater. The dozens of plays (accounts fall either just shy of or just over sixty) that he wrote in the space of nineteen years, many of them for the era's top stars; the affair with Oscar Wilde, who supposedly threw him over when Lord Alfred Douglas came along; the collaboration with Edith Wharton on a play of *The House of Mirth* and near-collaboration with Puccini on an opera—is none of this sufficient to earn Fitch a permanent spot in the history books?

The sheer pace with which he wrote, along with his lavish lifestyle and his habit of maintaining it by contriving popular happy endings to his plays, kept Fitch from ever being truly embraced by the critics. But the audiences came in droves. He had four shows running simultaneously on two different occasions, a feat not matched for another sixty years (by Neil Simon).

ABOVE: A 1925 musical adaptation of *Captain Jinks* had music by Lewis Gensler and Stephen Jones, a book by Frank Mandel and Laurence Schwab, and lyrics by B. G. DeSylva. It ran for 167 performances at the Martin Beck Theater.

OPPOSITE PAGE: Ethel Barrymore (sister of John and Lionel) as Madame Trentoni, c. 1901. The role, which she played again in the 1907 revival at the Empire Theater, made her a star. *Burr McIntosh, Library of Congress*

Fitch had a knack for writing sturdy vehicles for top-drawing actors, among them Richard Mansfield and Helena Modjeska. His biggest star-making play was *Captain Jinks of the Horse Marines*, which starred a twenty-one-year-old Ethel Barrymore as an American opera singer rechristened Madame Trentoni, "the Primy Donner what the young Prince of Wales says is a A one-er."

Fitch didn't want her in the part, but his regular producer Charles Frohman insisted, and Barrymore quickly became the biggest star on Broadway. (Less impressive was her younger brother, John Barrymore, who performed in the show briefly when the company went to Philadelphia. When John forgot his lines, the cast was forced to improvise until the Act I curtain went down. Nonetheless, Frohman liked what he saw and told John, "With a better memory, you might make a comedian someday.")

Of all of his plays, Fitch himself preferred 1909's *The City*, best known today for the first onstage usage of the word "goddamn." (The audience went berserk on opening night.) But *Captain Jinks* has charm and a foolproof romantic resolution, as well as a great role for an actress of a certain age as the title character's disapproving mother. The piece was last revived in 1938, running in repertory with Shaw, O'Neill, and Shakespeare. It ran a total of four performances. It was the last mounting of a Clyde Fitch play on Broadway.

THE CARETAKER

BY HAROLD PINTER

Playwright Terence Rattigan to Harold Pinter about *The Caretaker*: "It's about the God of the Old Testament, the God of the New and Humanity, isn't it?"

Pinter: "No, Terry, it's about a caretaker and two brothers."

Rattigan's impulse is an understandable one. Like Pinter's most apparent influence, Samuel Beckett, and his most obvious disciple, David Mamet, Pinter created narrative and linguistic gaps that cried out to be filled. (Mamet's much-discussed refusal to supply his actors with characters' "back stories," or usable sets of background information, stems from Pinter.)

And just as Beckett used such well-known comedians as Buster Keaton and Bert Lahr in his scorched-earth parables, Pinter forced audiences to find mirth as well as menace in his terse, elliptical works. "As far as I'm concerned, *The Caretaker* is funny up to a point," Pinter wrote of the play, his first to reach New York. "Beyond that point it ceases to be funny, and it was because of that point that I wrote it."

DATES:
October 4, 1961–February 24, 1962 at the
Lyceum Theater (165 performances)

SYNOPSIS:
Harold Pinter's quote pretty much sums it up.

AWARDS:
None

NOTED REVIVALS
AND ADAPTATIONS:
Broadway revivals in 1986 and 2003; movie
version in 1963

ORIGINAL STARS:
Robert Shaw, Alan Bates, Donald Pleasance

Admittedly, such boundaries were difficult to map out from the very beginning. The *New York Times*' Howard Taubman described portions of the play in 1961 as "sardonic comedy, beatnik style," the first and presumably last time the word *beatnik* was ever used to describe Harold Pinter. And the Act II monologue in which Aston—the gentler of the two brothers who take in the volatile tramp Davies—describes the shock treatment he received as a young man ("I knew they had to get me back on the bed because if they did it while I was standing up, they might break my spine") has few equals in its sparse, tragic majesty. But that same act opens with a three-man slapstick sequence that could have come straight from Laurel and Hardy (or from *Waiting for Godot*).

Not surprisingly for a playwright who would ultimately change the metabolism of Western theater, Pinter had to ply his trade in the more forgiving precincts of off-Broadway for the next several years. By the time he returned to Broadway in 1967 with *The Homecoming*, audiences still had difficulty filling in the gaps—but they were eager to try.

ABOVE: The character of Davies is abrasive and manipulative, as well as hungry for power.

OPPOSITE PAGE: Alan Bates (Mick), Donald Pleasance (Davies), and Robert Shaw (Aston) in the original Broadway production of *The Caretaker*, 1960.

CAROUSEL

BY RICHARD RODGERS AND OSCAR HAMMERSTEIN II

Jean Darling (Carrie), John Raitt (Billy), and Jan Clayton (Julie) in the original production.

Richard Rodgers and Oscar Hammerstein II's previous musical, *Oklahoma!*, is rightly hailed for ushering in any number of innovations. But first does not necessarily mean best, and *Carousel*—which found nearly as many new ways to tell a story through song and dance—continues to delight and devastate seventy years later.

Decades before Stephen Sondheim explored ambivalence in songs like "Sorry-Grateful" and "The Road You Didn't Take" (from *Company* and *Follies*, respectively), his mentor Hammerstein led viewers through the extended, tortured thought process of the none-too-bright Billy Bigelow in his stunning eight-minute "Soliloquy." (John Raitt, the original Billy, was handed the lyrics on a five-foot-long sheet of paper.) *Oklahoma!* used a dream ballet to convey mood; *Carousel* used one, again choreographed by Agnes de Mille, to

Carousel, based on the play *Liliom* and directed by Rouben Mamoulian, transferred the play's Budapest setting to late-nineteenth-century Maine.

DATES:

April 19, 1945–May 24, 1947 at the Majestic Theater (890 performances)

SYNOPSIS:

A New England carnival barker named Billy Bigelow falls hard for Julie Jordan, but their relationship is cut tragically short by circumstances and by Billy's own decisions. It takes the intervention of a heavenly Starkeeper to give Billy and his broken family a second chance.

AWARDS:

None

NOTED REVIVALS AND ADAPTATIONS:

Broadway revivals in 1949 and 1994; movie version in 1956; TV version in 1967

ORIGINAL STARS:

John Raitt, Jan Clayton, Christine Johnson

actually introduce a major character. Sondheim later said that the extended opening "bench scene," in which the lead characters fall in love, was "probably the single most important moment in the revolution of contemporary

musicals." And those innovations don't even include the fact that Billy is a womanizer and a wifebeater.

But even if *Carousel* hadn't moved the art form an inch, the sheer force of its score would provide ample reward. Musical rationalizations don't get any sadder than "What's the Use of Wond'rin'?," and lyrics don't get any kinder than "When today is a long time ago / You'll still hear me say / That the best dream I know is you" (from "When the Children Are Asleep"). Throw in a truly throat-catching finale in "You'll Never Walk Alone," and it becomes clear why Ferenc Molnár—the author of the source material, the 1909 play *Liliom*—allowed Rodgers and Hammerstein to adapt the piece after refusing Giacomo Puccini and Kurt Weill.

Of the "Big Five" Rodgers and Hammerstein musicals, *Carousel* had the shortest run by a wide margin. In this writer's opinion, it is also the best of the five by no less wide of a margin.

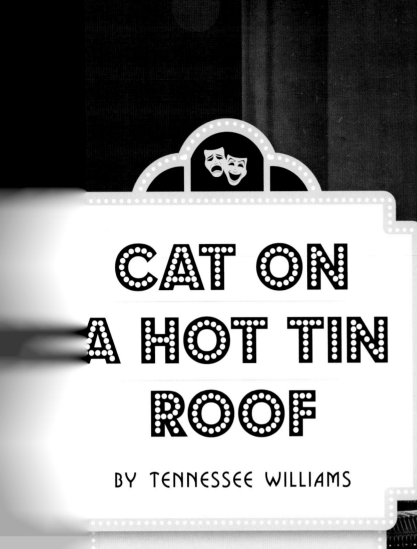

CAT ON A HOT TIN ROOF

BY TENNESSEE WILLIAMS

DATES:
March 24, 1955–November 17, 1956 at the Morosco Theater (694 performances)

SYNOPSIS:
Tempers and (with one notable exception) passions run high at Big Daddy Pollitt's Mississippi estate. Beloved son Brick is drinking himself to death, and Brick's wife Maggie is desperate to get pregnant; both share a murky sexual past with Brick's friend Skipper. Big Daddy himself might not be long for this world.

AWARDS:
Pulitzer Prize

NOTED REVIVALS AND ADAPTATIONS:
Broadway revivals in 1974, 1990, 2003, 2008, and 2013; movie version in 1958; TV versions in 1976 and 1984

ORIGINAL STARS:
Barbara Bel Geddes, Ben Gazzara, Burl Ives, Mildred Dunnock

Playwrights are often not to be trusted when it comes to naming their own favorite works, but it's hard to second-guess Tennessee Williams' choice: *Cat on a Hot Tin Roof*. Still, that hasn't stopped plenty of people from trying to fix what was anything but broken.

Elia Kazan, the original director, was known for putting his playwrights through their paces, and he successfully lobbied for an entirely new, redemption-heavy Act III. (Kazan, coming off a massive success with the film *On the Waterfront*, had considerable leverage over Williams, who was reeling from 1953's dismally received *Camino Real*.) Yet Kazan's changes paled in comparison to those mandated for the 1958 film adaptation, in

ABOVE: In addition to his prolific stage and film career, Burl Ives, a folk singer, recorded more than one hundred albums and had a repertoire of over three thousand traditional ballads.

OPPOSITE PAGE: Ben Gazzara and Barbara Bel Geddes as Brick and Maggie the Cat in the original production. Brick, a one-time football star, has injured his ankle while jumping hurdles on the high school athletic field.

which the central theme of Brick's homosexuality was all but ignored. Williams reportedly begged audiences lining up at the movie box office to go home.

He got his revenge in 1974 during a regional production of the play in Connecticut. Williams dove back into his original notes, even granting the actors license to sift through his drafts and suggest additions. To this day, revivals that use the 1974 text will elicit gasps of surprise from theatergoers used to the earlier versions.

Even in *Cat*'s various expurgated forms, Brick's closeted homosexuality was pretty racy stuff for the 1950s; it's worth noting that both the original Broadway production and the blockbuster film came up empty on awards night, despite receiving a combined ten Tony and Academy Award nominations. The Pulitzer Prize, which *Cat* did win, only came about when the chairman of the Pulitzer board cajoled his peers into shifting their support away from Clifford Odets' *The Flowering Peach*.

The main roles—thunderous Big Daddy, tremulous Big Mama, sultry Maggie, sodden Brick, even black-sheep relatives Gooper and Mae—are absurdly rich morsels for actors of all stripes. Maggie the Cat, in particular, has proven fruitful for the negligee-clad likes of Kathleen Turner, Elizabeth Taylor, Sanaa Lathan, Scarlett Johansson, Natalie Wood, Kim Stanley, Jessica Lange, Elizabeth Ashley, and many others.

With three Broadway revivals in the last twelve years, public opinion seems to have caught up with Williams.

CATS

BY ANDREW LLOYD WEBBER AND (POSTHUMOUSLY) T. S. ELIOT

DATES:
October 7, 1982–September 10, 2000 at the Winter Garden Theater (7,485 performances)

SYNOPSIS:
A gaggle of cats gathers in a junkyard to see who will be chosen to ascend to the Heaviside Layer (i.e., heaven). Will it be Rum Tum Tugger or Bustopher Jones? Mungojerrie or Munkustrap? Grizabella or Skimbleshanks?

AWARDS:
7 Tony Awards

NOTED REVIVALS AND ADAPTATIONS:
TV version in 1998

ORIGINAL STARS:
Betty Buckley, Terrence Mann, Harry Groener, Ken Page, Stephen Hanan

"Now and Forever." Over the eighteen years during which *Cats* ran on Broadway, that tagline struck some as a promise and some as a threat. Here are three of the many, many people for whom the former applied.

Marlene Danielle grew up in a West Village railroad flat with her mother and sister. The rent was $35 a month, and the three of them slept in bunk beds. She became an actress, spent a few years in France, had a son, came back to New York, and finally got hired in a handful of shows, even understudying Debbie Allen in a *West Side Story* revival. But the jobs never lasted more than a few months. Danielle had just received her final unemployment check when she landed *Cats*, again as an understudy—this time for several characters. When one of those roles (the glamorous Bombalurina) became available in 1984, the part was hers. It stayed hers until the final performance, some seven thousand shows later.

Valerie Eliot, T. S. Eliot's widow, gave Andrew Lloyd Webber permission to adapt the poems from her husband's 1939 collection *Old Possum's Book of Practical Cats* for the stage, on the condition that the text consist solely of Eliot's poems, with no explanatory dialogue. Now, the process of writing a musical usually involves extensive changes to the book, lyrics, and music, but two of those were off limits. You can't change what you don't have in the first place, and T. S. Eliot was not available for rewrites. Valerie did provide some unpublished verses, including one that paved the way for the immortal song "Memory." The royalties from *Cats* allowed her to set up an arts charity called Old Possum's Practical Trust.

OPPOSITE PAGE: The cats on Broadway. Among the actors who have played Grizabella are Betty Buckley, Elaine Paige, Lea Salonga, and Stephanie J. Block. Judi Dench was cast in the role for the original West End production but was injured during rehearsals and had to leave the production.

BELOW: John Napier won the Tony for Best Costume Design for his work on *Cats*. (Other Tonys went to the musical itself, Andrew Lloyd Webber, Betty Buckley, Trevor Nunn, David Hersey for lighting, and, posthumously, T. S. Eliot, who won the award for Best Book of a Musical.)

John Scanlan, my grandfather, was an actor who never appeared in *Cats* or saw a dime from it. During its record-breaking run, he was starring in regional productions of *The Gin Game* and *A Christmas Carol* and taking the occasional bit part in movies. By 1993, his energies were waning; his last stage appearance, a Shakespeare in the Park production of *As You Like It* in 1992, featured him being carried onto the stage. A year later, he and I attended our first show together. It was *Cats*. He recoiled with delight when one cat wriggled past him. (It might have been Bombalurina.) He couldn't stop talking about the performers' stamina. "So much energy," he said more than once. *Cats* was also the last show we attended together: while the musical had many more years left in it at the time, my grandfather did not. Years later, after Danielle and the rest of the cast took their last bow, the show's props were publicly auctioned off. I purchased an oversize cigarette box. It is the only piece of theater memorabilia I own.

CHARLEY'S AUNT

BY BRANDON THOMAS

DATES:
Opened October 2, 1893 at the Standard Theater (closing date not known)

SYNOPSIS:
Oxford undergraduates Charley Wykeham and Jack Chesney have no chance of making time with their lady friends without a chaperone. Luckily, their friend Lord Fancourt Babberley has come into possession of a dowager costume and can pass (sort of) as the title character, Donna Lucia d'Alvadorez. Unluckily, the real Donna Lucia is on her way.

AWARDS:
None

NOTED REVIVALS AND ADAPTATIONS:
Broadway revivals in 1906, 1925, 1940, 1953, and 1970; movie versions in 1915, 1925, 1930, 1940, and 1941

ORIGINAL STAR:
Etienne Girardot

ETIENNE GIRARDOT

AS

CHARLEY'S AUNT

It's hard to lament the fading of fox hunts as a pastime, yet the local hunt of Bury St. Edmunds in West Suffolk, England, could proudly take credit for at least one achievement. It commissioned a play each year for its annual "Hunt Bespeak," and 1892's offering was *Charley's Aunt*, which Brandon Thomas wrote as a vehicle for a D'Oyly Carte Opera Company veteran named W. S. Penley. Before the year was out, the farce had toured England and settled into what would become an unprecedented four-year London run. Penley's performance as Babberley/Donna Lucia came to be the talk of the town. (At the risk of sounding catty, the fact that Penley was in his forties when he assumed the role might have helped his college-age character's subterfuge as a dowager.)

By that point, Thomas had joined the cast. Penley, meanwhile, had a renewable seven-year contract as producer of the play. Legal squabbles between the two over royalties and Penley's liberties with the text scuttled a planned American run in 1898, and

ABOVE: Ray Bolger played the title character in *Where's Charley?* The original Broadway production, directed by George Abbott and choreographed by George Balanchine, ran for 792 performances.

OPPOSITE PAGE: Etienne Girardot as Lord Fancourt Babberley in *Charley's Aunt*, 1906. *Library of Congress*

Thomas and New York producer Charles Frohman contracted London-born actor Etienne Girardot to play Babberley on Broadway. It was a hit there, too, though accounts vary as to just how big of a hit. The most dependable accounts put it at about two hundred performances.

Charley's Aunt gets extra points for spawning Frank Loesser and George Abbott's sparkling 1948 musical

Where's Charley? Like *My Fair Lady, Carousel,* and *The Producers,* it's a show that's not afraid of either borrowing heavily from its source material or boldly rejiggering it. Turning one of the two suitors into the cross-dresser boosted the farcical possibilities considerably. Ray Bolger's performance as the title character—both title characters, actually—literally stopped the show: audiences demanded that he sing his charming "Once in Love With Amy" a second time, and then joined in.

Bolger was also in his forties at the time. Given the material, in which middle-aged men can play college students passing as middle-aged women, suspension of disbelief appears to be a nonissue with all things *Charley's Aunt.* At the end of the 1952 movie of *Where's Charley?,* the cast members come out for "curtain calls."

CHICAGO

BY JOHN KANDER, FRED EBB, AND BOB FOSSE

DATES:
June 3, 1975–August 27, 1977 at the 46th
Street Theater (936 performances)

SYNOPSIS:
Can the slickster lawyer Billy Flynn keep
Roxie Hart and Velma Kelly out of the
gallows—and in the spotlight? Are the front
pages of Chicago's papers big enough for
two murderous showgirls? Ain't there no
decency left?

AWARDS:
None

NOTED REVIVALS AND ADAPTATIONS:
Broadway revival in 1996; movie version in
2002

ORIGINAL STARS:
Gwen Verdon, Chita Rivera, Jerry Orbach,
Barney Martin

How does one of the losingest shows in Tony Awards history become the most popular revival in Broadway history? Bob Fosse was never one for half measures, and *Chicago*—which bears his visual and philosophical signature more than any other show—encapsulates his swing-for-the-fences view of life, show business, and the folly of trying to separate the two.

Fosse spent years trying to get the stage rights to *Chicago* from journalist Maurine Dallas Watkins, who covered a pair of high-profile Windy City murder trials in the 1920s and (with the help of director George Abbott) turned her experiences into a popular play. But Watkins had become a born-again Christian, and she fended Fosse off; it wasn't until after her death in 1969 that her estate agreed to sell the rights.

It's not hard to see why Watkins soured on the material. Deeply, even ostentatiously cynical, *Chicago* hammers home the notion that everything, and everyone, in Cook County is for sale. "If Jesus Christ lived in Chicago today," crows the slick lawyer Billy Flynn, "and he had come to me and he had five thousand dollars, let's just say things would have turned out differently." Fosse didn't need a shyster lawyer; he had the perfect Roxie Hart in his wife, Gwen Verdon, and the perfect songwriting team in John Kander and Fred Ebb, who had just joined Fosse in reimagining *Cabaret* for the smashingly effective film version.

Fosse had a heart attack during rehearsals—and returned angrier than ever. ("I'm going to make this darker and meaner," he said during the show's Philadelphia tryout.) Then it was Verdon's turn to be hospitalized, after a freak onstage incident required emergency vocal cord surgery, although this actually became a windfall for the show when Liza Minnelli did her *Cabaret* team a favor and took over as Roxie for a month. Finally, *Chicago* had the bad luck of opening just a few weeks before *A Chorus Line*, the biggest musical of the decade. It lost all nine of the Tony Awards for which it was nominated, with Fosse, Kander, Ebb, Verdon, and her costar Chita Rivera all going home empty-handed.

Chicago nonetheless stuck around for 936 performances—which looks like a healthy run until you compare it with its first and only Broadway revival. That production opened during the Clinton administration, and it's still razzle-dazzling audiences. The bare-bones staging, which began as part of the acclaimed Encores! series of staged concerts, starred two women with rock-solid Fosse credentials—Ann Reinking and Bebe Neuwirth—before degenerating into an endless series of stunt casting. (Christie Brinkley! Melanie Griffith! Ashlee Simpson!) The enormously profitable results continue to prove Billy Flynn right: there's no such thing as bad publicity.

THE CHILDREN'S HOUR

BY LILLIAN HELLMAN

Robert Keith, Anne Revere, Florence McGee, Katherine Emery, and Katherine Emmett in the original production of *The Children's Hour*. Hellman based her play on an early-nineteenth-century incident in Edinburgh, Scotland, when a boarding school student accused her teachers of having an affair.

Nearly every major theater award is cloaked in secrecy, with one exception: the New York Drama Critics Circle Award. For the last decade or so, each member's vote has been tabulated and, within hours, posted on the website for all to see. This group officially formed in 1935, boasting the voluble likes of Walter Winchell and Robert Benchley; it was largely established in response to the Pulitzer Prize committee and its inscrutable ways. The final straw appears to have come that year, when *The Old Maid*, adapted from Edith Wharton, won the Pulitzer over Lillian Hellman's scandalous drama *The Children's Hour*.

Far better known from its film versions, Hellman's play—her first, and the one that quickly made her a literary celebrity—instantly set tongues wagging. Her boyfriend at the time, detective novelist Dashiell Hammett, steered her toward an early-nineteenth-century scandal, when two Scottish headmistresses were accused of having an affair. The women took their case to court and won, but by that point, their school had been all but abandoned.

More than one hundred years later, homosexuality was still illegal to depict—or even discuss—on stage in New York, though the law seems not to have been enforced in the case of *The Children's Hour*. When Hellman signed on to write the screenplay for the 1936 film version, she didn't even bat an eye when asked to completely expunge any mention of lesbianism. (The rumors became about one teacher sleeping with the other's fiancé.) Not even the play's title would get past the Production Code—it went by *These Three* instead.

Why was Hellman so cavalier in making the changes? She was prescient in seeing how the specifics of the accusation paled in comparison to the accusation itself—and to the susceptibility of those within earshot. The date of the play's only Broadway revival thus far is instructive: it opened in December 1952, just a month after Senator Joseph McCarthy was re-elected on the wave of his much-publicized "list" of Communists working in the US government, and just a month before Arthur Miller's *The Crucible* opened. Hellman had clearly understood just how loud whispers could become.

DATES:
November 20, 1934–July 1936 at Maxine Elliott's Theater (691 performances)

SYNOPSIS:
Accusations engulf an all-girls school when one pupil accuses her two headmistresses of carrying on a lesbian affair.

AWARDS:
None

NOTED REVIVALS AND ADAPTATIONS:
Broadway revival in 1952; movie versions in 1936 and 1961

ORIGINAL STARS:
Katherine Emery, Anne Revere, Florence McGee

The 1952 Broadway revival, at the Coronet Theater, starred Patricia Neal as Martha Dobie and Kim Hunter as Karen Wright. Hellman staged the production.

A CHORUS LINE

BY MARVIN HAMLISCH, EDWARD KLEBAN, JAMES KIRKWOOD JR., AND NICHOLAS DANTE

ABOVE: *A Chorus Line* dancers (a replacement cast during the fifteen-year original Broadway run) perform "One."

RIGHT: Michael Bennett with the *Chorus Line* cast in rehearsal. Bennett had choreographed *Promises, Promises, Company,* and *Follies* by the time he developed, directed, and choreographed *A Chorus Line.*

DATES:
July 25, 1975–April 28, 1990 at the Shubert Theater (6,137 performances)

SYNOPSIS:
Seventeen aspiring dancers are asked/forced to talk about themselves while auditioning for a Broadway musical. Only eight will be chosen.

AWARDS:
9 Tony Awards; Pulitzer Prize

NOTED REVIVALS AND ADAPTATIONS:
Broadway revival in 2006; movie version in 1985

ORIGINAL STARS:
Donna McKechnie, Robert LuPone, Kelly Bishop, Priscilla Lopez, Sammy Williams

Depending on whom you talk to, *A Chorus Line* is the show that saved Broadway, saved the Public Theater, turned finessing the *New York Times* into an art form, or did all of the above.

First, the least important of these claims: a possibly-but-probably-not apocryphal story holds that director/choreographer/mastermind Michael Bennett went with the name *A Chorus Line* instead of just *Chorus Line* so that the "A" would put it first in the *Times*' alphabetical listings of shows. (Bennett was in a bit of a directorial dogfight with Bob Fosse at the time, and without that "A," Fosse's project at the time—*Chicago*—would have landed just above *Chorus Line*.)

Bennett, along with such former collaborators as Harold Prince and Stephen Sondheim, was at the forefront of creating what has become known as the "concept musicals." These are shows in which the interweaving of dance, music, and text works in the service of an overarching metaphor or concept; there is no conventional plot. Bennett knew he had a concept worth developing when he was invited to sit in on a series of tape-recorded workshop discussions with a group of Broadway dancers. James Kirkwood Jr. and Nicholas Dante adapted the reminiscences into monologues, and soon Bennett had brought eight of the participants into more formalized rehearsals.

Joe Papp at the Public Theater offered space, money, and, most important, a lengthy period of time to develop the project. Soon Marvin Hamlisch—fresh off winning three Oscars in 1974, when he was still in his twenties—was writing melodies like "One," "What I Did for Love" (which one of the show's creators, lyricist Edward Kleban, found maudlin and unnecessary), and "The Music and the Mirror," a nine-minute solo tour de force for Bennett's peerless muse, Donna McKechnie.

The 101 Public performances were sold out well before opening night. Exactly three months later, *A Chorus Line* transferred to Broadway's Shubert Theater, where it would stay for the next fifteen years. Bennett's dizzying blend of cinematic techniques and song-and-dance verve set a new standard for directorial seamlessness, and the show has served as a paycheck, as well as a promise, for dancers around the world. *A Chorus Line* may end with a once-again anonymous group kicking in unison (and, given Bennett's decision to bring the curtain down mid-dance, seemingly in perpetuity) behind an unseen star. But though they fade back into being just "One," they are and always will be a great many.

The seventeen auditionees are told that four women and four men will make the final cut.

CITY OF ANGELS

BY CY COLEMAN, DAVID ZIPPEL, AND LARRY GELBART

DATES:
December 11, 1989–January 19, 1992 at the Virginia Theater (879 performances)

SYNOPSIS:
Hapless novelist Stine struggles to bring his hardboiled detective character, Stone, to the silver screen in 1940s Hollywood. Stine's travails (lots of rewrites) and those of his creation (lots of beatings) begin to overlap, until Stone finally bursts from the page to confront his creator.

AWARDS:
6 Tony Awards

NOTED REVIVALS AND ADAPTATIONS:
None

ORIGINAL STARS:
Gregg Edelman, James Naughton, Randy Graff, Dee Hoty, Rachel York

Jazz and Broadway have had a complicated, only partially requited love affair from the beginning. Jazz musicians have long treated the standards of musical theater as a melodic sandbox, from Miles Davis' atmospheric subversions of the *Porgy and Bess* score to John Coltrane's hopscotching riffs on "My Favorite Things" to the Trotter Trio's repeated forays into the Sondheim canon. When the touring circuit was less entrenched, top jazz names like Wynton Marsalis and Hank Jones spent time playing in Broadway pit orchestras.

But during much of its history, Broadway has regarded jazz primarily as a way to repackage preexisting material, often with a racial overlay to the packaging. (Titles like *The Swing Mikado* practically use "swing" as code for "black.") It wasn't until 1989 that a seasoned Broadway hand delivered an original jazz score to the stage.

That man was Cy Coleman, who had already done time as a jazz pianist as well as a Broadway composer (*Sweet Charity*, *Little Me*). His swinging score to *City of Angels* was easy to overlook at the time, surrounded as it was by a whip-smart book by Larry Gelbart (my pick for the funniest bookwriter in Broadway history, with apologies to Michael Stewart and George S. Kaufman); comparably ear-catching lyrics by a newcomer, David Zippel; and a mesmerizing production, during which

Michael Blakemore and his wizardly design team depicted half of the action in color and half in film noir–style black and white.

Time, however, has proven extremely kind to noir-drenched ballads like "With Every Breath I Take" and "Lost and Found." The jazz community had embraced Coleman's pop standards as far back as the 1950s ("Witchcraft" and "The Best Is Yet to Come" among them); if his heavenly *City of Angels* score had debuted a decade or two earlier, big chunks of it would sit very comfortably alongside those timeless tunes in the Great American Songbook. That was his loss, but it is also ours.

OPPOSITE PAGE: James Naughton (the detective Stone) and Gregg Edelman (the novelist Stine) in *City of Angels*.

BELOW: Both Dee Hoty and Randy Graff played dual roles in the original production.

CLYBOURNE PARK

BY BRUCE NORRIS

The first act of *Clybourne Park* takes place in 1959. From left, Christina Kirk, Jeremy Shamos, Annie Parisse, Brendan Griffin, Damon Gupton, and Crystal A. Dickinson in the 2010 off-Broadway production at Playwrights Horizons. © *Joan Marcus*

There's an old joke that makes many actors wince with recognition. A guy gets hired to play the gravedigger in *Hamlet*, and when he's asked about the play, he says, "It's about a gravedigger whose life is changed when he meets this prince."

The viewpoint-flipping strategy has yielded some surprisingly durable pieces of theater, among them *Wicked* (about this witch whose life changes when her sister gets crushed by a girl's house) and *Rosencrantz and Guildenstern Are Dead* (about these two classmates whose lives end after they reconnect with the same guy that gravedigger met). *Clybourne Park* is a little different. It owes its existence to Lorraine Hansberry's *A Raisin in the Sun*, and many theaters have programmed the two plays side by side (*see entry on* A Raisin in the Sun). But for every *Clybourne* audience member who chuckles knowingly at the arrival of Karl Linder, the earlier play's villain, there seem to be just as many who don't know the first thing about *Raisin*. And both sets appear to enjoy *Clybourne* about the same.

DATES:

April 19–September 2, 2012 at the Walter Kerr Theater (157 performances)

SYNOPSIS:

A working-class home in Chicago is seen in two different eras: first in 1959, as a white family is unwittingly about to sell the home to an African American family, and then in 2009, when a white couple is looking to move into the now predominantly black neighborhood.

AWARDS:

1 Tony Award; Pulitzer Prize

NOTED REVIVALS AND ADAPTATIONS:

None

ORIGINAL STARS:

Jeremy Shamos, Crystal A. Dickinson, Damon Gupton, Christina Kirk, Annie Parisse, Frank Wood

Perhaps "enjoy" isn't quite the right word. Bruce Norris, who saw the film of *Raisin* in junior high school and realized that he came from a background similar to the largely unseen antagonists, forces us to ask some very tricky questions about race and resentment, both then and now. "It is a play for white people," he once said, yet it plays better in front of a mixed-race audience "because it makes white people even more uncomfortable."

Jeremy Shamos, who memorably created the roles of two loathsome men (including Karl Linder, the only *Raisin* carryover) with uncomfortably valid opinions, told me once that *Clybourne Park*'s greatest strength is that everyone in it makes sound points—and then keeps talking for several sentences after he or she should have stopped. This might be a recipe for bad neighbors, and we see plenty of those in *Clybourne Park*. But it also makes for very, very good theater. It certainly makes for the funniest and probably best play to reach Broadway so far this century.

The second act is set in the same home, fifty years later. From left, Gupton, Dickinson, Parisse, and Shamos. © *Joan Marcus*

COMPANY

BY STEPHEN SONDHEIM AND GEORGE FURTH

DATES:
April 26, 1970–January 1, 1972 at the Alvin Theater (705 performances)

SYNOPSIS:
It's Bobby's thirty-fifth birthday, and his married friends have gathered to surprise him. So, when will Bobby settle down and join their ranks? Are any of those girls he's been seeing good enough for him? And where is he, anyway?

AWARDS:
6 Tony Awards

NOTED REVIVALS AND ADAPTATIONS:
Broadway revivals in 1995 and 2006; TV versions in 2007 and 2011

ORIGINAL STARS:
Dean Jones (briefly), Larry Kert, Elaine Stritch, Susan Browning, Donna McKechnie

When *Company* came along in 1970, laying waste to decades' worth of traditions and tendencies, it gave Broadway something it had rarely encountered in a musical: ambivalence. Bobby, the thirty-five-year-old bachelor at its center, as well as virtually every one of his "good and crazy" friends pinwheel between conflicting emotions and desires. Bobby asks his male pals whether marriage is worth the complications; their response is "Sorry-Grateful." The women get cold feet at the altar ("Getting Married Today"), vacillate about whether to skip work ("Barcelona"), and realize too late that their vodka-fueled contempt is aimed at themselves more than at their fellow "Ladies Who Lunch." An early version of Bobby's final song, "Being Alive," used as its title a perfect distillation of this skittish intimacy: "Marry Me a Little."

Nothing in Stephen Sondheim's Playbill bio thus far had prepared audiences for the scouring, virtuosic material he and George Furth put together. Lyrics that rhyme "personable" with "coercin' a bull"? Mile-a-minute patter songs, including one about a bride floating in the Hudson River with the other garbage? Songs that comment on the (in)action with a Brechtian sense of distance? (Actually, director Harold Prince had prepared audiences for that four years earlier with *Cabaret*.) Many kept Sondheim and his jaded, unsettling worldview at arm's length. "I left *Company* feeling rather cool and queasy," Walter Kerr wrote in the *New York Sunday Times*, "whatever splendors my head may have been reminding me of."

The nonlinear structure stemmed in part from Sondheim's realization that the men and women in *Company* are the

OPPOSITE PAGE: Dean Jones as Robert, with the cast of *Company*.

BELOW: From left (standing), George Coe, Charles Braswell, Beth Howland, Larry Kert, Teri Ralston, Charles Kimbrough, Barbara Barrie, and John Cunningham with, seated, Elaine Stritch and Merle Louise in the original Broadway production of *Company*. Kert, who had created the role of Tony in *West Side Story*, replaced Jones after only two weeks.

kinds of people who don't sing. So, what are they doing in a musical? And why can't they just relax and try to enjoy themselves? (If it's any consolation to them, the show hasn't always been easy on the people in it. Dean Jones, the original Bobby, was going through a divorce and had to be begged to stay through opening night and the cast recording. Speaking of that recording, which was turned into the marvelous documentary *Original Cast Album: Company*, fans of Elaine Stritch's flinty, no-bullshit style will find the sequence devoted to her *many* takes of "The Ladies Who Lunch" to be excruciatingly essential viewing.)

Well, to quote Prince, "Who says you can't do plays about empty vessels? The world is full of walking empty vessels." By boldly plunking such a character in its center, *Company* allowed its gifted young creators (including the peerless orchestrator Jonathan Tunick) to flood the stage with wit, rage, and a kind of astringent lyricism that still leaves traces almost a half-century later.

THE CRUCIBLE

BY ARTHUR MILLER

Arthur Kennedy (John Proctor) and Beatrice Straight (Elizabeth Proctor) in *The Crucible*, 1953. Kennedy was also in the original Broadway productions of the Arthur Miller works *All My Sons*, *Death of a Salesman*, and *The Price*.

"**I** have seen too many frightful proofs in court— the Devil is alive in Salem, and we dare not quail to follow wherever the accusing finger points!"

First off, Arthur Miller was neither a pioneer nor a historian when it came to telling the tale of the Salem witch trials of 1692. He did his share of homework, but not nearly as much as a slew of scholars had before him. Those so inclined can find fault with any number of factual glitches in *The Crucible*, from the archaic speech patterns to the love-triangle-friendly ages of John Proctor, the play's flawed hero, and Abigail Williams, its central accuser. (The real Abigail wasn't even a teenager at the time of the trials, while Proctor was actually in his sixties.)

Yet Miller got an incredible amount right in his unsparing morality play—about the events three hundred years earlier *and* about the Communist witch hunt unspooling around him in 1953. This had taken on personal significance a year earlier when his *Death of a Salesman* director, Elia Kazan, named Clifford Odets and seven other members of the influential

The 2002 revival at the Virginia Theater starred Liam Neeson, left, as John, and Laura Linney as Elizabeth. Right of Neeson is Brian Murray (Deputy Governor Danforth). © Joan Marcus

DATES:
January 22–July 11, 1953 at the Martin Beck Theater (197 performances)

SYNOPSIS:
An affair between the upstanding John Proctor and conniving Abigail Williams in seventeenth-century Salem, Massachusetts, results in Proctor's wife being accused of witchcraft. Before long, more than a dozen townspeople are dead.

AWARDS:
2 Tony Awards

NOTED REVIVALS AND ADAPTATIONS:
Broadway revivals in 1964, 1972, 1991, and 2002; movie versions in 1957, 1958, and 1996

ORIGINAL STARS:
Arthur Kennedy, Beatrice Straight, Walter Hampden, Madeleine Sherwood

Group Theater in front of the House Un-American Activities Committee.

Miller and Kazan wouldn't speak to each other for a decade. Their artistic output, however, spoke volumes. In rapid succession came *The Crucible*, in which innocent men and women are hanged and literally crushed by a tribunal; the 1954 film *On the Waterfront*, Kazan's defense of informing as a moral act; and Miller's fascinating 1955 play *A View from the Bridge*, which takes a far more nuanced position than either of the previous works, depicting the central informant as a principled but damaged—and ultimately tragic—figure.

Critic Eric Bentley wrote that "one never knows what a Miller play is about: politics or sex." *The Crucible* never asks us to choose. The nightmarish web of accusations and deaths is woven as much out of John Proctor's affair with Abigail as it is from moonlight dances in the forest and petty skirmishes over land rights. "There are wheels within wheels in this village, and fires within fires!" cries one character. In *The Crucible*, the wheels turn as inexorably as the ones that threatened Miller (who was refused a routine passport renewal to attend the play's London premiere). The fires are why it is still relevant today.

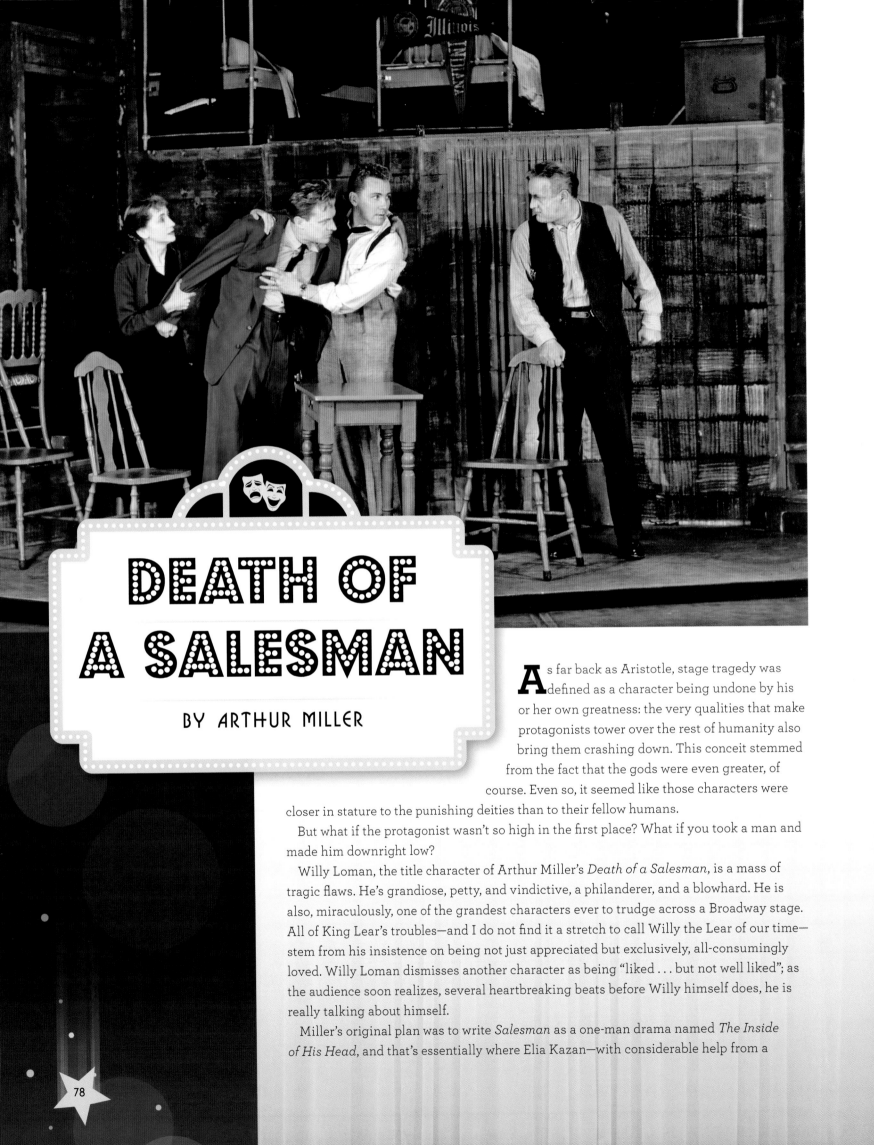

DEATH OF A SALESMAN

BY ARTHUR MILLER

As far back as Aristotle, stage tragedy was defined as a character being undone by his or her own greatness: the very qualities that make protagonists tower over the rest of humanity also bring them crashing down. This conceit stemmed from the fact that the gods were even greater, of course. Even so, it seemed like those characters were closer in stature to the punishing deities than to their fellow humans.

But what if the protagonist wasn't so high in the first place? What if you took a man and made him downright low?

Willy Loman, the title character of Arthur Miller's *Death of a Salesman*, is a mass of tragic flaws. He's grandiose, petty, and vindictive, a philanderer, and a blowhard. He is also, miraculously, one of the grandest characters ever to trudge across a Broadway stage. All of King Lear's troubles—and I do not find it a stretch to call Willy the Lear of our time—stem from his insistence on being not just appreciated but exclusively, all-consumingly loved. Willy Loman dismisses another character as being "liked . . . but not well liked"; as the audience soon realizes, several heartbreaking beats before Willy himself does, he is really talking about himself.

Miller's original plan was to write *Salesman* as a one-man drama named *The Inside of His Head*, and that's essentially where Elia Kazan—with considerable help from a

DATES:

February 10, 1949–November 18, 1950 at the Morosco Theater (742 performances)

SYNOPSIS:

After thirty-four years on the road, Willy Loman is slowing down. He basks in the glow of his two sons, refusing to acknowledge how damaged they are; suffers multiple indignities at work; and lashes out at anyone who tries to help him. Only a $20,000 insurance policy offers hope for the rest of the family.

AWARDS:

6 Tony Awards; Pulitzer Prize

NOTED REVIVALS AND ADAPTATIONS:

Broadway revivals in 1975, 1984, 1999, and 2012; movie version in 1951; TV versions in 1966, 1985, and 2000

ORIGINAL STARS:

Lee J. Cobb, Mildred Dunnock, Arthur Kennedy, Cameron Mitchell

creative team that included set and lighting designer Jo Mielziner—set the play, in a dazzling kitchen-sink-meets-the-cosmos conception. That head is a wonderful place to be. It is at once mesmerizing and infuriating, and it has attracted the likes of Dustin Hoffman, George C. Scott, and Philip Seymour Hoffman. (And that's not even mentioning the phenomenal performers who have tackled the roles of Willy's long-suffering wife Linda and tormented son Biff.) It's widely acknowledged that actors like to make sure they play Hamlet before they're too old, and then stick around the stage long enough for Lear. Between that prince and that king, a sixty-three-year-old traveling salesman from Brooklyn is waiting for them.

OPPOSITE PAGE: Mildred Dunnock (Linda Loman), Arthur Kennedy (Biff), Cameron Mitchell (Happy), and Lee J. Cobb (Willy Loman) in the original production.

BELOW: Jo Mielziner's groundbreaking set did away with solid boundaries, creating a skeletal space dwarfed by the apartment buildings looming in the background.

A DELICATE BALANCE

BY EDWARD ALBEE

Jessica Tandy (Agnes) and Hume Cronyn (Tobias) in
A Delicate Balance, 1966. Other actresses who have played
Agnes include Rosemary Harris, Katharine Hepburn, Eileen
Atkins, and Glenn Close. Tobias has been played by George
Grizzard, Paul Scofield, John Standing, and John Lithgow.

Elaine Stritch (as Claire, Agnes' sister) and George Grizzard in the 1996 Broadway revival of *A Delicate Balance*, which ran for 185 performances at the Plymouth Theater. © Joan Marcus

Ifirst read *A Delicate Balance* in my early twenties, and I couldn't decide whether I adored it or hated it. I had just moved to New York, not exactly fleeing the suburbs but certainly putting some distance between me and them. The idea of a well-heeled couple practically chaining themselves to a suburban manse made no emotional or theatrical sense to me. The fact that Albee's script deploys some of the most dogmatic, micromanaging stage directions since Eugene O'Neill didn't help the reading experience, either.

It took the 1996 Broadway revival, with its cast steeped in Albee's rhapsodic, biting style, to shift me firmly into the "adore it" camp. More than three decades earlier, Elaine Stritch had been hired to give Uta Hagen the matinees off during the original run of *Who's Afraid of Virginia Woolf?* George Grizzard, meanwhile, had done all of the *Virginia Woolf* performances. (The bug also bit such Albee newbies as Rosemary Harris and Mary Beth Hurt, who have gone on to tackle more of his plays since appearing in that 1996 revival.)

DATES:

September 22, 1966–January 14, 1967 at the Martin Beck Theater (132 performances)

SYNOPSIS:

An affluent suburban couple's typical evening of martinis and erudite verbiage is interrupted by an insistent—and, it turns out, indefinite—request from their neighbors to move in. What are the neighbors trying to escape? And will the couple's home really offer a refuge?

AWARDS:

1 Tony Award; Pulitzer Prize

NOTED REVIVALS AND ADAPTATIONS:

Broadway revivals in 1996 and 2014; movie version in 1973

ORIGINAL STARS:

Hume Cronyn, Jessica Tandy, Rosemary Murphy, Marian Seldes

Subsequent Albee works would give us talking lizards, fractured timelines, and man-goat relationships. But in *A Delicate Balance*, Albee rooted his singular oddness in the most anodyne of settings: a beautifully appointed living room, straight from the fizzy 1930s drawing-room comedies of, say, S. N. Behrman or Philip Barry. The long-married Tobias and Agnes are surrounded by character types that could have swanned over from *The Philadelphia Story*: the tippling sister, the quirky neighbors, the pouty daughter. (The effect would have been even more pronounced if Albee had succeeded in casting the reigning stage couple from that earlier era, Alfred Lunt and Lynn Fontanne, as Tobias and Agnes. But Lunt and Fontanne insisted on a shorter run and a London premiere, neither of which the producers wanted; another married couple, Hume Cronyn and Jessica Tandy, was cast.)

But not so fast. The existential terror that descends on this impeccable home in the form of those persistent neighbors speaks to something deeper and, in its own way, more subversive than the matrimonial blood sport of *Virginia Woolf?* As Agnes describes it:

> Time happens, I suppose. To people. Everything becomes . . . too late, finally. You know it's going on . . . up on the hill; you can see the dust, and hear the cries, and the steel . . . but you wait; and time happens. When you *do* go, sword, shield . . . finally . . . there's nothing there . . . save rust; bones; and the wind.

Maybe that's not what one is ready for at the age of twenty-two. Or ever.

THE DIARY OF ANNE FRANK

BY FRANCES GOODRICH AND ALBERT HACKETT

Susan Strasberg as Anne Frank. Strasberg grew up in a theater-royalty household: her father, Lee Strasberg of the Actors Studio, pioneered Method acting.

Meyer Levin is maybe the most famous playwright who never was. An American journalist who founded an experimental marionette theater in Chicago in the 1930s, Levin played a pivotal role in getting Anne Frank's diary published in the United States. After he wrote a glowing review of it in the *New York Times*, he began corresponding with Otto Frank, Anne's father, and then secured the rights to adapt the diary for the stage. That's when things got messy.

Although accounts vary on why Levin's pass at the *Diary of Anne Frank* adaptation was rejected, many contend that his version was deemed too overtly Jewish to appeal to a wider audience. Lillian Hellman and Carson McCullers were among the replacement writers discussed before producers settled on the husband-and-wife team of Albert Hackett and Frances Goodrich, best known for such Hollywood screenplays as the *Thin Man* series. Their result captivated audiences and put Susan Strasberg, who played Anne, on the cover of both *Life* and *Newsweek*.

Anne Frank wrote, "You only really get to know a person after a fight," and by this token, Levin, Goodrich, and Hackett got to know one another very, very well. Levin spent the next thirty years in a morass of conspiracy theories, memoirs, and lawsuits over whose Anne Frank deserved to lodge herself into the world's conscience.

If the producers had opted for Levin's version instead of commissioning a more secular one, would its impact have been muted? If Levin hadn't corresponded with Otto Frank and gotten the stage rights, would we even know who Anne Frank was?

For that matter, if Richard Rodgers and Oscar Hammerstein II hadn't added a new song called "Oklahoma!" to their struggling musical *Away We Go!*—and changed the title accordingly—would their show have been successful enough to change the way we think of the Broadway musical? If Jerome Robbins hadn't attended the out-of-town tryout of *A Funny Thing Happened on the Way to the Forum* and suggested a slapstick opening number, which became "Comedy Tonight," would *that* show have been popular enough to launch the career of its first-time Broadway composer, Stephen Sondheim? Broadway is stuffed with counterfactuals, glimpses of what might or should have been.

But so is everywhere else. On November 3, 1943, a fourteen-year-old girl in Amsterdam, bristling with self-pity after being unfairly scolded by her father, wrote in her diary, "Who else but me is ever going to read these letters?"

DATES:

October 5, 1955–June 22, 1957 at the Cort Theater and Ambassador Theater (717 performances)

SYNOPSIS:

Otto Frank, the only surviving member of his family, returns to the attic in Amsterdam where his family spent more than two years in hiding before being caught by the Nazis. There he finds the diary left by his teenage daughter, Anne. Her entries become the rest of the play.

AWARDS:

1 Tony Award; Pulitzer Prize

NOTED REVIVALS AND ADAPTATIONS:

Broadway revival in 1997; movie version in 1959

ORIGINAL STARS:

Susan Strasberg, Joseph Schildkraut

The original cast included, clockwise from left, Gusti Huber, Joseph Schildkraut, Susan Strasberg, Eva Rubinstein, and Jack Gilford. Garson Kanin (the *Born Yesterday* playwright) directed.

DINNER AT EIGHT

BY GEORGE S. KAUFMAN
AND EDNA FERBER

Constance Collier (Carlotta Vance), left, and Ann Andrews (Millicent Jordan) in *Dinner at Eight*, 1932. George S. Kaufman directed the original Broadway production.

A phrase began to gain traction in the 2000s: "First World problems" points out the absurdity of some inconveniences that only the affluent are lucky enough to be in a position to suffer. One illustrative online Venn diagram featured "hunger," "cholera," and "rape" on one side of the chart, while the other featured "too much goat cheese in salad," "had to park far from door," and "your show isn't in HD."

In October 1932, the Depression had been ravaging America for several years, and the election of Franklin D. Roosevelt was still a month away. It would seem like just about the worst possible time for George S. Kaufman and Edna Ferber to write a play all about a woman's fraying plans for a society dinner. But *Dinner at Eight*, which features

The 2002 revival at the Vivian Beaumont Theater. Christine Ebersole (center, in yellow) played Millicent Jordan and Marian Seldes (center foreground) was Carlotta Vance. © *Joan Marcus*

DATES:

October 22, 1932–May 1933 at the Music Box Theater (232 performances)

SYNOPSIS:

Society dinners are never easy to put together, even without a fading matinee idol, a vulgar mistress, and a romantic maid to contend with. No wonder Millicent Jordan is getting a bit agitated.

AWARDS:

None

NOTED REVIVALS AND ADAPTATIONS:

Broadway revivals in 1966 and 2002; movie version in 1933; TV version in 1989

ORIGINAL STARS:

Ann Andrews, Constance Collier, Conway Tearle, Judith Wood

Millicent Jordan claiming to have had "the most hellish day that anybody ever had" on account of an unsuitable aspic, became a hit in both its stage and screen incarnations. To be fair, the aspic is only the first in a litany of woes that Millicent spills out in one of the stage's greatest slow burns. And part of the play's genius is that legitimate problems—insolvency, alcoholism, and even suicide—gradually creep in without ever hobbling the breezy action (or overshadowing Livingston Platt's sets, among the most opulent that Broadway had seen at the time).

Kaufman moved from project to project quickly—he had directed one Broadway play and contributed to another revue in the seven weeks prior to the *Dinner at Eight* opening. He never seemed to mind too much when Hollywood inevitably had its way with his work. MGM head David O. Selznick had a trio of new screenwriters file away any number of *Dinner*'s rough edges for his stable of stars, which included a pair of Barrymores, John and Lionel; the rising starlet Jean Harlow, who proved a surprisingly dab hand at comedy; and the incomparable Marie Dressler, who had become Hollywood's top box-office star well after her sixtieth birthday.

Still, for a full double-barreled blast of caustic, cynical comedy, Kaufman and Ferber's original *Dinner* plans are hard to beat.

A DOLL'S HOUSE

BY HENRIK IBSEN

A Doll's House originally premiered in Copenhagen in 1879 with, from left, Peter Jerndorff, Betty Hennings (Nora), Agnes Gjørling, and Emil Poulsen (Torvald). Toward the end of Act II, Nora dances the tarantella wildly, "as if it were a matter of life and death," notes another character.

DATES:
Opened December 21, 1889 at Palmer's Theater (number of performances unknown)

SYNOPSIS:
Over the holidays, the seemingly idyllic Helmer family—doting husband Torvald, pampered wife Nora, three adoring children—begins to splinter as facts surface about an illicit loan that Nora took to help an ailing Torvald. These facts force Nora to realize that there may be more to life than being a wife and mother.

AWARDS:
None

NOTED REVIVALS AND ADAPTATIONS:
Broadway revivals in 1894, 1902, 1905, 1907, 1908, 1918, 1937, 1971, 1975, and 1997; movie versions in 1923 and (twice) 1973; TV versions in 1959, 1974, and 1992

ORIGINAL STAR:
Beatrice Cameron

Janet McTeer as Nora in the 1997 Broadway revival at the Belasco Theater, directed by Anthony Page. McTeer won the Tony Award for her performance.

The door slam heard around the world, as Nora's departure at the end of *A Doll's House* has famously been called, was strangely muted when the play made its first US appearance in Louisville, Kentucky, in 1883. The result was something close to indifference.

This was not the usual response to Henrik Ibsen's 1879 masterpiece, which earned him a scandalized reputation as a man singlehandedly out to destroy the institution of marriage. (*A Doll's House* couldn't even appear in London until two men wrote an adaptation with the dreadful title *Breaking a Butterfly*.) But here in Kentucky was the esteemed Polish actress Helena Modjeska, who had performed Shakespeare the night before and would perform Dumas the following night. Ibsen's ending in the context of such chestnuts gave her cold feet; she changed it to allow Nora to remain at home, forgiven and adored. Despite (or perhaps because of) this modification, the first Louisville performance was also the last. "Our experience seemed to prove that the public was not yet ripe for Ibsen," Modjeska later said.

It was another six years before New York had its look at the play, in what proved to be a career-defining role for first Beatrice Cameron and, later, Minnie Maddern Fiske. For all the attention both women received, their combined runs only added up to fifty-five or so performances of the play. But Mrs. Fiske, as she was known, dragged the public behind her until it was ready for Ibsen, performing several of his other works on Broadway and repeatedly comparing him (in many ways favorably) to Shakespeare in the media. Her efforts paid off: as the above list of early-twentieth-century revivals makes clear, any resistance to *A Doll's House* wasn't from lack of exposure. As recently as 2006, it was named the most frequently performed play in the world.

DOUBT

BY JOHN PATRICK SHANLEY

ABOVE: Brían F. O'Byrne (Father Flynn) and Cherry Jones (Sister Aloysius) in *Doubt*, 2005. © *Joan Marcus*

OPPOSITE PAGE: John Patrick Shanley at the Walter Kerr Theater. *Frank Franklin II, Associated Press*

Well, did he or didn't he? Running a brief ninety minutes, *Doubt* left plenty of time for audiences to head out into the street and pick up where John Patrick Shanley cunningly left off.

Shanley, who had seen more than a dozen of his plays open off-Broadway over the previous twenty years, struck gold with this lean, twisty, compelling parable. (The subtitle "A Parable" was added upon publication.) He imbued Father Flynn, the priest whose guilt is in question throughout the play, with the sort of affable, right-minded qualities that audiences would have recognized from a Bing Crosby movie. Sister Aloysius, by comparison, was rigid and mirthless, the kind of person who recoils at the suggestion of including "Rudolph the Red-Nosed Reindeer" in a Christmas pageant.

If Sister Aloysius' suspicions about Father Flynn's actions involving a young student are correct, then no response would be too severe on her part. If she's wrong—and we see her prejudices cloud her judgment on more than one occasion—the accusations would be ruinous to Flynn and to others, including the boy's family. (We meet only his mother, in a scene that packs more pathos and confusion into twelve minutes than most plays do during their entire length.) What is poor Sister James, the audience surrogate plunked in the middle, to think?

Only Shanley and Brían F. O'Byrne, the original Father Flynn, knew whether the character was guilty. They used that uncertainty to their advantage from night to night. *Doubt* begins with a Father Flynn sermon, and O'Byrne gauged the audience's response to him during the scene. If he sensed that they were looking at him and seeing a pedophile, he would approach that performance as someone who was innocent; if they assumed the best of him, he would give them his worst.

That balance was hard to attain in the film version, in part because of the medium's one-off nature and in part because of Philip Seymour Hoffman's decidedly creepy take on Father Flynn. Only on stage do the questions and assumptions and doubts fly back and forth with the appropriate level of ambivalence. Shanley included his email address in the *Doubt* Playbill and got about fifteen queries a day. He gave each one a response—but not an answer.

DATES:
March 31, 2005–July 2, 2006 at the Walter Kerr Theater (525 performances)

SYNOPSIS:
A young nun at a Bronx parochial school in 1964 finds herself torn between two formidable figures: the kindly, progressive Father Flynn and the severe Sister Aloysius, who suspects Father Flynn of acting inappropriately toward one of his students.

AWARDS:
4 Tony Awards; Pulitzer Prize

NOTED REVIVALS AND ADAPTATIONS:
Movie version in 2008

ORIGINAL STARS:
Cherry Jones, Brían F. O'Byrne, Adriane Lenox, Heather Goldenhersh

EAST LYNNE

BY CLIFTON W. TAYLEUR

Any time theaters in the provinces needed to goose their box office in the late nineteenth century, the sign went up: "Next week, *East Lynne*." It has been estimated that one version or another of this Victorian melodrama—and there were many—was seen every Saturday night for more than forty years in North America and England. New York alone had three different versions competing for audiences in 1863; the one listed

ABOVE: *East Lynne,* 1881. The English novelist Ellen Wood, author of the novel that inspired countless theatrical productions, wrote more than thirty novels. *Library of Congress*

OPPOSITE PAGE: Mary Blair (Lady Isabel and Madame Vine) and Stanley Howlett (Sir Francis Levison and the production's codirector) in the 1926 Broadway revival of *East Lynne.*

DATES:

Opened October 18, 1869, at Niblo's Garden (approximately 20 performances)

SYNOPSIS:

Led astray by a caddish aristocrat, beautiful young Isabel Vane abandons her family. When the affair ends, she disguises herself as a governess and goes to work for her own husband, who has since remarried.

AWARDS:

None

NOTED REVIVALS AND ADAPTATIONS:

Broadway revival in 1926; movie versions in 1913, 1916, 1925, and 1931; TV versions in 1982 and 1987

ORIGINAL STARS:

Lucille Western, James A. Herne

above is the only one of the three to qualify as a Broadway production, even by the era's looser definition. These theaters didn't concern themselves with securing the rights, as the period was a free-for-all from a copyright perspective, with new adaptations popping up left and right. Some would tweak the title a bit; others wouldn't even do that.

What was the fuss all about? Ellen Wood's *East Lynne* began as one of the more popular examples of the "sensation novels" that flooded the market in the 1860s and 1870s. (Wilkie Collins' *The Woman in White* is perhaps the best-remembered example today.) They spurred the clergy to new levels of denunciation, which didn't stop Joseph Conrad, King Edward VII, and hundreds of thousands of other readers from devouring *East Lynne*.

True to form, the plot features murder, bigamy, and several handkerchiefs' worth of betrayals. (When Edna Ferber wanted to depict a prototypical stage melodrama in her novel *Show Boat*, she chose *East Lynne*.) The best-known line from the stage versions—it's not in the novel—gives a sense of what audiences thrilled and sobbed to well into the twentieth century: "Dead! Dead! And never called me mother!" What modern-day theater wouldn't kill to have something like that at the ready on a week's notice?

EVITA

BY ANDREW LLOYD WEBBER AND TIM RICE

You graduate from the first class of Juilliard's new drama division and parlay that into four years of touring with the prestigious Acting Company. You touch down on Broadway for a pair of repertory runs with that group, earning a Tony nomination for one of them. You hook up with a promising young playwright named David Mamet and create a few roles for him. You get the lead in one Broadway-bound musical that never makes it there. Another musical does—and closes after three weeks.

Then, just seven years after graduating, you land the title role in London's new smash hit musical,

The original Broadway production, starring Patti LuPone (Eva Perón), Bob Gunton (Perón), and Mandy Patinkin (Che).

Mandy Patinkin, the original Che (for which he won the Tony Award), would later create roles in *Sunday in the Park with George* and *The Secret Garden*.

when it is announced that Actors' Equity won't allow its star to repeat the role in New York. The chance of a lifetime, right?

"*Evita* was the worst experience of my life. I was screaming my way through a part that could only have been written by a man who hates women."

That was Patti LuPone describing the role of Eva Perón, which vaulted her into the pantheon of Broadway superstars. (Her costar, a slightly younger Juilliard grad named Mandy Patinkin, came out of it okay, too.) To be fair, LuPone gave that quote after she and Andrew Lloyd Webber, the writer in question, had tangled in court over another show, *Sunset Boulevard*. Still, the role of Eva has gained a reputation for being among the toughest in the Broadway canon, both musically and emotionally.

While Webber and Tim Rice had envisioned the show as a stage musical from the beginning, *Evita* originated in 1976 as a successful concept album, which had audiences entering the theater already familiar with songs like "Don't Cry for Me, Argentina" and "Another Suitcase in Another Hall." That might have been part of the issue. The recording studio allows for multiple takes. There are no dance numbers or costume changes. Albums don't require replication eight or even six times a week. (Most Evas are now given the matinees off.)

Evita's audio origin also put the onus on the director, who had to take a blueprint that audiences already knew—one in which a lot more is described than depicted—and build a musical around it. The producers waited two years until director Harold Prince was available. It was a smart decision: Prince surrounded his three principals with scaffolding, pitch-black shadows, film, placards, and all sorts of other visual dazzlements. Turning the bed-hopping wife of a South American dictator into a sympathetic protagonist couldn't have been easy, but Prince and his anguished, gifted star pulled it off.

DATES:
September 25, 1979–June 26, 1983 at the Broadway Theater (1,567 performances)

SYNOPSIS:
Eva Duarte, a poor fifteen-year-old girl from rural Argentina, comes to Buenos Aires in 1934 and eventually meets the up-and-coming military officer and politician Juan Perón. Documenting their rise to power is a cynical one-man Greek chorus named Che.

AWARDS:
7 Tony Awards

NOTED REVIVALS AND ADAPTATIONS:
Broadway revival in 2012; movie version in 1996

ORIGINAL STARS:
Patti LuPone, Mandy Patinkin, Bob Gunton

FALSETTOS

BY WILLIAM FINN AND JAMES LAPINE

In 1981, not long before the off-Broadway premiere of *March of the Falsettos*—William Finn and James Lapine's one-act musical about a gay man trying to cobble together something like a family with his wife, son, and new lover—Finn mentioned a new topic he wanted to incorporate. "I said to Lapine, 'There's this new disease—I feel we should include it,'" Finn said years later.

"It" was the as-yet-unnamed AIDS virus, which had just begun leveling the gay community. It presented Finn and Lapine with a reason to revisit the family in 1986 (actually a re-revisit for Finn, who had introduced several of the characters in another one-act musical, *In Trousers*, in 1979). The result was *Falsettoland*, set two years after *March* and depicting the death of the lover (now ex-lover).

By 1992, of course, the world was all too familiar with AIDS, which had claimed such essential voices of the theater as Michael Bennett, Charles Ludlam, Howard Ashman, and Ethyl Eichelberger. *March* and *Falsettoland* came together to form *Falsettos*, whose ultimately loving, decidedly non-nuclear family felt weird and practically unmanageable and very real. Like its ad campaign, a pitch-perfect logo by Keith Haring, the show had style and an enormous heart.

Finn's irrepressible, why-the-hell-not style of writing benefited enormously from Lapine's exacting ministrations, and songs like "Everyone Hates His Parents" and "Four Jews in a Room Bitching" were a welcome dose of cantankerousness in a Broadway

OPPOSITE PAGE: From left, Stephen Bogardus (Whizzer), Barbara Walsh (Trina), Chip Zien (Mendel), Jonathan Kaplan (Jason), Michael Rupert (Marvin), Heather MacRae (Charlotte), and Carolee Carmello (Cordelia) in the original Broadway production. © Carol Rosegg

ABOVE: © Carol Rosegg

climate packed with British megamusicals. *Falsettos* also features a personal favorite line from a musical, spoken by a psychiatrist eager to wrap up a session and get back to wooing the young patient's mother: "Drop it and smile." This has always struck me as the cleanest, drollest encapsulation imaginable of Lapine's precise yin and Finn's ebullient yang. Somehow, miraculously, an AIDS musical managed to be a lot of fun.

DATES:
April 29, 1992–June 27, 1993 at the John Golden Theater (486 performances)

SYNOPSIS:
Marvin is a confused New Yorker who has left his wife, Trina, and their son, Jason, to be with another man, Whizzer. Marvin's psychiatrist ends up treating Jason and marrying Trina. Two years later, Jason's bar mitzvah plans become intertwined with Whizzer's sudden—and initially unexplained—illness.

AWARDS:
2 Tony Awards

NOTED REVIVALS AND ADAPTATIONS:
None

ORIGINAL STARS:
Michael Rupert, Stephen Bogardus, Chip Zien, Barbara Walsh

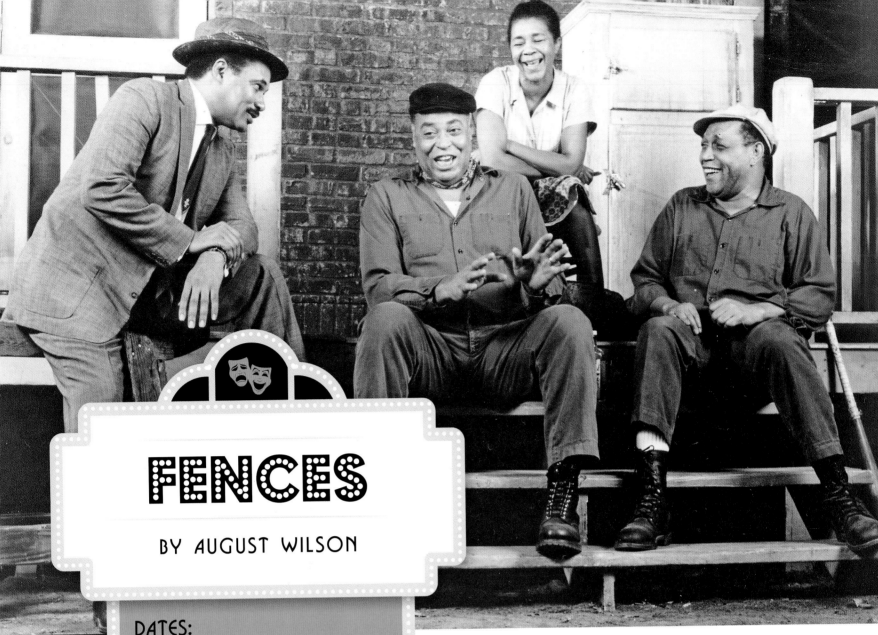

FENCES

BY AUGUST WILSON

DATES:
March 26, 1987–June 26, 1988 at the 46th Street Theater (525 performances)

SYNOPSIS:
Troy Maxson, a Pittsburgh garbageman and former baseball star in the Negro leagues, rules over his family with a mix of entitlement and (at times well-hidden) love. His son's ascension as a promising high school athlete adds jealousy and long-simmering resentment into the mix, with wrenching consequences.

AWARDS:
4 Tony Awards; Pulitzer Prize

NOTED REVIVALS AND ADAPTATIONS:
Broadway revival in 2010

ORIGINAL STARS:
James Earl Jones, Mary Alice, Courtney B. Vance

Only once during August Wilson's phenomenally ambitious ten-play cycle, in which each play is set in a different decade of the twentieth century, did a work have commercial success to rival its critical acclaim. *Fences* ran for over a year, owing in part to star James Earl Jones' marquee appeal, in part to the prizes it picked up along the way, and in part to its subject matter. By contrast, Wilson's last five plays to reach Broadway had a combined 565 performances, just about five weeks longer than *Fences*' run.

With their "binding spells" and 285-year-old matriarchs, Wilson's pieces stretch far beyond the 1900s, offering theatergoers a tantalizing glimpse at the complicated lore of African mythology. *Fences* is different: both it and his second-most popular play, *The Piano Lesson*, focus predominantly on a family unit, albeit with the typical Wilson strain of misfit neighbors and cronies dropping by. It is about a proud, gifted, deeply flawed man and the family members who tremble in his wake, seething, forgiving, and (in one case) fleeing.

August Wilson, 1987. Wilson won his first Pulitzer for *Fences*, and his second for 1990's *The Piano Lesson*. *Fences* was the third play written for the ten-part "Pittsburgh Cycle," and the sixth in the cycle's chronological order. The first, *Gem of the Ocean* (2003), depicts the first decade of the twentieth century; the cycle culminates with *Radio Golf* (2005), set in the 1990s.

James Earl Jones came to the world's attention in 1967 as a boxer toiling under potentially ruinous circumstances in the play *The Great White Hope*. Now he was a broken-down version of that same man. Baseball had not yet been integrated during Troy's heyday; his skin color stood between him and greatness, and between him and hope.

"Your daddy wanted you to be everything he wasn't," explains Rose, Troy's wife (an extremely difficult role that can easily be overshadowed by the actress' costar), "and at the same time he tried to make you into everything he was." This is parenthood in a nutshell, and it goes a long way toward describing why—though not excusing the fact that—*Fences* is the only one of August Wilson's works to win the Tony Award for Best Play.

ABOVE: Jones as Troy. Kenny Leon, who directed the 2010 revival of *Fences* (starring Denzel Washington), told *Vogue* that Troy is "on a scale with Othello, Lear, Willy Loman."

OPPOSITE PAGE: Charles Brown (Lyons), James Earl Jones (Troy Maxson), Mary Alice (Rose), and Ray Aranha (Jim Bono) in *Fences*, 1987.

FIDDLER ON THE ROOF

BY JERRY BOCK, SHELDON HARNICK, AND JOSEPH STEIN

Every lover of musical theater can point to a seminal moment when the form vaults upward in scope and ambition, permanently putting to rest (at least in his or her mind) any talk of jazz hands and power ballads. Rose's shattered and shattering aria at the end of *Gypsy* looms as Exhibit A of this phenomenon, with Billy Bigelow's "Soliloquy" in *Carousel* and the Act I finale of *Sunday in the Park with George* not far behind. But for this viewer, the moment in *Fiddler on the Roof* when Tevye runs out of hands trumps them all.

Fiddler follows the tragicomic story of Tevye, who is able to withstand the weight of his milk cart when his lame horse takes the day off, but who is less successful at shouldering the era's shifting mores. The "Tradition" that has sustained him and the rest of the shtetl, Anatevka, through increasingly difficult times also forces him to grapple with the marriage proposals that his two oldest girls have received through untraditional means. Each time, he weighs the pros and cons through a seesawing monologue. On the one hand, this; on the other hand, that; on the *other* hand, another thing; etc.

Finally, however, his third daughter, Chava, announces that she has eloped—with a non-Jew. This occasions the most agonized of Tevye's monologues, which ends, "If I try to bend that far, I will break. On the other hand . . . there is no other hand. No, Chava." With that pronouncement, the people of Anatevka sing an ominously robust chorus of "Tradition," crossing the stage as they do so. When they leave, Chava is gone from the stage, and from her father.

For almost a decade, *Fiddler* was the longest-running show in Broadway history. "Sunrise, Sunset" was heard at so many weddings that it was often mistaken for a folk song. (Not only is it contemporary, but lyricist Sheldon Harnick even gave the lyrics a pair of optional tweaks in 2011, to make the song applicable to same-sex weddings.) Zero Mostel's capering, often script-averse style may not have been for all tastes—he and director-choreographer Jerome Robbins drove each other to distraction—and most subsequent Tevyes have been a good bit more subdued. But *Fiddler* is one of those rare titles that allows for almost limitless amounts of comedy as well as pathos. It is very nearly a perfect musical.

OPPOSITE PAGE: The sets of *Fiddler on the Roof*, designed by Boris Aronson, were reminiscent of the paintings of Marc Chagall. Aronson, a six-time Tony Award winner, was born in Kiev in 1898, seven years before *Fiddler on the Roof*'s Russian setting and four years after Sholem Aleichem (who was also from present-day Ukraine) published his stories about the dairyman Tevye.

BELOW: "Tradition," being rehearsed by Zero Mostel and company.

DATES:

September 22, 1964–July 2, 1972 at the Imperial Theater, Majestic Theater, and Broadway Theater (3,242 performances)

SYNOPSIS:

Tevye, an impoverished milkman with five daughters in the shtetl of Anatevka, struggles to reconcile his Jewish faith with the changing times and values of Czarist Russia.

AWARDS:

9 Tony Awards

NOTED REVIVALS AND ADAPTATIONS:

Broadway revivals in 1976, 1981, 1990, and 2004; movie version in 1971

ORIGINAL STARS:

Zero Mostel, Maria Karnilova, Beatrice Arthur, Austin Pendleton

FINIAN'S RAINBOW

BY BURTON LANE, E. Y. HARBURG, AND FRED SAIDY

ABOVE: David Wayne won the first Tony Award for Best Featured Actor in a Musical for his performance as leprechaun Og, who is enamored of Sharon (Ella Logan).

OPPOSITE PAGE: Bretaigne Windust directed, and five-time Tony Award winner Michael Kidd choreographed, the original production.

George S. Kaufman famously opined that "satire is what closes on Saturday night." So what happens to a satirical work on Sunday morning or the following Tuesday—or a few decades later?

Finian's Rainbow is hardly the only musical to traffic in satire for comic effect. The early revues of the 1910s and 1920s were constantly poking around for new hairstyles, dance crazes, matinee idols, and the like to lampoon. But just as old *Bugs Bunny* cartoons can baffle young (and some not-so-young) viewers with their references to Jerry Colonna and George Raft, shows with torn-from-the-headlines subject matter run the risk of feeling as old as those rapidly yellowing headlines.

That might explain why *Rainbow*, despite its enchanting score and ingenious lyrics, is performed so infrequently. (Well, that and the blackface. We'll get to that part.) For every bit with a leprechaun set loose on the American South or a dancing mute sister, there's a reference to the Tennessee Valley Authority or such noted 1940s politicians as Theodore Bilbo and John Rankin. (Those two were amalgamated into one Senator Billboard Rawkins, declarer of the unforgettable line, "My whole family's been havin' trouble with immigrants ever since we *came* to this country!")

If anyone could make these lessons go down easy, it was lyricist/colibrettist E. Y. "Yip" Harburg, who himself had a

bit of the leprechaun in him. Harburg took on women's rights in *Bloomer Girl* and the Communist blacklist (something he knew about all too well) in the far less successful *Flahooley*. Here he couched his liberal sentiments in some wickedly funny dialogue (see earlier) and lyrics:

> When the Begat got to gettin' under par,
> They Begat the Daughters of the D.A.R.
> They Begat the Babbitts of the bourgeoisie
> Who Begat the misbegotten G.O.P.

This is sung by a black quartet that features the newly African-Americanized Rawkins; the plot point (involving a magical pot of gold) allows for some of *Rainbow*'s sharpest humor but also makes it a difficult sell these days. A 2009 revival, with a black actor taking over the role of Rawkins midshow, came and went quickly. *Rainbow* has had more success of late in concert stagings, where classic songs like "That Old Devil Moon" and "How Are Things in Glocca Morra?" are emphasized over the more overtly satirical ones. (Composer Burton Lane was a protégé of George Gershwin, and it shows.) Still, any enterprising director looking for a provocative title to revive will find a gold mine in *Finian's Rainbow*.

DATES:
January 10, 1947–October 2, 1948 at the 46th Street Theater (725 performances)

SYNOPSIS:
Finian McLonergan and his daughter, Sharon, lug their pot of gold all the way from Glocca Morra, Ireland, to Missitucky in the American South. There they encounter a strapping union organizer, a stowaway leprechaun, a racist senator, and a group of dancing sharecroppers.

AWARDS:
3 Tony Awards

NOTED REVIVALS AND ADAPTATIONS:
Broadway revivals in 1960 and 2009; movie version in 1968

ORIGINAL STARS:
Ella Logan, David Wayne, Donald Richards, Albert Sharpe

FOLLIES

BY STEPHEN SONDHEIM
AND JAMES GOLDMAN

Follies' "Loveland" sequence harks back to the sumptuousness of the old *Ziegfeld Follies* productions.

It is by no means a knock on *Follies* to say that there will likely never again be a perfect production of it. In many ways, that is a compliment.

Extraordinarily ambitious, ruinously expensive, unsparingly angry, this arsenic-laced valentine to the *Ziegfeld Follies*–style entertainments of yesteryear has collected a fan base of people who remember the lavish original production with ferocious affection. For one thing, it included among its cast actual performers from the *Follies* era, among them the formidable Ziegfeld veteran Ethel Shutta. In *Follies*, at the age of seventy-three, Shutta wowed the crowds nightly with the seen-it-all classic "Broadway Baby." An egregiously truncated cast recording only helped to burnish a sense of nostalgia among those who saw the original production. (And stayed to the end. There were a lot of walk-outs.)

But as the show's characters would be the first to tell you (through a barrage of withering one-liners, which

DATES:

April 4, 1971–July 1, 1972 at the Winter Garden Theater (522 performances)

SYNOPSIS:

The living veteran showgirls of Dimitri Weissman's *Follies* series convene for a bittersweet reunion just before the Weissman Theater is torn down, triggering alternately pleasant and painful memories (and flashbacks). Ben and Sally attempt to rekindle a decades-old romance while their respective spouses, Phyllis and Buddy, look on.

AWARDS:

8 Tony Awards

NOTED REVIVALS AND ADAPTATIONS:

Broadway revivals in 2001 and 2011

ORIGINAL STARS:

Alexis Smith, Dorothy Collins, John McMartin, Gene Nelson, Yvonne De Carlo, Ethel Shutta

Spectral chorus girls dance alongside their older counterparts, including Mary McCarty (Stella Deems) and Alexis Smith (Phyllis Rogers Stone).

librettist James Goldman tinkered with until his death in 1988), nostalgia can be costly. The production closed at a loss of almost $800,000 despite running well over a year, and the two Broadway revivals had even shorter runs. And while stripped-down revivals have worked out well enough for Stephen Sondheim—Broadway has seen ten reimaginings of his shows in the last twenty years—*Follies* is a separate breed. In order for the characters' older, sadder, angrier days to fully resonate, their memories need to pale in comparison to the bright and beautiful possibilities they let slip away. The impact of their follies on us hinges on the impact of the *Follies* on them.

Codirectors Harold Prince and Michael Bennett created a ghostly physical production that rivals that of any Broadway musical before or since. And not many composers would dare to take on the likes of George Gershwin and Cole Porter in a pastiche-heavy score; even fewer would have the gall to arguably better those predecessors, as Sondheim did with "Losing My Mind" and "The Story of Lucy and Jessie," respectively.

For all these reasons, *Follies* will continue to lure the glamorous and the nostalgic and the sadder-but-wiser—qualities the theater world is unlikely to lack anytime soon. People like to talk about the Mount Rushmore of basketball players or pizzerias or whatever. Well, for many, *Follies* is the Mount Everest of Broadway musicals: people don't feel like they've conquered the genre until they've scaled its heights. Still, they'll never be Edmund Hillary.

THE FRONT PAGE

BY BEN HECHT AND CHARLES MACARTHUR

As someone who has spent two decades in and out of newsrooms, I can confirm that roughly two-thirds of all journalists claim to have a job experiences–based screenplay and/or memoir in the works. Sorry, gang: Ben Hecht and Charles MacArthur beat you to it about eighty-five years ago.

The Front Page has served as a virtual instruction manual for generations of go-getter writers and tyrannical editors. Its so's-your-old-man wisecracks and dyspeptic view of the newspaper business, based on the authors' time at two Chicago news outlets, ring uncomfortably true even now. Hecht, meanwhile,

ABOVE: The first Broadway revival of *The Front Page* was produced in 1946 at the Royale Theater. Coauthor Charles MacArthur directed. From left, Roger Clark, Jack Arnold, Ray Walston, Bruce MacFarlane, Benny Baker, Lew Parker (Hildy Johnson), and Pat Harrington.

OPPOSITE PAGE: Lee Tracy (front) as Hildy Johnson and Osgood Perkins as Walter Burns in the original Broadway production.

maintained that theirs was a sanitized version of what really went down. He claimed to have once plugged up the chimney of a grieving mother's house and, once the smoke drove her out of her home, sneaked in to grab a photo of the dead daughter.

Tennessee Williams called *The Front Page* the play that "uncorseted the American theater with its earthy, two-fisted vitality." The seductive overtones are not inappropriate. The diabolical Walter Burns ("I was in love once, with my third wife") behaves like a spurned lover when his star reporter, Hildy Johnson, announces his intention to get married and leave the *Herald Examiner*. No wonder Howard Hawks hit pay dirt when he suggested making Hildy a woman: the more overt love affair, along with a dizzying pace of 240 words per minute, resulted in the sublime 1940 film *His Girl Friday*, with Cary Grant and Rosalind Russell. (Playwright John Guare, whose gimlet-eyed fondness for ink-stained wretches was on display in his underappreciated *Sweet Smell of Success* libretto, adapted *His Girl Friday* for the stage in 2012.)

The days of eight newspapers duking it out in one city are long gone, as are the inescapable thickets of cigar smoke in the workplace. Some have wondered whether the entire newspaper business will follow suit. Journalism schools looking to stem the tide could do worse than present a touring company of *The Front Page*. It's a hell of a recruitment tool.

DATES:
August 14, 1928–April 1929 at the Times Square Theater (276 performances)

SYNOPSIS:
Chicago's Criminal Court Building is even more chaotic than usual in anticipation of an execution. But when the (not-so-) guilty party sneaks into the pressroom, it falls to *Herald Examiner* star reporter Hildy Johnson and his devious editor, Walter Burns, to keep the accused under wraps until they can get the exclusive story.

AWARDS:
None

NOTED REVIVALS AND ADAPTATIONS:
Broadway revivals in 1946, 1969, and 1986; movie versions (under various names) in 1931, 1940, 1945, 1974, and 1988

ORIGINAL STARS:
Osgood Perkins, Lee Tracy

GIRL CRAZY

BY GEORGE GERSHWIN, IRA GERSHWIN, GUY BOLTON, AND JOHN McGOWAN

With an opening-night pit orchestra that included Benny Goodman, Glenn Miller, Gene Krupa, Tommy Dorsey, and Jack Teagarden—all being conducted by George Gershwin, no less—it would be hard to imagine the audience at *Girl Crazy* even noticing the mere mortals up on the stage. Except that nobody overshadows Ethel Merman.

Merman, who had already attained a moderate amount of attention for her nightclub and vaudeville appearances, auditioned for Gershwin at his apartment on Manhattan's Riverside Drive. After he played one of the songs he had in mind for her, a tune called "I Got Rhythm" that hadn't made the cut for a show two years earlier, he said, "If there's anything about this you don't like, I'll be happy to change it." The twenty-one-year-old Merman's response: "That'll do very nicely, Mr. Gershwin."

And it did, with the opening-night audience yelling for several encores after Merman held a high C for sixteen bars. The *New Yorker* critic called her "imitative of no one," and one of Broadway's most iconic stars was born.

Incredibly, the other main female role in *Girl Crazy* also launched both a career and a partnership. In 1930, Merman was a seasoned pro compared to Ginger Rogers, who was just nineteen at the time, with one Broadway musical and one failed marriage under her belt. Merman may have had rhythm, but Rogers had both "Embraceable You" and "But Not for Me," two of Gershwin's most beloved songs. The "Embraceable You" dancing needed a little polishing, though, so Gershwin's longtime producer Alex A. Aarons brought in a guy

by the name of Fred Astaire to work with Rogers. That also did very nicely.

With that kind of firepower both on and below the stage, it's no wonder that people have been wary of reviving *Girl Crazy*. It wasn't until 1992 that it returned to Broadway, in the form of the effervescent *Crazy for You*. Ken Ludwig did a gut renovation on the book, adding other Gershwin songs and jettisoning the forced Eddie Cantor and George Jessel imitations. The "revisal," as these overhauls have increasingly become known, may not have created any overnight stars, but Susan Stroman's torrent of clever, prop-heavy dances won her the first of several Tony Awards and put her on an extremely short list of go-to choreographers.

LEFT: Well before collaborating with his brother Ira on *Oh, Kay!*, *Strike Up the Band*, *Porgy and Bess*, and others, a teenage George Gershwin played piano for a music publisher on Tin Pan Alley. *Library of Congress*

BELOW: Jodi Benson and Harry Groener in *Crazy for You*, which ran for 1,622 performances at the Shubert Theater.

OPPOSITE PAGE : Ethel Merman in *Girl Crazy*, her first Broadway show, 1930.

DATES:
October 14, 1930–June 6, 1931 at the Alvin Theater (272 performances)

SYNOPSIS:
A New York playboy hops a cab all the way to Custerville, Arizona, where he quickly converts a dude ranch into a club packed with showgirls, gambling tables, and mobsters.

AWARDS:
None

NOTED REVIVALS AND ADAPTATIONS:
Broadway "revisal" in 1992; movie versions in 1932, 1943, and 1965

ORIGINAL STARS:
Willie Howard, Ginger Rogers, Ethel Merman, Allen Kearns

THE GLASS MENAGERIE

BY TENNESSEE WILLIAMS

Anthony Ross (Jim O'Connor), Laurette Taylor (Amanda Wingfield), Eddie Dowling (Tom Wingfield), and Julie Haydon (Laura Wingfield), the entire original cast of *The Glass Menagerie*.

Serious actors tend to make their way from Hamlet to King Lear, typically with a Richard III or a Macbeth along the way. For actresses, the predominant generation-mapping roles can arguably be found in the stifling, sweltering South of Tennessee Williams' plays. (Juliet's Nurse and Gertrude notwithstanding, Shakespeare did better with the younger female roles.) Maggie the Cat is optional early on, but all roads tend to lead first to Blanche DuBois and then to Amanda Wingfield, the sympathetic monster at the center of *The Glass Menagerie*.

Williams' first major success, *Menagerie* is perhaps his most autobiographical work, which is saying something; it is also his greatest work, which is *really* saying something. By

DATES:

March 31, 1945–August 3, 1946 at the Playhouse Theater and the Royale Theater (563 performances)

SYNOPSIS:

Tom Wingfield recalls life in a St. Louis tenement with his overbearing mother, Amanda, and his debilitatingly shy sister, Laura. The hope of salvation—false hope, it turns out—comes when Tom brings home a gentleman caller to meet Laura.

AWARDS:

None

NOTED REVIVALS AND ADAPTATIONS:

Broadway revivals in 1965, 1975, 1983, 1994, 2005, and 2013; movie versions in 1950 and 1987; TV versions in 1966 and 1973

ORIGINAL STARS:

Laurette Taylor, Eddie Dowling, Julie Haydon, Anthony Ross

Dowling and Haydon. Dowling, a *Ziegfeld Follies* alum, coproduced and codirected (with Margo Jones) *The Glass Menagerie*.

refracting his own upbringing through the fictional Wingfield family, Williams illustrated with haunting lucidity just what had kept him at home, and what finally forced him to leave. And in Amanda, whom he described in the stage directions as "a little woman of great but confused vitality clinging frantically to another time and place," he hewed so closely to his mother, Edwina Williams, that the legendary Laurette Taylor, who created the role, reportedly greeted Edwina by saying, "Well, Mrs. Williams, how did you like yourself?" (As if immortalizing her wasn't enough, Williams also gave Edwina one half of his *Menagerie* royalties.)

The absent father, the numbing work in a St. Louis shoe factory, the withering mother: Williams and Tom Wingfield, the play's narrator, had much in common. Each also had a broken sister. While the fictional Laura's ailments are confined to crippling shyness and a limp, Rose Williams was less fortunate. The year before Williams wrote *Menagerie*, Rose—who had been diagnosed with schizophrenia—suffered a botched prefrontal lobotomy. She remained hospitalized for the rest of her life.

In 1938, when Rose's mental state worsened considerably, Williams wrote in his diary, "God must remember and have pity some day on one who loved as much as her little heart could hold—& more!" With *The Glass Menagerie*, Williams saw to it that both Rose and Edwina would be remembered for a very long time.

GLENGARRY GLEN ROSS

BY DAVID MAMET

ABOVE: Robert Prosky and Joe Mantegna in *Glengarry Glen Ross*, directed by Gregory Mosher.

OPPOSITE PAGE: The original Broadway production. The play's US debut took place earlier that year at Chicago's Goodman Theater.

"The truth, George. Always tell the truth. It's the easiest thing to remember." That's pretty much the operating philosophy for so many of David Mamet's hustlers, grifters, and snake-oil salesmen, and its wisdom is proven both when it is followed and when it is ignored. The line could just as easily have come from the deadbeat junk-shop denizens of his *American Buffalo* (1975) or the Hollywood barracudas of *Speed-the-Plow* (1988). But it is said in *Glengarry Glen Ross* by Ricky Roma, the giant among dwarves in a Chicago real estate office (not unlike one where Mamet himself had worked a decade earlier).

Like such other all-American masterpieces as *Angels in America* and Wallace Shawn's *The Designated Mourner*, *Glengarry* had its world premiere in London. Audiences on both sides of the Atlantic took to Mamet's juicy argot with relish.

The three man-to-man dialogues that make up Act I—the references to women in the play are, shall we say, less than complimentary—serve as a master class in misdirection, in getting what you want by not asking for it:

> AARONOW: Yes. I mean are you actually talking about this, or are we just . . .
> MOSS: No, we're just . . .
> AARONOW: We're just "talking" about it.
> MOSS: We're just speaking about it. (pause) As an idea.

Mamet, whose right-wing politics and other works (notably *Oleanna*) would seem to distance him from anything resembling political correctness, took out disparaging comments about Indian customers for the 2012 revival starring Al Pacino. (What he did not remove was the "coffee's for closers" speech that Alec Baldwin made famous in the 1992 film version. The reason he did not remove it was because it was never in the play to begin with, much to the confusion of many theatergoers.)

But there's still plenty to unsettle in *Glengarry*, both on a word-by-word level (with more than 150 variations on one particular four-letter word) and in its unsparing look at late-twentieth-century capitalism. Decency is in short supply among these two-bit salesmen—and what little there is invariably works against them.

DATES:
March 25, 1984–February 17, 1985 at the John Golden Theater (378 performances)

SYNOPSIS:
Four salesmen at a third-rate real estate agency plot, plead, plunder, and otherwise act less than admirably in their efforts to always be closing.

AWARDS:
1 Tony Award; Pulitzer Prize

NOTED REVIVALS AND ADAPTATIONS:
Broadway revivals in 2005 and 2012; movie version in 1992

ORIGINAL STARS:
Joe Mantegna, Robert Prosky

GREASE

BY JIM JACOBS AND WARREN CASEY

DATES:
February 14, 1972–April 13, 1980 at the Eden Theater, Broadhurst Theater, Majestic Theater, and Royale Theater (3,388 performances)

SYNOPSIS:
Rydell High School's graduating class of 1959 has a new transfer student, the virginal Sandy Dumbrowski. Danny Zuko, leader of the tough-talking Burger Palace Boys, falls hard for her.

AWARDS:
None

NOTED REVIVALS AND ADAPTATIONS:
Broadway revivals in 1994 and 2007; movie version in 1978

ORIGINAL STARS:
Barry Bostwick, Carole Demas, Adrienne Barbeau, Timothy Meyers

The glut of rock musicals to reach Broadway in the wake of *Hair*—almost two dozen, the majority of them quite bad—had older audiences itching to experience something different. Two distinct paths emerged. The better-known path involved the erudite, adult concept musicals, exemplified by such Stephen Sondheim and Harold Prince collaborations as *Company* and *Follies*. But this was also the time of faux-naif works like *Godspell* and *Grease*, the latter of which constructed an entire song ("Those Magic Changes") around the amateur-guitarist-friendly chords of doo-wop.

Remember, this was before the likes of *American Graffiti* and *Happy Days* had entrenched 1950s nostalgia as a major strain of pop culture. (The closest thing Broadway had seen was *Bye Bye Birdie*, which looked at the Danny Zukos of the world with a mix of condescension and horror.) The tens of thousands of subsequent high school and summer stock productions of *Grease*, nearly all of which use a sanitized version of the book, have obscured just how bawdy it was in 1972. *Grease* looked and sounded old, but it worked hard to act as pugnacious and carefree—okay, almost as pugnacious and carefree—as the hippies in *Hair*. The result ran for more than eight years, becoming the longest-running show in Broadway history until *A Chorus Line* supplanted it.

The original production became famous for the talents that would emerge from it: John Travolta, Richard Gere,

Patrick Swayze, Treat Williams, and Peter Gallagher all did time at Rydell High. The 1994 revival, by contrast, was all about the talents (and sometimes "talents") who had come from other realms entirely: Monkee Micky Dolenz, *Exorcist* star Linda Blair, Twist expert Chubby Checker, gymnast Dominique Dawes. By 2007, the likes of *American Idol* had redefined the parameters of stardom, and for the next *Grease* revival, America got to play casting director. Sandy and Danny were chosen over the course of an eleven-week NBC reality-television show. (Actually, judging from the solid work Laura Osnes has done since winning, America didn't do a bad job of it.)

Critics have never had much use for *Grease*'s pastiche melodies, its juvenile book, or its morally questionable finale. Nonetheless, what began as a nostalgia trip for former greasers has become an all-but-obligatory credential for young performers whose grandparents were barely alive in 1959. *Grease* was the third most popular musical in US high schools in 2010.

OPPOSITE PAGE: Barry Bostwick and Carole Demas, the original Danny Zuko and Sandy Dumbrowski. *Bill Ray, The LIFE Picture Collection, Getty Images*

BELOW: The 1978 film adaptation of *Grease*, starring Olivia Newton-John and John Travolta, is the highest-grossing movie musical of all time. © *Paramount Pictures, courtesy Photofest*

GUYS AND DOLLS

BY FRANK LOESSER, JO SWERLING, AND ABE BURROWS

Broadway loves New York. From *Pal Joey* to *West Side Story* to *Company* to *Rent* to *In the Heights*, dozens of musicals have drawn inspiration from their own backyard, peddling the idea of a raffish, glamorous town with plenty of wit and even more heart. And no New York musical has more of those two attributes than *Guys and Dolls*.

Nobody ever really spoke the way early-twentieth-century newspaperman Damon Runyon—on whose short stories *Guys and Dolls* was based—said they did, which is a damn shame: "It's no use, Nathan. I have succeeded in your not being able to upset me no more." This less-than-convincing vow comes from Miss Adelaide, the nightclub dancer who has been engaged to no-goodnik Nathan Detroit for fourteen years and has the psychosomatic illnesses to prove it. ("If she's getting a kind of name for herself, / And the name ain't his, / A person can develop a cough," according to "Adelaide's Lament," maybe the greatest comic song in the history of musical theater.)

Getting Runyon's syntax right isn't easy, and it proved too much for the original bookwriter, Jo Swerling. By the time Abe Burrows came in as a replacement, Frank Loesser had already written fourteen very good songs, including "If I Were a Bell,"

"A Bushel and a Peck," and "Sit Down, You're Rocking the Boat." So Burrows wrote a new book that fit these songs and Runyon's voice like a glove. The result, directed by George S. Kaufman, was so seamless that some critics barely noticed Loesser's ingenious score: John Chapman of the *New York Daily News* congratulated the songs for being "so completely lacking in banality."

Burrows saved this show and several others; "Get me Abe Burrows!" became shorthand among Broadway producers for when they needed help. But he also inadvertently prevented *Guys and Dolls* from winning the Pulitzer Prize for Drama in 1951. An anti-Communist pamphlet called *Red Channels* had printed the names of 151 entertainment and journalism figures, implying heavily that they were aligned with "the Red Fascists and their sympathizers." Burrows was on the list, which was enough for the trustees of Columbia University to veto the awarding of the prize that year.

The Manhattan of Nicely-Nicely Johnson and Big Jule and Angie the Ox may be just as fictional as Brigadoon or Camelot. But it feels like it could have existed, if only those mugs and molls had had a fraction of the genius of their besotted creators.

OPPOSITE PAGE: The guys in the original Broadway production, playing craps during "Luck Be a Lady."

BELOW: The dolls, aka The Hot Box Girls, led by Miss Adelaide (Vivian Blaine, with a basket) and admired by Nicely-Nicely Johnson (Stubby Kaye).

DATES:

November 24, 1950–November 28, 1953 at the 46th Street Theater (1,200 performances)

SYNOPSIS:

The oldest established permanent floating crap game in New York is poised to make Nathan Detroit a killing—*if* he can lure Sky Masterson to join in. Among the many complications is a wager that Sky can successfully woo Sarah Brown of the Save-a-Soul Mission.

AWARDS:

5 Tony Awards; almost the Pulitzer Prize

NOTED REVIVALS AND ADAPTATIONS:

Broadway revivals in 1976, 1992, and 2009; movie version in 1955

ORIGINAL STARS:

Sam Levene, Vivian Blaine, Robert Alda, Isabel Bigley, Stubby Kaye

GYPSY

BY JULE STYNE, STEPHEN SONDHEIM, AND ARTHUR LAURENTS

DATES:
May 21, 1959–March 25, 1961 at the Broadway Theater and Imperial Theater (702 performances)

SYNOPSIS:
The vaudeville circuit is tough on Rose and her two daughters, Baby June and Louise, in the early 1920s. When Baby June finally splits, the formidable Rose gets it into her head to make Louise the new headliner. Her wish comes true in ways nobody could have predicted.

AWARDS:
None

NOTED REVIVALS AND ADAPTATIONS:
Broadway revivals in 1974, 1989, 2003, and 2008; movie version in 1962; TV version in 1993

ORIGINAL STARS:
Ethel Merman, Jack Klugman, Sandra Church

ABOVE: Ethel Merman as Rose and Maria Karnilova as Tessie Tura, one of the strippers who advises that "You Gotta Get a Gimmick." (Tessie's is that she can strip while doing ballet.)

OPPOSITE PAGE: Jerome Robbins rehearses with the Gypsy cast.

This is as good a time as any to talk about overtures, something younger readers might not know much about. Audiences used to enter Broadway theaters and see a curtain covering the stage. They'd sit and flip through their Playbills until the lights dimmed. Then the orchestra—typically one a *lot* bigger than what you'd encounter today—would play what was essentially a medley of the songs to be performed. Four or five minutes later, the curtain would rise, and the show would begin. These brassy, boisterous, often shrewdly arranged orchestral works served as a transition from the outside world to the new one about to be conjured—and they gave latecomers a little nudge to get to their seats quickly.

Several Broadway musicals are famous for their superb overtures, among them *South Pacific*, *Bye Bye Birdie*, and *My Fair Lady*. Others, like *Candide* and *Mack & Mabel*, never quite live up to the promises made in those first few minutes. But the greatest overture ever, perhaps not so coincidentally, belongs to what many feel is the greatest musical ever, *Gypsy*. Jule Styne's vaudeville- and burlesque-inflected score is such an embarrassment of riches that the overture doesn't even have room for such standards as "Let Me Entertain You" or "Together, Wherever We Go."

Arthur Laurents' merciless book and Stephen Sondheim's gut-punch lyrics combined to create one of the American stage's great gorgons: Rose, with her relentless drive to make a star out of first her older daughter and then the meek girl who would become Gypsy Rose Lee, the most famous stripper in American history. (Laurents based his book on Lee's memoirs.)

Styne got the job only after Irving Berlin and Cole Porter turned it down. Sondheim initially refused to write just the lyrics, until Oscar Hammerstein II convinced him otherwise. One of Sondheim's *Gypsy* lyrics sounds so timeless that it's easy to forget somebody actually sat down and wrote it: "Everything's coming up roses." Yet director Jerome Robbins was not a fan of it at first. "Everything's coming up Rose's *what*?" he asked.

Louise's progression from kind afterthought to reluctant leading lady, and then to aloof stripper, is contrasted with Rose's propulsive forward motion—at least until her final aria of recrimination, "Rose's Turn." Ethel Merman, who wasn't exactly known for her subtlety, pounced on the musically and emotionally complicated material. Angela Lansbury and Bernadette Peters are just two of the actresses to make major impressions in the role in later years. But then, they had one hell of a road map to guide them, one whose glories were apparent before the curtain even went up.

HAIR

BY GALT MACDERMOT, JAMES RADO, AND GEROME RAGNI

If director Tom O'Horgan had had his way, the cast of *Hair* would have lived in the Biltmore Theater, with audiences walking past makeshift clotheslines holding the performers' laundry. Much of the theater community at the time gladly would have seen them stay in there, and never come out. The generation gap was felt all over the country in 1968; Broadway joined the tussle upon the opening of this "American tribal love-rock musical," as it called itself. The production began life at the brand-new New York Shakespeare Festival and made an underwhelming pit stop at a nightclub named Cheetah, before reaching the unlikely environs of Broadway.

These days, it's hard to imagine just how incendiary the sight of a group of performers burning their draft cards and getting high (and, yes, disrobing) was at the time. *Hair* touring companies—which proliferated at an unheard-of rate, with itineraries determined in part by the company astrologer—issued an eight-page document to cast members, describing what to say and what not to say if they were pulled over by the local police. Injunctions and bomb threats followed the show as it crossed the country, and two separate cases involving regional productions made their way to the Supreme Court. And while *Hair* went on unmolested in New York City, where student protests at Columbia University came to a violent end just hours after opening night, the contempt displayed toward it during the Tony Awards was palpable.

What exactly was the problem? People tended to blame the nudity, which was brief and dimly lit—and, let's face it, extremely marketable. (The producers later offered cast members an extra $1.50 a performance to strip.) The show's anti–Vietnam War sentiments and cavalier treatment of the US flag also rankled many. And Galt MacDermot's eclectic, vamp-heavy score, frontloaded with provocative titles like "Sodomy" and "Colored Spade," threw down a gauntlet to audiences. Plenty happily picked it up, storming the stage at the finale each night for four years.

DATES:

April 29, 1968–July 1, 1972 at the Biltmore Theater (1,750 performances)

SYNOPSIS:

Conflicted Claude Bukowski and "psychedelic teddy bear" Berger lead a group of hippies through a series of protests, japes, acid trips, and rebellions, with the specter of the Vietnam War waiting to claim Claude.

AWARDS:

None

NOTED REVIVALS AND ADAPTATIONS:

Broadway revivals in 1977 and 2009; movie version in 1979

ORIGINAL STARS:

James Rado, Gerome Ragni, Lynn Kellogg, Lamont Washington

MacDermot, who looked like a Midwestern gym teacher but has a funky streak a mile wide, made for a winning contrast to his hirsute cowriters, James Rado and Gerald Ragni (who also starred as Claude and Berger). It's unclear who exactly wrote which lyrics. The show was seemingly being rewritten nightly, with a fair amount of doggerel coming and going along the way. But *somebody* is responsible for such ingenious songs as "Easy to Be Hard," "Good Morning Starshine," and the irresistible "Frank Mills."

The creative team's pioneering insertion of rock and roll into Broadway put the cast recording atop the *Billboard* album chart for thirteen consecutive weeks, with everyone from The 5th Dimension to Barbra Streisand to Nina Simone recording songs from *Hair*. Bob McGrath even sang "Starshine" to a group of puppets on *Sesame Street*. Who needs those old fogeys when you've got the toddler audience?

OPPOSITE PAGE: The original Broadway production. *Hair* premiered at Joseph Papp's New York Shakespeare Festival off-Broadway before eventually moving to the Biltmore Theater.

BELOW: The 2009 revival, starring Gavin Creel as Claude. Diane Paulus directed and Karole Armitage choreographed the production, which, like the original, transferred to Broadway after a Public Theater production (at the Delacorte Theater in Central Park). © *Joan Marcus*

HARVEY

BY MARY CHASE

Elwood P. Dowd, the bibulous eccentric who may or may not have an invisible six-foot-three-and-a-half-inch-tall rabbit named Harvey for a friend, is and always has been a tricky part to cast. The first person to learn this was *Harvey* producer Brock Pemberton, a former press agent who, in 1947, would host the first Antoinette Perry Awards ceremony and offhandedly refer to one award as a "Tony," giving Broadway's biggest award its all-but-official name. His quest for the perfect Elwood went through Harold Lloyd, Edward Everett Horton, and Pemberton's fellow Algonquin

Round Table wit Robert Benchley, all of whom turned him down. Finally, a desperate Pemberton cast Frank Fay, who at one time was the top earner in vaudeville but had since fallen prey to the talkies and the bottle.

Between vacations and trips to kick off road companies of Mary Chase's effervescent bit of whimsy, however, Fay would leave the show for weeks at a time. And so Pemberton needed additional Elwoods. His second replacement? James Stewart, fresh from World War II service and eager to return to the stage for the first time since 1935. Stewart, of course, would go on to star in the 1950 film version as well as a 1970 revival, by which point he was arguably a more suitable age for the role.

Directed by Antoinette "Tony" Perry herself, *Harvey* was the biggest nonmusical hit of the decade. Postwar America basked in the sheer congeniality of it all, but tucked away under the play's affable surface was a series of tweaks at the psychiatry profession—Elwood's sister is inadvertently committed to the local sanitarium instead of him—that would soon give way to more overtly anti-establishment works like *One Flew Over the Cuckoo's Nest* and *Anyone Can Whistle*. As Elwood explains to one of the doctors at the sanitarium, "I wrestled with reality for forty years, and I am happy to state that I formally won out over it."

ABOVE: James Stewart in the 1970 Broadway revival, at the ANTA Playhouse. Stewart starred alongside Helen Hayes.

OPPOSITE PAGE: Frank Fay as Elwood P. Dowd. Fay, a tremendously popular vaudevillian in the 1920s, is considered to have been the first stand-up comedian. He was not as popular offstage, however. According to Milton Berle, "Fay's friends could be counted on the missing arm of a one-armed man."

THE HEIRESS

BY RUTH AND AUGUSTUS GOETZ

Peter Cookson (Morris Townsend, a suitor with questionable motives) and Wendy Hiller (the shy, awkward heiress Catherine Sloper) in *The Heiress*.

DATES:

September 29, 1947–September 18, 1948 at the Biltmore Theater (410 performances)

SYNOPSIS:

Plain, naïve Catherine Sloper prepares to flout the wishes of her father and marry for love in 1850s New York City. But what if her father's fears about her dashing suitor are accurate?

AWARDS:

1 Tony Award

NOTED REVIVALS AND ADAPTATIONS:

Broadway revivals in 1950, 1976, 1995, and 2013; movie version in 1949

ORIGINAL STARS:

Wendy Hiller, Basil Rathbone, Peter Cookson

"Splendid," "breathtaking," and "revelatory" were just some of the adjectives used to describe Cherry Jones as Catherine in the 1995 revival of *The Heiress*. Jones and Philip Bosco (Dr. Austin Sloper) starred alongside Jon Tenney as Morris.

Patience is a virtue—or, at the very least, a consolation. This was true for Catherine Sloper, whose melancholy revenge on fortune hunter Morris Townsend takes years to unspool in the 1880 Henry James novel *Washington Square*. It was true for playwrights Ruth and Augustus Goetz, who had to endure numerous requests for a happy ending on their way to bringing James' story to the stage as *The Heiress*. (It took an unsuccessful Boston tryout with a happy ending to convince the Goetzes to trust their instincts and revert to the original script.) And it was true for the play itself, which saw its reputation soar almost fifty years after its premiere on the strength of a sublime director/actor pairing.

To be clear, it was a big success in 1947, as was the film version two years later. Henry James may have hated *Washington Square*, dismissing it as one of his "unhappy accidents," but the very qualities that seemed to draw his enmity—a crisply defined narrative, with romantic complications that would have delighted Jane Austen—have made *The Heiress* a durable fan favorite. The Goetz' sturdy adaptation gave the noted Shaw performer Wendy Hiller arguably her crowning role as the newly christened title character, and Basil Rathbone's performance as her chilly, unyielding father earned him one of the first Tony Award nominations.

But it took director Gerald Gutierrez, fresh from a pared-down Broadway revival of *The Most Happy Fella* the year before, to dust off the title and give it new life in 1995. Cherry Jones left critics stumbling for superlatives in a career-launching performance, and the bold staging of Catherine's betrayal, which took place in near darkness, marked Gutierrez as one of the most inventive directors of his day. Another mid-1940s drama, J. B. Priestley's *An Inspector Calls*, was also being revived on Broadway at the time, in a production that shattered the scenery, summoned mute supernumeraries from the wings, and demanded to be noticed. *The Heiress*, by contrast, dimmed the lights and asked us to lean in. Henry James, the exemplary realist who desperately sought success as a playwright but was literally hissed off the stage, might have approved.

HELLO, DOLLY!

BY (OFFICIALLY) JERRY HERMAN AND MICHAEL STEWART

Carol Channing, "resplendent in scarlet gown embroidered with jewels and a feathered headdress . . . sings the rousing title song with earthy zest," raved Howard Taubman of the *New York Times* when *Hello, Dolly!* premiered.

O f the more than forty new musicals to open on Broadway between 2010 and 2014, how many of their titles ended with exclamation points? Four, nine, twelve, or eighteen?

The answer is actually none of the above: the forgettable 2011 jukebox musical *Baby, It's You!* was the only such show to open during those years. *Hello, Dolly!* has an awful lot to do with why you might well have assumed that the number was on the upper end of that scale.

The traditional (and rather reductive) description of the way musicals work is that people talk until mere words aren't up to the task of describing how they feel, at which point they sing instead. The exclamation point is the typographic equivalent of that surge, capping off a title that is too big to not have one. The difference between *Fiorello* and *Fiorello!* is both very small and enormous.

Hello, Dolly! was hardly breaking new ground. Irving Berlin contributed two songs to *Hullo, Ragtime!* in 1912, George Gershwin was partial to exclamatory punctuation, and Jerome Kern had three exclamation points in 1918's *Oh Lady! Lady!!* But it could be argued that Jerry Herman's big musical—with all those stairs and all those waiters and all that dress and all that Carol Channing—did as much as any show to encode the exclamation point into the public perception of what a Broadway show is and does. If not for it, *Friends*

Gower Champion's choreography shone in the Act II "Waiters' Gallop." Anticipating the return of the beloved Dolly, the waiters at the Harmonia Gardens Restaurant in New York City determine to make their lightning-speed service even faster.

DATES:

January 16, 1964–December 27, 1970 at the St. James Theater (2,844 performances)

SYNOPSIS:

When Yonkers matchmaker Dolly Levi gets it into her head to make herself the match for the "half-a-millionaire" Horace Vandergelder at the turn of the twentieth century, it's off to New York City, with a quartet of ingénues in tow.

AWARDS:

10 Tony Awards

NOTED REVIVALS AND ADAPTATIONS:

Broadway revivals in 1975, 1978, and 1995; movie version in 1969

ORIGINAL STARS:

Carol Channing, David Burns, Eileen Brennan, Mary Jo Catlett, Jerry Dodge, Charles Nelson Reilly

and *SCTV* might not have given the world *Freud!* and *Indira!*, respectively.

It took several capable hands to steer *Hello, Dolly!* through a rocky gestation period: the tyrannical producer David Merrick, known as "the Abominable Showman"; the librettist Michael Stewart, whose comic concision remains severely underrated; the director-choreographer Gower Champion, with his stylish riffs on period movement; and a handful of songwriters brought in to help Herman flesh out the score, including Bob Merrill, Charles Strouse, and Lee Adams. (Thornton Wilder's airtight source material, the play *The Matchmaker*, also deserves a mention, as does whoever decided to change the title from *Dolly, a Damned Exasperating Woman*.)

But any mental image of *Hello, Dolly!* begins and ends with Channing, the saucer-eyed, frog-voiced wonder who would play the marvelously meddlesome Dolly Levi more than five thousand times. Channing, who got the part after both Ethel Merman and Mary Martin turned it down, won one of the play's ten Tony Awards—a record that wasn't broken until the twenty-first century. (Merman and Martin both did play the role eventually.) Channing was still at it in 1995, when she once again earned midperformance standing ovations on Broadway. If any performer deserves an exclamation point, it's her!

H.M.S. PINAFORE

OR, THE LASS THAT LOVED A SAILOR

BY W. S. GILBERT AND ARTHUR SULLIVAN

DATES:
December 1–27, 1879 at the Fifth Avenue Theater (28 performances)

SYNOPSIS:
Ralph Rackstraw's love for Captain Corcoran's daughter, Josephine, is imperiled by his status as a lowly seaman. Complicating and/or abetting matters are the dastardly Dick Deadeye; the haughty Sir Joseph Porter; and Little Buttercup, a dockside vendor with a secret.

AWARDS:
None

NOTED REVIVALS AND ADAPTATIONS:
Dozens of Broadway revivals; TV versions in 1939, 1973, 1981, and 1997

ORIGINAL STARS:
Hugh Talbot, Blanche Roosevelt, Signor Brocolini, J. H. Ryley, Furneaux Cook, Alice Barnett, Jessie Bond, W. S. Gilbert

The CAPTAIN and SWEET LITTLE BUTTERCUP.

BUTTERCUP: "How sweetly he carols forth his melody to the unconscious moon"

H.M.S. PINAFORE

ABOVE: "The Captain and Sweet Little Buttercup," below an unconscious moon and other scenes from *H.M.S. Pinafore*, c. 1879. *A.S. Seer Print, Library of Congress*

OPPOSITE PAGE: A "juvenile" production of *H.M.S. Pinafore*, c. 1879. *Strobridge & Co. Lith., Library of Congress*

In Anne Washburn's astonishing 2013 play *Mr. Burns*, a group of postapocalyptic survivors is desperately trying to piece together a synopsis of a *Simpsons* episode, apparently the last surviving bit of Western culture. As it happens, this particular episode—in which the villainous aesthete Sideshow Bob prepares to slaughter the Simpson family—is a sort of two-for-one. Given a last request, Bart stalls for time by asking Sideshow Bob to sing the entire score of *H.M.S. Pinafore*.

Back in 1878 and 1879, the idea of *Pinafore*'s resilience would not have been so surprising. The dates listed at left for the show's premiere are actually misleading—by the time Arthur Sullivan, W. S. Gilbert (who also sang in the chorus), and impresario Richard D'Oyly Carte brought the piece to America, about 150 unauthorized productions had beaten them to the punch. Yiddish-language versions, minstrel-show versions, cross-dressing versions, all-children versions: "the *Pinafore* craze," as it was called, was in full swing in America before the show's creators tried to get a piece of the profits.

The attempt proved to be surprisingly unsuccessful. Having already been offered multiple *Pinafore*s within a few blocks of one another, audiences didn't show much interest in the genuine article. Gilbert and Sullivan fielded a solid group of singers, including the redoubtable Alice Barnett and a former baseball player now named Signor Brocolini, but they only managed a few weeks of performances before shifting their focus to their next show, *The Pirates of Penzance*. (That show premiered in New York immediately after *Pinafore* closed. They had learned their lesson about US copyright laws.)

The idea of using *Pinafore* to ward off evil, as Bart Simpson does, has some precedent. In the late nineteenth century, the theater was viewed—not entirely inaccurately—as a debauched fleshpot, and ministers frequently denounced it from the pulpit. But Gilbert and Sullivan's confection, brimming with good-natured parodies and charming melodies, was something even the clergy could get behind. Its enormous popularity, along with that of *The Mulligan Guards' Ball* and a musical farce called *The Brook*, has inspired many to call 1878–1879 the genesis of what we think of today as musical theater.

THE HOMECOMING

BY HAROLD PINTER

Carolyn Jones (Vivien Merchant's replacement as Ruth) and Jerry Mickey (a replacement for Teddy) in *The Homecoming*, 1967. The play centers on Teddy and Ruth's visit to London, where Ruth meets her husband's father and brothers.

Plotless or structurally ingenious? Married or not really married? Feminist or misogynist? Those famous Harold Pinter pauses give audiences plenty of time—though not nearly enough time—to mull these questions during *The Homecoming*, which has emerged as perhaps Pinter's finest play.

It took people a while to appreciate the murky genius of this work, in which the arrival of a prodigal son and his wife triggers round after round of psychosexual jockeying. One of the critics who did get it right away was Penelope Gilliatt, who, after the play's 1965 London premiere, wrote, "The drama in *The Homecoming* is not the plot. In Pinter it never is. It consists in the swaying of violent people as they gain minute advantages."

But even minute advantages can add up, and the upheavals that Pinter depicted still pack a punch almost a half-century later. And in creating Ruth, the lone female in a family that both desperately needs one and doesn't deserve one, he set in motion a series of debates that still rage on. The homecoming in question is arguably hers: though she has never been to her husband Teddy's childhood home before, and is in fact mistaken at first for a prostitute he has brought there, her acceptance into the family implies a sort of morally dubious deliverance.

The original production helped launch the career of Ian Holm, who played the slithery middle son Lenny and frequently returned to Pinter, giving a stellar performance thirty-five years later as the play's patriarch, Max. (Vivien Merchant, Pinter's wife at the time, was reportedly no slouch either in what is a phenomenally complicated role even under less fraught circumstances.)

Among the more unlikely supporters of Pinter's bracing new voice was someone who would appear to be his theatrical opposite. In a letter he wrote to Pinter after seeing *The Homecoming*, Noël Coward saluted the "arrogant but triumphant demands you make on the audience's imagination." Over the decades, those demands have become less arrogant and more commonplace in the theater—which only makes them more triumphant.

DATES:

January 5–October 14, 1967 at the Music Box Theater (324 performances)

SYNOPSIS:

A philosophy professor brings his wife back to his North London home, only to see his father and brothers try to enlist her in one of the family businesses: prostitution.

AWARDS:

4 Tony Awards

NOTED REVIVALS AND ADAPTATIONS:

Broadway revivals in 1991 and 2007; movie version in 1973

ORIGINAL STARS:

Paul Rogers, Vivien Merchant, Ian Holm, Michael Craig

1965 Royal Shakespeare Company production, with Michael Bryant (left) as Teddy, Vivien Merchant as Ruth, and Ian Holm as Lenny. Sir Peter Hall directed the original London production, which was restaged by Rosemary Beattie. Hall also directed the 1973 film. *Keystone, Hulton Archive, Getty Images*

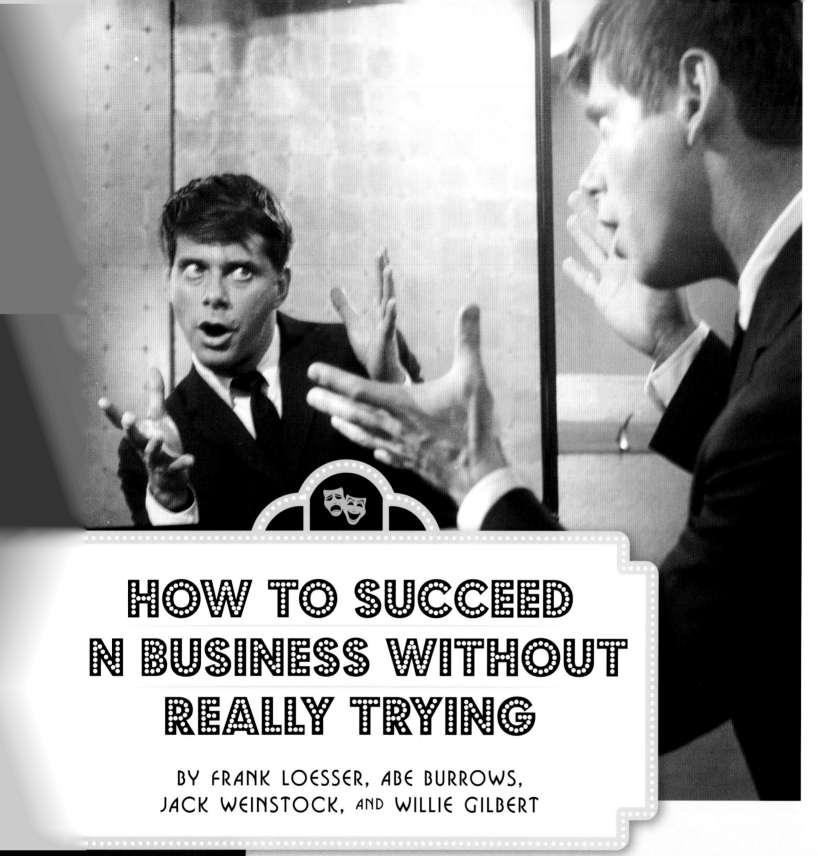

HOW TO SUCCEED IN BUSINESS WITHOUT REALLY TRYING

BY FRANK LOESSER, ABE BURROWS, JACK WEINSTOCK, AND WILLIE GILBERT

A choreographer in way over his head. A supporting performer insistent on crooning a few songs he had popularized twenty-five years earlier. A libretto that had lain around for years. And, most daring of all, a satirical tone more commonly found in the far less audience-pleasing environs of off-Broadway.

The triumph of *How to Succeed in Business Without Really Trying* was as unlikely as the ascent of J. Pierrepont Finch, the endearing sociopath at its center, from window washer to chairman of the board. "Ponty" does it in the space of two weeks, whereas it took quite a bit longer for the musical, which had humble beginnings and gradually accumulated a blue-chip team of showmen.

Jack Weinstock and Willie Gilbert had adapted the book of the same name, a nonfiction bestseller from 1952 by Shepherd Mead. But their nonmusical version went nowhere until producers Cy Feuer and Ernest Martin signed on and enlisted the help of their *Guys and Dolls* team of Frank Loesser and Abe Burrows. Loesser's lyrics manage to be both heartfelt and deeply cynical, somehow making workplace chauvinism ("Her pad is to write in / And not spend the night in") and domestic chauvinism ("Home to be loved by a man I respect / To bask in the glow / Of his perfectly understandable neglect") almost endearing.

Robert Morse had a lot to do with this. He turned Ponty into the kind of back-stabbing climber you root for, even as he delivered his big love song ("I Believe in You") to himself in a mirror. Singer Rudy Vallée was a draw at the box office, but at a cost; Loesser walked off the show when Vallée balked at singing one of the composer's songs and insisted on adding a few old hits. Feuer lured Loesser back three days later by promising to punch Vallée out as soon as the show closed. (Apparently the promise was never fulfilled.)

And once the creative team realized that their choreographer had an extremely small bag of tricks, they brought in Bob Fosse, who replaced every dance but one (and refused to take credit as the new choreographer).

The Pulitzer Prize that *How to Succeed* received might have been a "make good" on the snub for Loesser and Burrows' *Guys and Dolls* a decade earlier (a result of Burrows' blacklisting). That show, maybe the greatest Broadway musical ever, was only Loesser's second. *How to Succeed*, easily the least romantic hit musical ever, was his fifth and final. No composer has ever accomplished so much in so few.

ABOVE: The original Broadway production ensemble performs "A Secretary Is Not a Toy."

OPPOSITE PAGE: Robert Morse as J. Pierrepont Finch in the film of *How to Succeed in Business Without Really Trying*, 1967. Morse later played Bertram Cooper on the TV series *Mad Men*. © *United Artists, courtesy Photofest*

DATES:
October 14, 1961–March 6, 1965 at the 46th Street Theater (1,417 performances)

SYNOPSIS:
With the help of his trusted self-help book, some quick thinking, and an adoring secretary, and without one iota of scruples, J. Pierrepont Finch makes a meteoric rise at the World Wide Wicket Company.

AWARDS:
7 Tony Awards; Pulitzer Prize

NOTED REVIVALS AND ADAPTATIONS:
Broadway revivals in 1995 and 2011; movie version in 1967

ORIGINAL STARS:
Robert Morse, Bonnie Scott, Rudy Vallée, Charles Nelson Reilly

THE ICEMAN COMETH

BY EUGENE O'NEILL

James Barton (Hickey) and Dudley Digges (Harry Hope) in the original Broadway production.

The Iceman Cometh has made it to Broadway four times, for a combined run of well under a year. But the impact of this bruising work, which devotes four hours to a group of men and women (but mostly men) confronting some extremely unpleasant realities, far surpasses its commercial success.

Commercial success on Broadway, that is. The most consequential production of *Iceman* actually took place a decade after its Broadway premiere, at Circle in the Square, then based in Greenwich Village. This off-Broadway production ran longer than any other Eugene O'Neill play had before—or ever would—and cemented the reputations of actor Jason Robards and director José Quintero as unparalleled O'Neill interpreters. It laid down a gauntlet for modern-day actors (most memorably Kevin Spacey, in the 1999 revival) not afraid to climb the rhetorical and psychological mountains O'Neill had built. No wonder he kept the play out of circulation for seven years after writing it.

Theodore "Hickey" Hickman is the topic of discussion for a good eighty minutes—longer than some full-length plays nowadays—before making his first appearance. Brimming with song and rounds of booze, Hickey is the eternal life of the party, equal parts traveling salesman and preacher. He hums with the zeal of a convert. But the life of the party is actually bringing a kind of death this time: a desire to snuff out the pathetic, alcohol-feuled "pipe dreams" that inspire each character to greet another grimy day. That is not what the constituency of Harry Hope's was expecting.

It may not have been what audiences were expecting either. *Iceman* was O'Neill's first Broadway play in twelve years, and during a press conference shortly before its opening, he alluded to the unease he thought the piece might generate. "The first act is hilarious comedy, *I think*, but then some people may not even laugh," he said. "At any rate, the comedy breaks up and the tragedy comes on."

The 1946 premiere might have had a bigger impact if Marlon Brando hadn't turned down the role of the anguished young anarchist Don—or if James Barton, the original Hickey, had consistently remembered his lines. The intervening decade before that Circle in the Square production also saw the likes of Ionesco and Genet and, especially, Beckett. By 1956, absurdist works like *The Bald Soprano* and *Waiting for Godot* had taught audiences how to laugh into the void. But O'Neill got there first.

DATES:
October 9, 1946–March 15, 1947 at the Martin Beck Theater (136 performances)

SYNOPSIS:
The denizens of Harry Hope's flophouse subsist on five-cent whiskeys and pipe dreams, until the charismatic Hickey arrives to rouse them out of their sodden stupors. But how did Hickey come upon his newfound wisdom?

AWARDS:
None

NOTED REVIVALS AND ADAPTATIONS:
Broadway revivals in 1973, 1985, and 1999; movie version in 1973; TV version in 1960

ORIGINAL STARS:
James Barton, Carl Benton Reid, Paul Crabtree, Dudley Digges

The 1999 revival of *Iceman* starred Kevin Spacey, who was "born to play" Hickey, according to Ben Brantley in the *New York Times*. © Joan Marcus

THE IMPORTANCE OF BEING EARNEST

BY OSCAR WILDE

1947 Broadway revival of *Earnest*, with, from left, Pamela Brown, John Gielgud, Robert Flemyng, and Margaret Rutherford. Gielgud directed the production.

Multiple pages could be devoted to quoting *The Importance of Being Earnest*, so let's confine the quotes to half of this entry.

"To lose one parent may be regarded as a misfortune . . . to lose both seems like carelessness."

"All women become like their mothers. That is their tragedy. No man does. That's his."

"Relations are simply a tedious pack of people, who haven't got the remotest knowledge of how to live, nor the smallest instinct about when to die."

"The truth is rarely pure and never simple."

"Thirty-five is a very attractive age. London society is full of women of the very highest birth who have, of their own free choice, remained thirty-five for years."

Oh, wait, that line, from the redoubtable Lady Bracknell, reminds me of an earlier one by Algernon, one of the play's two-faced gentlemen: "Really, if the lower orders don't set us a good example, what on earth is the use of them?"

DATES:

Opened April 22, 1895 at the Empire Theater
(fewer than 20 performances)

SYNOPSIS:

Jack and Algernon's penchant for creating alternate
identities comes back to haunt them during a trip
to woo Gwendolen and Cecily in the countryside.
Among the hurdles is Cecily's mother, the formidable
Lady Bracknell. Another is the women's preference
for the doppelgangers over the genuine articles.

AWARDS:

None

NOTED REVIVALS AND ADAPTATIONS:

Broadway revivals in 1902, 1910, 1921, 1926, 1939,
1947, 1977, and 2011; movie versions in 1952, 1992,
and 2002; TV versions in 1964, 1974, and 1986

ORIGINAL STARS:

Ida Vernon, William Faversham, Henry Miller,
Viola Allen

Oscar Wilde, c. 1882. *Napoleon Sarony, Library of Congress*

These lines probably conjure a very specific image for many of you—which is likely the exact same image they conjure for everyone else. Beyond the occasional casting of a man as Lady Bracknell, I can't think of a play that has inspired less directorial tampering than what Oscar Wilde dubbed his "Trivial Comedy for Serious People." Has anyone ever tried an *Earnest* set in the Middle East or outer space or the Wild West, or anywhere other than late-Victorian England?

The prejudices and posturings of 1890s English society seep from every syllable of the play. ("Never speak disrespectfully of Society, Algernon. Only people who can't get into it do that.") They certainly carried over to the audience in London when it premiered there a few months before the Broadway opening. The Marquess of Queensberry—the father of Wilde's lover, Alfred "Bosie" Douglas—was barred from entering the theater by policemen, owing to his stated plan to throw a bouquet of rotten vegetables onto the stage.

The feud between Wilde and Queensberry quickly escalated into a series of fateful lawsuits. Four days after *Earnest* opened on Broadway, Wilde's trial for gross indecency (the Victorians' euphemistic name for homosexuality) began; by the time he was found guilty and sentenced to two years of hard labor, the show had already closed.

Fine, one last quote: "The good ended happily, and the bad unhappily. That is what Fiction means."

IN DAHOMEY

BY WILL MARION COOK, JESSE A. SHIPP, AND PAUL LAURENCE DUNBAR

In 1894, Bert Williams—once described by W. C. Fields as "the funniest man I ever saw"—and his partner George Walker were enlisted to impersonate Africans from Dahomey (now part of Benin) at the Midwinter Exposition in San Francisco, until the real ones got there. When the Dahomeans did arrive, Williams and Walker stuck around and spent some time with them.

This odd encounter likely informed the creation of *In Dahomey*, which flipped the trajectory and had Americans travel to Africa. In doing so, the creators made a pivotal trip of their own, creating the first musical written and performed by black men and women to be staged in a legitimate Broadway theater.

More than twenty songs by other composers found their way into *In Dahomey* at one point or another. All existing scripts and programs of the show list fewer than half the numbers that were ultimately in it. (Not every composer, it seems, knew his material had been added.) A bit of a Meyerbeer opera called *L'Africaine* even popped up. The constantly morphing results were more than a bit reminiscent of the operatic conventions of eighteenth-century Italy.

The strains of minstrelsy were consistent through all versions, though. The hugely popular team of Williams & Walker referred to themselves as the "Two Real Coons," in contrast to white actors who wore blackface at the time—although they wore it, too. Composer Will Marion Cook, who had trained at Oberlin and studied with Dvořák, worked hard to bypass and/or subvert the genre's more despicable elements, but there are enough there to give pause to any but the most daring modern-day theater companies. (The noted writer Paul Laurence Dunbar had by far the highest profile among the creative team, but he appears to have played a relatively small role in the show's creation.)

In Dahomey brought a level of prestige well beyond what its fifty-three-performance Broadway record might indicate. The show toured England and America for years, including a command performance at Buckingham Palace. After its historic run ended, Williams became the only black member of the *Ziegfeld Follies*, a title he held for several years. When the white actors balked at Williams' inclusion, Flo Ziegfeld informed them that every performer in the show was replaceable—except Williams.

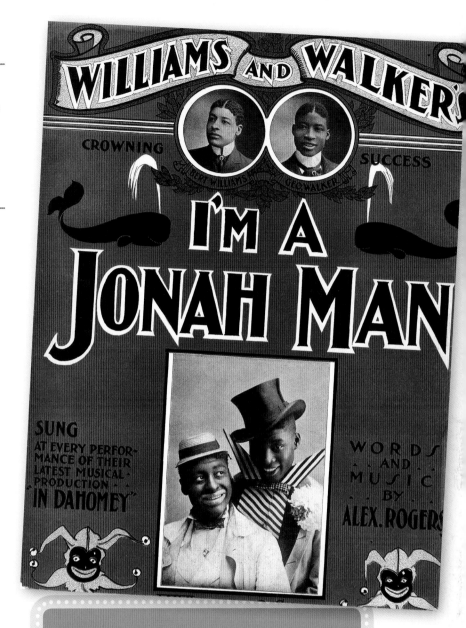

DATES:
February 18–April 4, 1903 at the New York Theater (53 performances)

SYNOPSIS:
Two swindlers, the shrewd Rareback Pinkerton and the reluctant Shylock Homestead, head off to Florida to recover a missing casket. A series of complications leads them to the African nation of Dahomey, where their access to rum makes them assistants to the king.

AWARDS:
None

NOTED REVIVALS AND ADAPTATIONS:
None beyond a return engagement in 1904

ORIGINAL STARS:
Bert Williams, George Walker

INHERIT THE WIND

BY JEROME LAWRENCE AND ROBERT E. LEE

We have two competitors for the title of Best Barn-Burning, Historical-Liberties-Taking Theatrical Anti-McCarthyism Parable. In the left corner, there's *The Crucible*, in which Arthur Miller looked back more than 250 years to the Salem witch trials. And in—well, it's probably accurate to call this one the left corner, too—there's *Inherit the Wind*, which gave its setting as "not too long ago."

"Not too long" meant thirty years ago, to be precise, when the 1925 Scopes monkey trial pitted the famous agnostic Clarence Darrow against the famous Presbyterian William Jennings Bryan in a proxy battle over the teaching of evolution. Throw in the presence of America's then-best-known cynic, the dyspeptic newspaperman H. L. Mencken—not to mention the shock of Darrow calling Bryan himself to the witness box—and you've got a setting crying out for a witty, withering battle of wills.

That's precisely what Jerome Lawrence and Robert E. Lee, whose collaborative career included everything from *Auntie Mame* to *The Night Thoreau Spent in Jail*, provided. The message had additional resonance amid Cold War–era threats to intellectual freedom, and audiences gobbled it up. *Inherit the Wind* ran four times longer than 1953's *The Crucible*, which had no cynical newspapermen in it. (Still, no jokes in *Inherit* can compete with the poster for the 1960 movie version, featuring a bespectacled chimp and the tagline, "IT'S ALL ABOUT THE FABULOUS 'MONKEY TRIAL' THAT ROCKED AMERICA!")

Lawrence and Lee changed the characters' names and stressed that *Inherit* was "not history," which will come as a surprise to credulous high school students everywhere. It's hard to deny that the play contributed to the historical record indirectly—the Scopes monkey trial only made it into *Encyclopedia Britannica* in 1957, and the play was mentioned in the listing.

The two lead roles are catnip for older actors with a taste for grandstanding, and the Darrow surrogate alone has attracted the likes of George C. Scott, Paul Muni, Kevin Spacey, Jack Lemmon, and Christopher Plummer. *Inherit* also tends to draw the attention of fundamentalist Christians, who have successfully lobbied for the cancellation of school productions as recently as 2013. Lawrence and Lee saw that coming. They wrapped up their introduction to the play with a closing argument that would do their dueling lawyers proud: "It might have been yesterday. It could be tomorrow."

DATES:

April 21, 1955–June 22, 1957 at the National Theater (806 performances)

SYNOPSIS:

When a high school teacher is jailed for teaching the theory of evolution in 1925, the small southern town of Hillsboro is overrun with reporters and gawkers gathering to see blue-chip lawyers Henry Drummond and Matthew Harrison Brady do battle.

AWARDS:

3 Tony Awards

NOTED REVIVALS AND ADAPTATIONS:

Broadway revivals in 1996 and 2007; movie version in 1960; TV versions in 1965, 1988, and 1999

ORIGINAL STARS:

Paul Muni, Ed Begley, Tony Randall

OPPOSITE PAGE: George C. Scott played Henry Drummond in the 1996 Broadway revival, at the Royale Theater.

BELOW: From left, Ed Begley (Matthew Brady), Tony Randall (E. K. Hornbeck), Paul Muni (Henry Drummond), and Louis Hector (the judge) in *Inherit the Wind*, 1955. The character of Matthew Brady was based on William Jennings Bryan, Hornbeck was based on H. L. Mencken, and Drummond was based on Clarence Darrow.

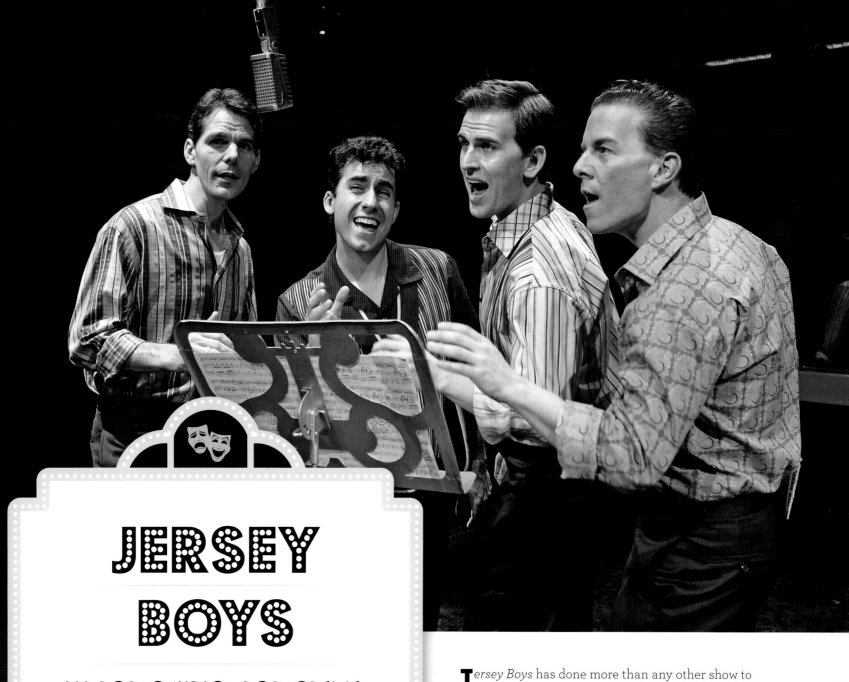

JERSEY BOYS

BY BOB GAUDIO, BOB CREWE, MARSHALL BRICKMAN, AND RICK ELICE

J. Robert Spencer, John Lloyd Young, Daniel Reichard, and Christian Hoff in *Jersey Boys*, 2005. © Joan Marcus

Jersey Boys has done more than any other show to validate the idea of the jukebox musical, a phrase that tends to be thrown around with a bit of a sneer.

Frankly, "jukebox musical" has never seemed quite right to me. Jukeboxes have lots of songs by lots of artists, allowing users to create their own playlists. With very few exceptions (*Rock of Ages* and *Motown* spring to mind), shows included under that umbrella term pull exclusively from one artist's or band's or songwriter's catalog. That would make for the most boring jukebox imaginable.

Anyway, the success of *Smokey Joe's Café* (music by songwriters Jerry Leiber and Mike Stoller), *Movin' Out* (Billy Joel), and especially *Mamma Mia!* (ABBA) spawned well over a dozen copycat shows. One of the trickiest parts of writing a musical—the music—was already taken care of! Just write a check for the rights to a batch of beloved songs, string them together, and start counting the box office receipts.

From left, Young, Reichard, Hoff, and Spencer perform "Walk Like a Man" as the Four Seasons. © Joan Marcus

DATES:
Opened November 6, 2005 at the August Wilson Theater (3,828 performances as of February 1, 2015)

SYNOPSIS:
An unremarkable 1950s rock band called the Variety Trio makes two key decisions: to bring in a singer named Frankie Castelluccio and to rename themselves after a local bowling alley. Oh, did I mention that Frankie would change his last name to Valli? And that the bowling alley was called the Four Seasons?

AWARDS:
4 Tony Awards

NOTED REVIVALS AND ADAPTATIONS:
Movie version in 2014

ORIGINAL STARS:
John Lloyd Young, Christian Hoff, Daniel Reichard, J. Robert Spencer

It wasn't that easy, of course. Theater never is. *Lennon*, *Good Vibrations*, *The Look of Love*, and *Holler If Ya Hear Me* are just some of the many titles to draw from the Top 40 well and come up dry, typically because of nonexistent and/or uninspired books. But *Jersey Boys* is different. Des McAnuff is one of the few established theater directors who truly gets rock music (he wrote his own rock opera at the age of nineteen, and would later direct what is by all accounts a much better one, *The Who's Tommy*); Marshall Brickman and Rick Elice's whip-smart book uses multiple narrators to create a *Rashomon*-style telling of the early days of Frankie Valli and the Four Seasons; and John Lloyd Young's ringing falsetto convinced audiences that Valli himself had returned to the stage. All of this resulted in the show becoming the first—and, at press time, the only—jukebox musical to win the Tony Award for Best Musical.

Less welcome are the spinoff concert acts made up of seemingly every *Jersey Boys* veteran except Young. A vigorous round of litigation saw to it that these oldies groups, which seem to have been created with PBS pledge drives in mind, couldn't use names too close to the original show. So they don't. In more ways than one, *Jersey Boys* stands alone.

JESUS CHRIST SUPERSTAR

BY ANDREW LLOYD WEBBER AND TIM RICE

ABOVE: Followers surround Jesus (Jeff Fenholt), while Judas (Ben Vereen) looks on in the original Broadway production of *Jesus Christ Superstar*. *John Olson, The LIFE Picture Collection, Getty Images*

OPPOSITE PAGE: Andrew Lloyd Webber and Tim Rice with their album of *Jesus Christ Superstar*, 1970. The two-disc set peaked at number 1 on the US *Billboard* 200 in 1971. *Bernard Gottfryd, Getty Images*

DATES:

October 12, 1971–July 1, 1973 at the Mark Hellinger Theater (711 performances)

SYNOPSIS:

The last week of Jesus' life unspools, with scenes familiar from the Gospels (the cleansing of the temple, Peter's denial) as well as newly fleshed-out tensions between him and Judas Iscariot.

AWARDS:

None

NOTED REVIVALS AND ADAPTATIONS:

Broadway revivals in 1977, 2000, and 2012; movie version in 1973

ORIGINAL STARS:

Jeff Fenholt, Ben Vereen, Yvonne Elliman

Jesus Christ Superstar made its world premiere to overflow crowds and standing ovations in New York. The cast of fifty basked in the applause, then found their parents after the show. Many of them still needed to be driven home.

One disadvantage to releasing your musical as a concept album first, as Andrew Lloyd Webber and Tim Rice did with Superstar, is that people can get around to staging it before you. That's what the senior humanities class at Southold High School, on the northeastern tip of Long Island, did in June 1971, having listened to the songs repeatedly on AM radio and their record players.

Musical theater had fallen out of favor among much of the younger set by 1971, but it's not hard to see why Southold high schoolers and hundreds of others in bootleg productions (many of which were forced to shut down) took a shine to Superstar. It had the first legitimate rock and roll score since Hair had premiered four years earlier, with swaggering funk riffs, electric guitars galore, and enough weird time signatures to satiate the biggest prog-rock fan. ("Everything's All Right" chugs along in 5/4, and the climactic "Trial Before Pilate" sequence has forty-one time signature changes.) And best of all, it was sufficiently irreverent—some would say sacrilegious—to earn the disapproval of authority figures. Perfect!

Producers hired Hair director Tom O'Horgan to adapt the album for the Broadway stage. Lloyd Webber liked the results about as much as he liked those bootleg student productions. Still, the show ran for almost two years, launched the career of Ben Vereen, and spawned a West End production that became London's longest-running musical for a time.

It lost every Tony Award it was nominated for, which didn't even include Best Musical. Twenty-four-year-old Lloyd Webber did, however, win a Drama Desk Award for Most Promising Composer. An earlier work that he and Rice had been commissioned to write for a preparatory school was quickly expanded into Joseph and the Amazing Technicolor Dreamcoat to piggyback on the success of Superstar, and two of musical theater's most financially (if not always critically) successful careers were on their way.

JOE TURNER'S COME AND GONE

BY AUGUST WILSON

Delroy Lindo (Herald Loomis, front), Ed Hall (Bynum Walker), and Mel Winkler (Seth Holly) in the Yale Repertory Theater production of *Joe Turner's Come and Gone*, 1987. The production was directed by Lloyd Richards. The play debuted on Broadway the following year with nearly all of the same cast. © *Joan Marcus*

Set in 1911, a time when slavery was a living memory for much of black America, *Joe Turner's Come and Gone* is the second oldest in the timeline of August Wilson's ten-play, ten-decade cycle. (*See also entry on* Fences.) Wilson originally planned to call it *Mill Hand's Lunch Bucket*, when the plan was to name each play in the cycle after a different Romare Bearden painting.

Pittsburgh, Pennsylvania, is a visceral presence in *Joe Turner*, as it is in virtually all of Wilson's plays; here we are uniquely aware of it as a way station as well as a destination. By the time the cycle reaches the 1940s (*Seven Guitars*) and 1950s (*Fences*), Wilson's characters may be trying to make sense of where they are—but at least they're already there. In *Joe Turner*, they are still moving, still searching, still lacking.

Herald Loomis is looking for his wife, whom he lost years earlier while toiling as part of the title character's chain gang. Other searchers are Rutherford Selig, a "People Finder" and the son of a fugitive slave hunter, and Martha Pentecost, who seeks in Christianity a sense of inclusion that still eludes her up north. Meanwhile, Walker Bynum—a clairvoyant young man whose song is capable of binding men and women together—says he "got so I used all of myself up in the making of that song. Then I was the song in search of itself." Wilson's relentless, masterfully deployed use of this theme allows *Joe Turner* to pinwheel between the everyday and the eternal more than just about any other of his works, culminating in Herald's literally paralyzing vision at the end of Act I.

The 2009 Lincoln Center Theater revival was noteworthy for two reasons. In addition to being only the second Wilson revival to reach Broadway (and the first after his death), it was directed by Bartlett Sher, who is white. This is a bigger deal than you might realize: Wilson, and later his estate, all but insisted that only African American directors be entrusted with major productions of his work. The hiring of Sher raised some eyebrows—frequent Wilson collaborator Marion

McClinton accused Lincoln Center Theater of "straight up institutional racism"—but Sher's gutsy production made converts out of nearly everyone.

Wilson needed no convincing when it came to the play itself: *Joe Turner* was his favorite of the ten plays. Mine, too.

Lindo (shown in the 1987 production) later directed a production of *Joe Turner* at Berkeley Rep in Berkeley, California, in 2008. © Joan Marcus

DATES:

March 27–June 26, 1988 at the Ethel Barrymore Theater (105 performances)

SYNOPSIS:

A Pittsburgh boardinghouse attracts a number of seekers partaking in the Great Migration. Among them are Herald Loomis, desperately hunting for his wife after seven years of hard labor, and a mysterious young man named Bynum Walker, whose "binding song" might come in handy.

AWARDS:

1 Tony Award

NOTED REVIVALS AND ADAPTATIONS:

Broadway revival in 2009

ORIGINAL STARS:

Delroy Lindo, Angela Bassett, L. Scott Caldwell, Ed Hall

JUNO AND THE PAYCOCK

BY SÉAN O'CASEY

If Séan O'Casey really is "Ireland's Shakespeare," as many have called him, *Juno and the Paycock* would be one of the whistling-past-the-graveyard problem plays, with a healthy (or unhealthy) double dose of the immortal Falstaff-like reprobate plunked down in the middle of it.

O'Casey—the last of thirteen children, eight of whom died in infancy—reportedly learned to read from a complete edition of Shakespeare's works. He grew up in a tumultuous era in Irish history, and the Easter Rising and resulting Irish Civil War play a central role in his career-making "Dublin Trilogy": *The Shadow of a Gunman*, *Juno and the Paycock*, and *The Plough and the Stars*. Several waves of immigration to the major cities of the northeastern United States, meanwhile, had resulted in New York City actually having more Irish-born citizens than Dublin. That population of New York flocked to Broadway comedies and musicals by the likes of George M. Cohan and the duo Harrigan & Hart.

Although O'Casey's works are considerably darker (his World War I play *The Silver Tassie* is just devastating), they leaven even the bleakest plot twists with a chatty, absurdist wit that holds up very well. "Isn't all religions curious?" muses *Juno and the Paycock*'s blustery "Captain" Jack Boyle, so nicknamed for the one trip he made as a seaman, and for his ever-present nautical cap. "If they weren't, you wouldn't get anyone to believe in them." Basically everything that could go wrong for the Boyle family does, and the play would never have seen four Broadway revivals within fifteen years if it hadn't been for Jack and his wastrel of a drinking buddy, Joxer Daly.

The Captain may have atrocious taste in the company he keeps, but *Juno and the Paycock* itself has attracted some illustrious fans over the years. Alfred Hitchcock filmed a remarkably sedate adaptation in 1930, while the consistently high-minded composer Marc Blitzstein took one last quixotic stab at Broadway in 1959 with *Juno*, which has attracted a cult following. Still, for Irish tragicomedy in its purest form, O'Casey's original *Juno* remains the one to beat.

OPPOSITE PAGE: Barry Fitzgerald ("Captain" Jack Boyle) and Sara Allgood (Juno Boyle) in the 1940 Broadway revival of *Juno at the Paycock*, at the Mansfield Theater. Both Fitzgerald and Allgood also starred in the play's 1924 debut production, in Dublin, and in the 1930 Alfred Hitchcock film adaptation.

BELOW: 1959's *Juno* starred Shirley Booth and Melvyn Douglas (both center). The musical, staged by José Ferrer and choreographed by Agnes de Mille, ran for sixteen performances at the Winter Garden Theater.

DATES:
Opened March 15, 1926 at the Mayfair Theater (74 performances)

SYNOPSIS:
Poor Juno Boyle. She's the only reason her family is still afloat, but not even the promise of an inheritance is enough to protect the rest of the family—particularly her vain husband, "Captain" Jack—from drunkenness and worse.

AWARDS:
None

NOTED REVIVALS AND ADAPTATIONS:
Broadway revivals in 1927, 1934, 1937, 1940, and 1988; movie version in 1930; TV versions in 1938, 1960, and 1980

ORIGINAL STARS:
Louise Randolph, Augustin Duncan, Claude Cooper

THE KING AND I

BY RICHARD RODGERS AND OSCAR HAMMERSTEIN II

Imagine an entire *Saturday Night Live* skit today devoted to the idea of someone succeeding, say, Idina Menzel in *Wicked* or John Lloyd Young in *Jersey Boys*. Unthinkable, right? That actually happened in 1987, when Phil Hartman played an actor in a defensive rage over assuming the role of the King of Siam in *The King and I*: "Listen, don't get me wrong. I'm not saying Yul Brynner wasn't good in the role. I'm sure he was. All I'm saying is that there's a guy by the name of Ross Treadway, and he's pretty good, too."

Such was the indelible mark that the hypnotic, effortlessly virile Brynner left on the role after 4,625 performances, including the entire original run, two Broadway revivals, several tours, the 1956 movie, and a short-lived TV show. (That works out to 578 weeks of performances, or more than eleven years.) Not bad for a guy who only got the part because Rex Harrison, Noël Coward, and Alfred Drake either weren't available or wanted too much money.

The role of Anna Leonowens, by comparison, was never under discussion. It was Gertrude Lawrence who approached Rodgers and Hammerstein about the project; she had purchased the rights to Margaret Landon's novel *Anna and the King of Siam*, a

fictionalized telling of Leonowens' time in Southeast Asia. The songwriters were concerned about the suitability of the material, and about Lawrence's singing voice, but they finally signed on. (For one thing, both of their wives were big fans of the idea.) The show went through extensive revisions out of town—the first preview was nearly four hours!—before reaching Broadway.

Lawrence's narrow vocal range, along with the inconvenient fact that the real-life King and Anna never canoodled, resulted in what might be the richest material ever allotted to a musical's secondary couple, a young slave intended to marry the King and her secret lover. (The lack of actual physical contact between the leads hardly gets in the way of a potent chemistry, as evidenced by the unforgettable moment when the King finally grabs Anna's waist in "Shall We Dance?") Songs like "I Have Dreamed" and "We Kiss in a Shadow" are ample compensation for bowing before the title characters do, even if Tuptim and Lun Tha are denied the juicy deaths they received in the novel.

Rodgers' canny, if intermittent, use of Asian musical idioms, such as open fifths and major seconds, beautifully straddled Western and Eastern styles, as did Jerome Robbins' mesmerizing "Small House of Uncle Thomas" ballet, with its traditional Siamese take on *Uncle Tom's Cabin*. *The King and I* was arguably the last time Rodgers and Hammerstein made a concerted effort to expand the boundaries of musical theater. Fair enough: with sixty-five years of combined Broadway experience at that point, they'd earned the right to play it a bit safer.

ABOVE: Jo Mielziner designed the grand sets of the original production, and Irene Sharaff was the costume designer. Mielziner and Sharaff also won Tonys.

OPPOSITE PAGE: Yul Brynner and Gertrude Lawrence as the King of Siam and Anna Leonowens in *The King and I*. Both won Tonys, as did the musical.

DATES:
March 29, 1951–March 20, 1954 at the St. James Theater (1,246 performances)

SYNOPSIS:
King Mongkut's attempt to westernize his country of Siam in the 1860s results in the hiring of a British schoolteacher, Anna Leonowens, to instruct his many children. Cultures clash, an unspoken love simmers in the background, et cetera, et cetera, et cetera.

AWARDS:
5 Tony Awards

NOTED REVIVALS AND ADAPTATIONS:
Broadway revivals in 1977, 1985, 1996, and 2015; movie version in 1956

ORIGINAL STARS:
Yul Brynner, Gertrude Lawrence

KISS ME, KATE

Y COLE PORTER, BELLA SPEWACK, AND SAMUEL SPEWACK

As literary-leaning gangsters, Jack Diamond and Harry Clark advised listeners, "If your blonde won't respond when you flatter 'er / Tell her what Tony told Cleopaterer."

Even bons vivants from Peru, Indiana, can learn new tricks. By the time Cole Porter began writing *Kiss Me, Kate*, he had spent more than thirty years writing delectable, detachable songs that could easily pop out of whatever show and be none the worse for it.

But then came *Oklahoma!*, changing—for good—the whole concept of what role songs should play in a musical comedy. People needed to have a reason to start singing, and the most beguiling triple rhyme or neologism no longer qualified as a reason. It was time to integrate. Porter, who had spent the last few years collaborating on misfires with the likes of Orson Welles, Salvador Dalí, and Igor Stravinsky, pounced on the opportunity.

DATES:

December 30, 1948–July 28, 1951 at the New Century Theater and Shubert Theater (1,077 performances)

SYNOPSIS:

A mislabeled bouquet of flowers, a pair of mobsters, a priggish politico, and some good old-fashioned narcissism conspire to make the divorce of Shakespearean actors Fred Graham and Lilli Vanessi a lot less amicable. Will *The Taming of the Shrew* ever be the same?

AWARDS:

5 Tony Awards

NOTED REVIVALS AND ADAPTATIONS:

Broadway revivals in 1952 and 1999; movie version in 1953; TV versions in 1958, 1964, 1968, and 2003

ORIGINAL STARS:

Alfred Drake, Patricia Morrison, Lisa Kirk, Harold Lang

Patricia Morison and Alfred Drake played Lilli Vanessi and Fred Graham, who in turn play Katherine and Petruchio in the show-within-a-show performance of *The Taming of the Shrew*. *Ralph Morse, The LIFE Picture Collection, Getty Images*

The beauty of it is that *Kiss Me, Kate*, easily the most structurally ambitious of his musicals, doesn't sacrifice one ounce of wit or charm along the way. On the contrary, by setting his tale of a recently divorced couple against the backdrop of a production of *The Taming of the Shrew*, Porter mixed Shakespeare and faux Shakespeare with almost obscene delight: "I come to thee a thoroughbred patrician / Still spraying my decaying family tree." (If the show within a show isn't metatheatrical enough for you, consider that Bella and Sam Spewack were separated when they wrote the show's book.)

The backstage milieu gave Porter a chance to go modern with sizzlers like "Too Darn Hot" and "Always True to You in My Fashion," while also taking his tongue out of his cheek for the ballad "So in Love." The mobsters who emerge from the action as unlikely Bardologists—and deliverers of one of the all-time great eleven o'clock numbers, "Brush Up Your Shakespeare"—serve as proxies for the audience. It's virtually impossible to come out of *Kiss Me, Kate* and not be so in love with the vain, fickle, glorious men and women who make theater.

LADY IN THE DARK

BY KURT WEILL, IRA GERSHWIN, AND MOSS HART

DATES:
Three blocks of performances at the Alvin Theater and Broadway Theater between 1941 and 1943 (total of 467 performances)

SYNOPSIS:
A "Glamour Dream," a "Wedding Dream," and a "Circus Dream": it is through these three extended sequences that magazine editor Liza Elliott and her psychoanalyst get to the bottom of her neuroses.

AWARDS:
None

NOTED REVIVALS AND ADAPTATIONS:
Movie version in 1944; TV version in 1954

ORIGINAL STARS:
Gertrude Lawrence, Danny Kaye, Macdonald Carey, Bert Lytell, Victor Mature

ABOVE: In *Lady in the Dark*, Gertrude Lawrence played Liza Elliott, an editor suffering from panic attacks and depression who tries to uncover the root of her troubles.

OPPOSITE PAGE: During the Circus Dream, Liza defends her indecisiveness in "The Saga of Jenny." The song describes a girl who, "inclined always to make up her mind," ends up an orphan, a hussy, and a boozer.

Any time somebody starts bellyaching about how musicals are so tired and predictable, steer them toward *Lady in the Dark*—with a few caveats. Not everything in it works, and the intervening decades haven't necessarily done its flaws any favors. But hoo boy, is it ambitious! "There has been nothing quite like it in the modern American theater," wrote the esteemed critic Elliot Norton during the show's Boston tryout.

Forget the fifty-six Russian composers that Danny Kaye rattled off in thirty-nine seconds in the song "Tchaikovsky," or the sight of grand Gertrude Lawrence on an acrobat's swing, or the then-unheard-of pair of turntables working simultaneously, or the fact that lyricist Ira Gershwin had come out of virtual retirement for the first time since his brother George's death in 1937. This was a musical about *psychoanalysis*. And not one sugared with time-traveling romance, like *On a Clear Day You Can See Forever*, or perfunctory sessions played for laughs, like *Falsettos*. Virtually the entire score was confined to three sprawling dream sequences experienced by Liza, Lawrence's character, each one triggered by a Freudian field day of a song called

"My Ship." (The song is supposed to evoke childhood memories, but some of the lyrics wouldn't be out of place in a bawdy blues club. "There's a paradise in the hold"?)

Kurt Weill's intricate, consistently surprising score earned him the praise of both Aaron Copland and Igor Stravinsky. (Gershwin described "The Saga of Jenny" as "a sort of blues bordello," words rarely connected with Weill.) But Moss Hart's book, which began as part of an abandoned Marlene Dietrich musical and then became an abandoned Katharine Cornell play, is glib and reductive; perhaps his own analyst's reported vetting of each draft of the script was to blame. Incidentally, Hart also all but offered Lawrence the lead role while it still technically belonged to Cornell. Did I mention that the event that sends Liza to the couch involves her having to decide between two magazine covers—and that "The Saga of Jenny" is about a woman who can't make up her mind?

No matter. In a 1940–1941 season that also featured such envelope-pushers as *Pal Joey* and *Cabin in the Sky*, *Lady in the Dark* pushed the hardest. Musical theater could use more of its type, warts and all.

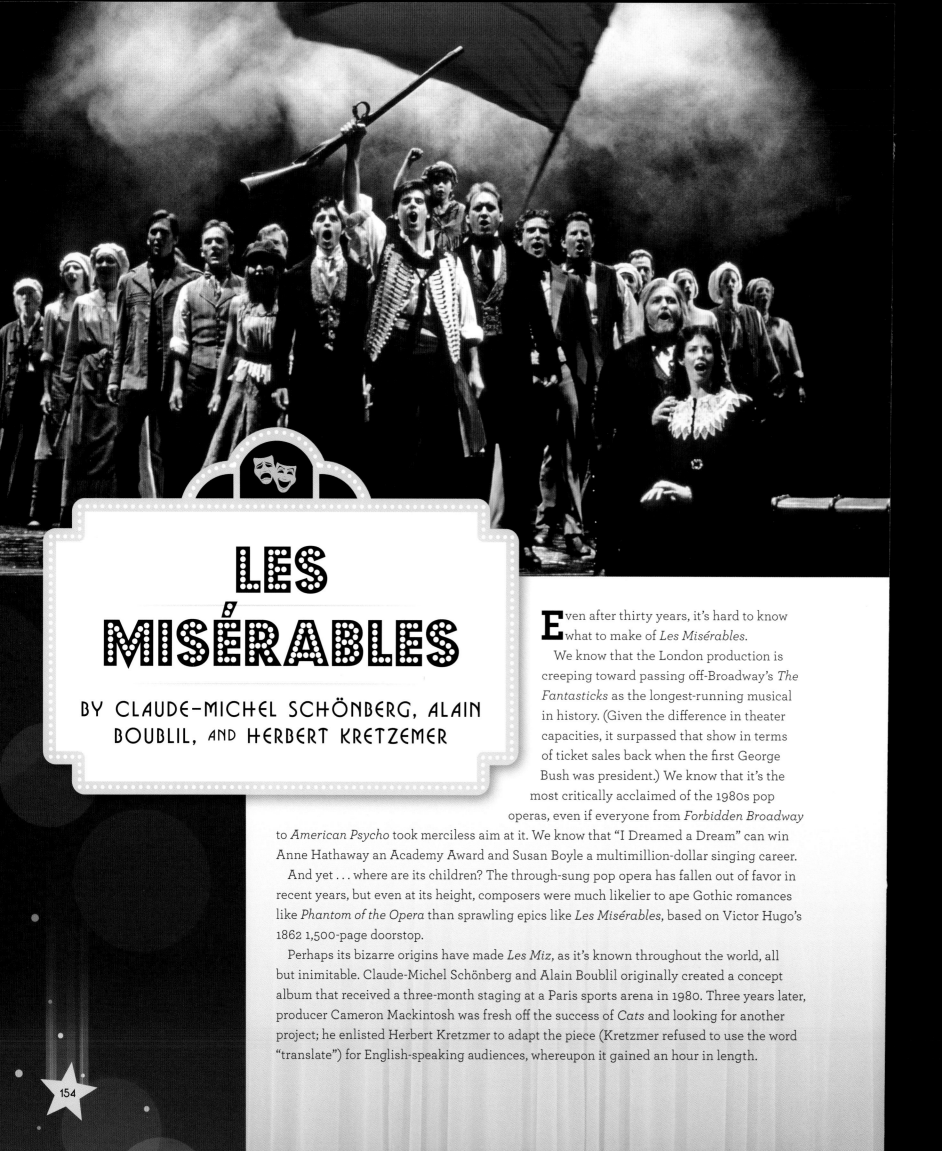

LES MISÉRABLES

BY CLAUDE-MICHEL SCHÖNBERG, ALAIN BOUBLIL, AND HERBERT KRETZEMER

Even after thirty years, it's hard to know what to make of *Les Misérables*.

We know that the London production is creeping toward passing off-Broadway's *The Fantasticks* as the longest-running musical in history. (Given the difference in theater capacities, it surpassed that show in terms of ticket sales back when the first George Bush was president.) We know that it's the most critically acclaimed of the 1980s pop operas, even if everyone from *Forbidden Broadway* to *American Psycho* took merciless aim at it. We know that "I Dreamed a Dream" can win Anne Hathaway an Academy Award and Susan Boyle a multimillion-dollar singing career.

And yet . . . where are its children? The through-sung pop opera has fallen out of favor in recent years, but even at its height, composers were much likelier to ape Gothic romances like *Phantom of the Opera* than sprawling epics like *Les Misérables*, based on Victor Hugo's 1862 1,500-page doorstop.

Perhaps its bizarre origins have made *Les Miz*, as it's known throughout the world, all but inimitable. Claude-Michel Schönberg and Alain Boublil originally created a concept album that received a three-month staging at a Paris sports arena in 1980. Three years later, producer Cameron Mackintosh was fresh off the success of *Cats* and looking for another project; he enlisted Herbert Kretzmer to adapt the piece (Kretzmer refused to use the word "translate") for English-speaking audiences, whereupon it gained an hour in length.

DATES:

March 12, 1987–May 18, 2003 at the Broadway Theater and Imperial Theater (6,680 performances)

SYNOPSIS:

How to make this brief? There's a cop named Javert who's actually sort of a bad guy, and he's chasing a criminal named Jean Valjean, who's actually a really good guy, and they get mixed up in a French revolution ("but not the big famous one, a little later one," as *Forbidden Broadway* memorably put it), along with a bunch of young people and a pair of scoundrels.

AWARDS:

9 Tony Awards

NOTED REVIVALS AND ADAPTATIONS:

Broadway revivals in 2006 and 2014; movie version in 2012

ORIGINAL STARS:

Colm Wilkinson, Terrence Mann, Judy Kuhn, Frances Ruffelle, Randy Graff

Then it was director Trevor Nunn's turn to work his magic. For the first (and, I maintain, only) time in the entire pop-opera era, Nunn saw to it that the spectacle—the turntable, the makeshift barricade, the sewers, the suicidal plunge from the bridge—was always in service of the story. That barricade is arguably more impressive than the chandelier in *Phantom* or the helicopter in *Miss Saigon*, but people don't talk about it in the same way. They're more interested in what's happening on it.

OPPOSITE PAGE: As Act I of *Les Misérables* closes, characters wonder what will happen with the arrival of "One Day More"—and with imminent uprising.

BELOW: The original production was the second-longest-running Broadway show at the time. As of early 2015, it was the fifth-longest of all time, after *The Phantom of the Opera, Chicago* (revival), *Cats,* and *The Lion King.* (The rest of the top ten? *A Chorus Line, Oh! Calcutta!* (revival), *Mamma Mia!, Beauty and the Beast,* and *Rent.*)

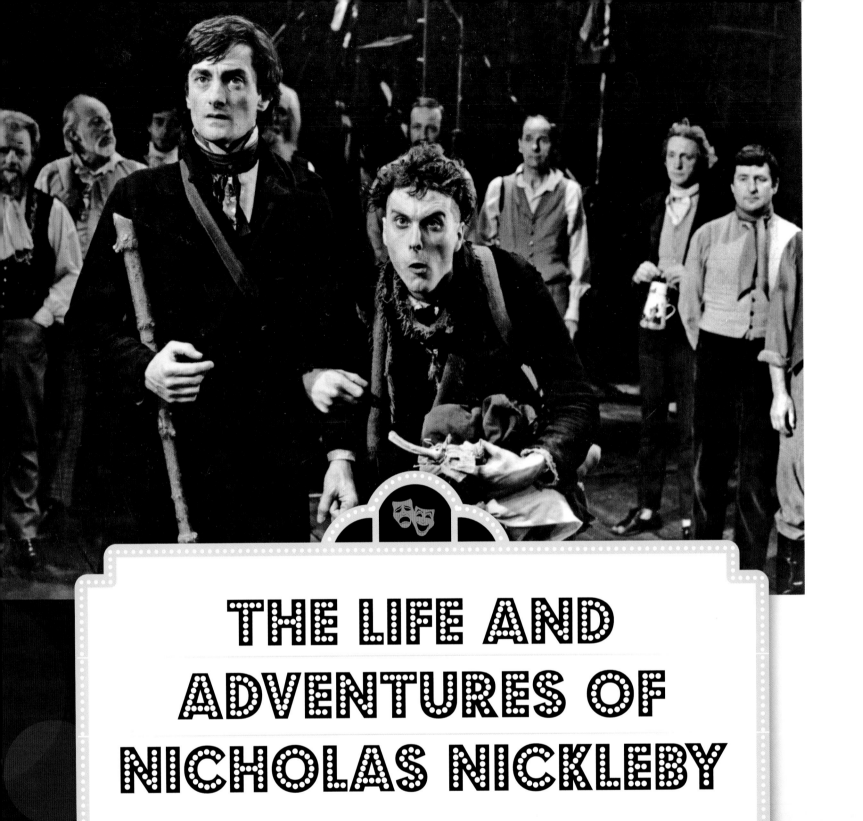

THE LIFE AND ADVENTURES OF NICHOLAS NICKLEBY

BY DAVID EDGAR

"**Y**ou will pay more than you ever thought possible for a theatre ticket. The experience will be priceless." So warned/boasted the advance ad in the *New York Times* for *The Life and Adventures of Nicholas Nickleby,* the cultural behemoth created by England's Royal Shakespeare Company. The price was $100 at a time when the going rate for a Broadway ticket was $30. For that sum you got two tickets—one for each half of the eight-and-a-half-hour production. Purchasing just one or the other was not an option. Virtually every ticket was sold before opening night.

DATES:

October 4, 1981–January 3, 1982 at the Plymouth Theater (49 performances)

SYNOPSIS:

The complete Charles Dickens novel on stage—*all* of it.

AWARDS:

5 Tony Awards

NOTED REVIVALS AND ADAPTATIONS:

Broadway revival in 1986; TV version in 1983

ORIGINAL STARS:

Roger Rees, David Threlfall, Suzanne Bertish, Alun Armstrong, Edward Petherbridge, Emily Richard, John Woodvine

OPPOSITE PAGE: Roger Rees (left, with David Threlfall as Smike) played Nicholas Nickleby, for which he received a Tony Award.

RIGHT: *The Life and Adventures of Nicholas Nickleby* had a cast of forty-two and a total run time of more than eight hours. *Ted Thai, The LIFE Picture Collection, Getty Images*

At the beginning of each segment, the cast assembled to confront the audience in a neutral stance before dissolving into Charles Dickens' bleak tale of power, money, and class disparity. It was an exhilarating combination of narration and locomotive storytelling, in which simple props became full-blown scenery and human bodies became landscapes to depict the novel's more than two hundred locales. RSC director Trevor Nunn's minimalist story-theater technique would later find its way into his (far more maximalist) junk piles of *Cats* and barricades of *Les Misérables*. Original star Roger Rees also revisited the style when he directed *Peter and the Starcatcher* some thirty years later.

Dickens' own love of theater and its denizens was fondly illustrated in *Nickleby* by the ragtag acting troupe known as the Crummles. Their depiction paid homage to the puffed-up acting style of the day, one that Dickens himself would display from time to time. The Crummles' generosity provides one of the few bright spots in the cruel world Nicholas and orphan Smike encounter.

Two rival theater owners, the Shubert Organization and the Nederlander Organization, put aside their differences to bring the complex production across the Atlantic Ocean. The entire RSC company of forty-two was imported from London—and there would be no replacements, which meant no extensions. (One cast member who did not make the journey was Ben Kingsley, who had originally played the sadistic schoolmaster Wackford Squeers but was tied up filming *Gandhi*.) In other words, the production would have to return its sizeable investment within a scant fourteen weeks. The result was the shortest run of any play to win the Tony Award for Best Play.

Was it great theater or a simply a great event? Most critics agreed that it was both. And *Nickleby* never compromised Dickens' outrage over social injustice. The indelible final image was of a defiant Nicholas holding aloft yet another wretched soul as the company sang "God Rest Ye Merry Gentlemen."

LIFE WITH FATHER

BY HOWARD LINDSAY AND RUSSEL CROUSE

ABOVE: Howard Lindsay, standing, played Father, alongside (clockwise from Lindsay), John Drew Devereaux, Richard Simon, Dorothy Stickney (as Vinnie), Larry Robinson, and Raymond Roe.

OPPOSITE PAGE: The author Clarence Day Jr. first began writing about his father in the *New Yorker*, and published the autobiographical book *Life with Father* in 1935. His stories inspired the play of the same name.

"Now, I love my wife just as much as any man, but that doesn't mean I should stand for a lot of folderol!"—Clarence Day Sr.

Way before Ward Cleaver and Gomez Addams and Archie Bunker and Phil Dunphy, TV audiences fell in love (albeit exasperated love) with Clarence Day, the title character in CBS' *Life with Father*, and his red-headed kids. The show was reasonably popular, but

DATES:

November 8, 1939–July 12, 1947 at the Empire Theater, Bijou Theater, and Alvin Theater (3,224 performances)

SYNOPSIS:

Clarence Day's status as the undisputed (yet unbaptized) master of his Madison Avenue brownstone is imperiled by various demands made upon him by his children—and by the accidental poisoning of his endlessly patient wife, Vinnie.

AWARDS:
None

NOTED REVIVALS AND ADAPTATIONS:

Movie version in 1947; TV series in 1953

ORIGINAL STARS:

Howard Lindsay, Dorothy Stickney

it can't compare to the play of the same name, which for twenty-five years was the longest-running show in Broadway history. To this day, it remains the most popular nonmusical.

The harried, obstreperous, but ultimately loving patriarch of Clarence Day Jr.'s *New Yorker* stories was no less archetypal in 1939—or in the late 1890s, when the play is set—than he is now. But with America teetering on the edge of a war that had already engulfed much of the world, a little Victorian rectitude went a long way, no matter how many maids Clarence went through or ailments he attempted to swear out of his system. ("Of course I yell! That's to prove to the headache that I'm stronger than it is.")

Life With Father came fairly early in the twenty-eight-year partnership between Howard Lindsay and Russel Crouse. Lindsay stepped into the title role (opposite his real-life wife, Dorothy Stickney) only after Alfred Lunt, among other bigger names, turned it down. Although opening night featured a variety of mishaps, from flubbed lines to dropped dishes, Lindsay and Stickney were still playing the same roles five years later.

A sequel called (of course) *Life With Mother* didn't fare as well, but then again, no other play ever has. *New York Times* theater critic Brooks Atkinson was hardly exaggerating when he wrote of the original piece, "Sooner or later everyone will have to see it." After its nearly eight years on Broadway, nearly everyone had.

THE LION KING

BY ELTON JOHN, TIM RICE, ROGER ALLERS, AND IRENE MECCHI

ABOVE: Director Julie Taymor also designed *The Lion King*'s costumes and, with Michael Curry, its puppets and masks. Richard Hudson was set designer. © *Disney Theatrical Productions, Joan Marcus*

OPPOSITE PAGE: *The Lion King* transferred to the Minskoff Theater nine years into its run. *ValeStock, Shutterstock.com*

NEXT PAGE: "The Circle of Life," *The Lion King*'s opening number, composed by Elton John with lyrics by Tim Rice. © *Disney Theatrical Productions, Joan Marcus*

It's easy to forget now, but there was a time not that long ago when the prospect of adapting Disney movies for Broadway was a novel one. The company kicked things off with a workmanlike *Beauty and the Beast* that was directed by a theme-park veteran and had kids fidgeting on the few occasions when it deviated from the film's screenplay. Still, it made pots of money, and Disney had no real incentive to tamper with the formula. Then came *The Lion King*.

Handing director Julie Taymor the beloved property and, essentially, a blank check was a huge gamble for the company, which also sunk tens of millions of dollars into refurbishing an old Ziegfeld palace called the New Amsterdam Theater for the show. Taymor had an avid following among the downtown theater scene, thanks to puppet-heavy pieces like the magic-realist "carnival mass" *Juan Darién*, but *The Lion King* was several degrees of magnitude bigger. Although the studio famously referred to the property as "*Hamlet* with fur," not even Shakespeare got around to murdering a lead character in an onstage wildebeest stampede.

Her solution involved a beguiling mix of modern technology and centuries-old puppetry styles. (She was also one of five composers and lyricists entrusted with fleshing out Elton John and Tim Rice's sparse but adequate film score.) Taymor flooded the stage, the aisles, and the balconies with stunning visuals, and even that stampede went off without a hitch.

One of Broadway's unlikelier collaborations was a booming success: *The Lion King* has earned more than $5 billion, more than the first six *Star Wars* films combined, and in 2014 it surpassed *The Phantom of the Opera* to become the biggest-selling musical in history. Believe it or not, though, the dividends should be even greater in the decades to come. Any kid who gets his or her first exposure to theater through *The Lion King* should be hooked for life.

LITTLE JOHNNY JONES

BY GEORGE M. COHAN

George M. Cohan's shadow looms large over Broadway, both figuratively and literally. The energy of today's musicals owes much to the former vaudevillian's "louder-faster-funnier" mantra, while his statue—the only one of its kind in Manhattan's Theater District—watches over the daily TKTS line for discount tickets.

With a family of performers to feed (and employ), the indefatigable Cohan wrote dozens of musicals and plays for the Broadway stage in the early twentieth century. And then he'd direct them, produce them, and star in them. *Little Johnny Jones* was the first example of this—and some hold it up as the first example of an integrated musical comedy, with book, music, and lyrics all serving one another.

Its title character, as in many of Cohan's shows, was a thinly veiled version of his own brash, patriotic

GIVE MY REGARDS TO BROADWAY

ONE OF THE
MUSICAL HITS
GEO. M. COHAN'S
LATEST PLAY

"LITTLE JOHNNY JONES"

Words &
Music by
GEO. M. COHAN

THE
YANKEE
DOODLE COMEDIAN

F. A. MILLS
48 WEST 29TH ST.
NEW YORK

ABOVE: "Give my regards to Broadway, / Remember me to Herald Square, / Tell all the gang at 42nd Street that I will soon be there," Johnny implores in one of *Little Johnny Jones'* hit songs. *Sheet music*

OPPOSITE PAGE: *Little Johnny Jones* Broadway cast members, with Ethel Levey (George M. Cohan's wife) far right, 1904. Levey played Goldie, Johnny Jones' sweetheart, who disguises herself as a man to investigate whether Johnny (played by Cohan) really loves her.

DATES:
November 7–December 24, 1904 at the Liberty Theater (52 performances)

SYNOPSIS:
In order to return to the States and reunite with the girl he loves, hotshot American jockey Johnny Jones must clear his name after being falsely accused of throwing the English Derby.

AWARDS:
None

NOTED REVIVALS AND ADAPTATIONS:
Broadway revivals in 1905, 1907, and 1982; movie versions in 1924 and 1929

ORIGINAL STARS:
George M. Cohan, Jerry Cohan, Nellie Cohan, Ethel Levey

persona. Future show business anthems like "Give My Regards to Broadway" and "Yankee Doodle Dandy" found a home in the hearts of immigrants who identified with the unapologetic sentiment of being the proudest American citizens possible. He spoke to them in a language they could understand.

With its mix of comedy, melodrama, music, and spectacle, *Johnny Jones* established the Cohan brand, becoming a model for the dozens of his shows that followed. More than its relative seamlessness, though, its energy and speed influenced other musical comedies and signaled the beginning of the end for the slower-moving operettas that dotted the Broadway landscape at the time. By the 1920s, musical comedy had become the dominant entertainment.

Johnny Jones was only a modest hit initially, but Cohan was not one to settle. After its Broadway premiere, he took it on the road and retooled it, bringing it back three times in as many years. Cohan's jingoism never endeared him to the critics (the show featured a song called "March of the Frisco Chinks"), yet he took pride that his typical audience was not the intelligentsia but, as he once described them, "the working man and his girl who sat in the balcony."

Nearly a century later, most people know Cohan either from that jaunty statue or from James Cagney's Academy Award–winning portrayal of him in the 1944 biopic *Yankee Doodle Dandy*, which includes a *Johnny Jones* sequence. Cohan, who was dying of abdominal cancer at the time, almost missed the film's release. His take on Cagney's performance after being given a private screening was, "My God, what an act to follow!" The same could be said for Cohan himself.

A LITTLE NIGHT MUSIC

BY STEPHEN SONDHEIM AND HUGH WHEELER

Glynis Johns, Laurence Guittard, Hermione Gingold, Patricia Elliott, and William Daniels (replacement for Len Cariou) in the original Broadway production, choreographed by Patricia Burch and designed by Boris Aronson.

For anyone who still clings to the notion of Stephen Sondheim as an unemotional songwriter whose tunes you don't hum on your way out of the theater, *A Little Night Music* will blow that assumption out of the water once and for all. First of all, his swirling, sardonic permutations on three-quarter time—best known as the accompaniment to waltzes—include by far his best-known song, "Send in the Clowns." And Sondheim himself has said that the roisterous Act I finale, "A Weekend in the Country," has so many reprises in part because he wanted to show audiences that sheer repetition was the secret to lodging a tune in the brain. It worked, and he also managed to cram massive amounts of plot into those reprises.

In adapting Ingmar Bergman's atypically sprightly film *Smiles of a Summer Night* (1955), Sondheim and Hugh Wheeler took a sumptuous but rueful look at love. Director/producer Harold Prince likened the result to "whipped cream with knives." (With its mistresses and cuckolds and botched seductions and even a pratfall into a hip bath, *A Little Night Music* is perhaps the most mature sex farce ever.) The puzzle fiend in Sondheim reveled in the complicated interweavings of characters; he introduced three characters through the virtuosic counterpoint of "Now/Later/Soon." But he also made room for poignant ballads like "Every Day a Little Death."

When Sondheim realized that the woman playing Desirée, Glynis Johns, had a hard time sustaining notes, he started writing a new song. Two days later, he returned with the wistful, haunting "Send in the Clowns," which uses a series of questions and line-ending consonants to keep each line short. Everyone from Sinatra to Streisand to Judi Dench to *The Simpsons*' Krusty the Clown ("Send in those soulful and doleful, / Schmaltz-by-the-bowlful clowns") has since had a go at it.

A Little Night Music capped off the greatest hot streak in the history of musical theater: Sondheim and Prince's *Company* had opened less than three years earlier, and in between came *Follies*, which many theater buffs call their favorite musical of all time. These days, composers are lucky if they can fit in one musical in that amount of time. (*Spring Awakening* took twice as long to put together, and that's hardly atypical.) Part of the problem may involve real estate. A run of 601 performances was considered pretty healthy in 1973. Today, as of press time, six different Broadway shows have had well over two thousand performances.

This may make for a healthy Broadway economy in the short run, but each megahit takes a theater off the market for years or even decades—and there are only forty theaters. If theater owners (who have a huge financial incentive to keep the lights on and the seats filled) had to keep finding new material, the barriers to entry would be far, far lower. Now, obviously, I'm not suggesting that there are a dozen *A Little Night Music*s out there circling the runway. But wouldn't it be nice to find out?

Daniels and Johns. "I knew I was writing a song in which Desirée is saying, 'aren't we foolish' or 'aren't we fools?'" Sondheim said of *A Little Night Music*'s most famous song. "Well, a synonym for fools is clowns."

DATES:

February 25, 1973–August 3, 1974 at the Shubert Theater and Majestic Theater (601 performances)

SYNOPSIS:

A weekend in a Swedish country house becomes the setting for a web of love affairs involving a child bride, a dragoon, a seminarian, and a maid. At its center is a long-dormant romance between Fredrik Egerman and Desirée, the glamorous actress whose mother is hosting the weekend.

AWARDS:

6 Tony Awards

NOTED REVIVALS AND ADAPTATIONS:

Broadway revival in 2009; movie version in 1977

ORIGINAL STARS:

Len Cariou, Glynis Johns, Hermione Gingold, Laurence Guittard, Patricia Elliott

LONG DAY'S JOURNEY INTO NIGHT

BY EUGENE O'NEILL

"**H**e would come out of his study at the end of a day gaunt and sometimes weeping. His eyes would be all red and he looked ten years older than when he went in in the morning."

That was how Carlotta O'Neill described the state of her husband, Eugene O'Neill, as he wrote *Long Day's Journey Into Night*. Eugene, for his part, called the piece "a play of old sorrow, written in tears and blood." If he had dipped a quill pen into his own vein enough times to write a four-act play, the results could scarcely have been more personal. The Connecticut summer home, the barnstorming miser of a father, the morphine-addicted mother, the dissolute older brother: all came directly from O'Neill's own childhood. No wonder he decreed that the play not be released to the public until twenty-five years after his death.

Carlotta jumped the gun by twenty-two years, as it happens, authorizing a production of the play just three years after O'Neill died. His life was still fresh enough to give *Long Day's Journey* a ghoulish resonance that originally overshadowed the work itself. It is often described as an autobiography in the form of a play. That is true up to a point, but it fails to take into full consideration the play's own lyrical, meandering, ultimately rending gifts.

The delusions that both bolster and cripple the Tyrone family are familiar from many of O'Neill's other works, from *The Emperor Jones* to *The Iceman Cometh*. But the exotic settings of those plays shielded audiences to some degree. The Tyrones, with their summer cottage and their summer maid, bore a much closer resemblance to the typical Broadway audience, which both thrilled and shuddered at what they saw in front of them.

Jason Robards Jr. and director José Quintero, who had helped reestablish the Nobel laureate as a major playwright with their off-Broadway production of *The Iceman Cometh* earlier that year, teamed up again for *Long Day's Journey*, joined by real-life couple Fredric March and Florence Eldridge as James and Mary Tyrone. O'Neill won his fourth Pulitzer Prize for the piece, the most any playwright has ever received. The award was posthumous, of course—though if O'Neill had had his way, it would have been a good bit more posthumous.

ABOVE: Florence Eldridge, Albert Morgenstern (Bradford Dillman's understudy and eventual replacement), Jason Robards, and Fredric March played the Tyrones in the original Broadway production of *Long Day's Journey Into Night*. The cast was rounded out by Katherine Ross as Cathleen.

OPPOSITE PAGE: Clockwise, Eldridge, Dillman, Robards, and March.

DATES:
November 7, 1956–March 29, 1958 at the Helen Hayes Theater (390 performances)

SYNOPSIS:
The Tyrones, a family of addicts (booze for the three men, morphine for their wife/mother), lurch between accusations, reconciliations, denials, and bitter memories over the course of a very long day at their seaside Connecticut summer home.

AWARDS:
2 Tony Awards; Pulitzer Prize

NOTED REVIVALS AND ADAPTATIONS:
Broadway revivals in 1962, 1986, 1988, and 2003; movie version in 1962; TV versions in 1973, 1982, 1987, and 1996

ORIGINAL STARS:
Florence Eldridge, Fredric March, Jason Robards Jr., Bradford Dillman

LOOK BACK IN ANGER

BY JOHN OSBORNE

Kenneth Haigh (Jimmy Porter) and Alan Bates (Cliff Lewis) in the original Broadway production. Haigh and Bates also costarred in the show's London premiere in 1956.

One side benefit of sequencing the plays and musicals in this book alphabetically, as opposed to chronologically or thematically, is the sometimes-surprising juxtapositions that pop up. A torrid Eisenhower-era look at closeted homosexuality (*Cat on a Hot Tin Roof*) sits right next to a group of felines looking to go a lot higher than a roof, all the way to the Heaviside Layer (*Cats*). But then we find *Look Back in Anger*, which opened just three months after *Long Day's Journey Into Night*, a play that could just as easily have used John Osborne's bristling title instead.

DATES:

October 1, 1957–September 20, 1958 at the Lyceum Theater and John Golden Theater (407 performances)

SYNOPSIS:

Jimmy Porter, a working-class Briton with a Buckingham Palace–sized chip on his shoulder, blames his class anxieties on his upper-crust wife, on women in general, and on mid-twentieth-century England.

AWARDS:

None

NOTED REVIVALS AND ADAPTATIONS:

Movie version in 1959; TV versions in 1980 and 1989

ORIGINAL STARS:

Kenneth Haigh, Mary Ure, Vivienne Drummond, Alan Bates

Both playwrights drew heavily from their own family situations, although Osborne—who scribbled *Look Back* in just over two weeks—would probably have turned his nose up at Eugene O'Neill's arduous writing habits. But then, there aren't many people up at whom Osborne's nose didn't turn. The "Angry Young Men" movement in British theater of the era may have been an unwieldy concept, lumping in all sorts of less deserving writers, but Osborne unquestionably belonged. He looked forward and sideways in anger, too.

To clear up a few of the legends that have accrued to the piece:

Did the play coin the phrase "angry young man"? No, although the *Look Back* press release did use it. The phrase actually came from the writer and educator Leslie Paul's autobiography several years earlier. Nonetheless, Osborne became known as the group's spiritual father—and he lived up/down to its name long after he qualified as young.

Did London audiences gasp at the sight of an ironing board on stage? Supposedly, yes. Terence Rattigan, the quintessential well-heeled British dramatist, was there on opening night and said afterward, "I think the writer is trying to say, 'Look how unlike Terence Rattigan I am, Ma!'" (One could argue that that single "Ma" packs more of a punch than many of Osborne's splenetic monologues.)

Did influential theater critic Kenneth Tynan write, "I doubt if I could love anyone who did not wish to see *Look Back in Anger*"? Yep.

There is one last myth, which is the hardest to prove; it's also the best one. When megaproducer David Merrick brought *Look Back* to Broadway, American audiences weren't nearly as scandalized by it, and they began to dwindle after just a few months. So Merrick supposedly paid a woman $250 to feign outrage at the main character's misogynistic diatribes, jump onto the stage, and slap actor Kenneth Haigh across the face. Business quickly picked up.

John Osborne, 1970. In 1958, Osborne and *Look Back in Anger* director Tony Richardson cofounded a film production company, which produced the film version of *Anger* and that of Henry Fielding's 1749 novel *Tom Jones*. Osborne's *Tom Jones* screenplay earned him an Oscar.

LOOT

BY JOE ORTON

DATES:

March 18–April 6, 1968 at the Biltmore Theater (22 performances)

SYNOPSIS:

Dennis and Hal store some stolen bank loot in the coffin that holds Hal's mother. The only problem is, they don't know where to stash her body. Well, and there's a nurse out to make Hal's dad Husband No. 8. And a psychotic police inspector investigating the robbery.

AWARDS:

None

NOTED REVIVALS AND ADAPTATIONS:

Broadway revival in 1986; movie version in 1970

ORIGINAL STARS:

George Rose, Kenneth Cranham, Carole Shelley, James Hunter, Liam Redmond

I am desired by the Lord Chamberlain to inform you that he will only consider granting a license for the above named play if certain scenes are rewritten so that:
The corpse is obviously a dummy.
The corpse remains fully clothed throughout the play and is not undressed, even behind a screen, at any time; and the accompanying dialogue is adjusted accordingly.
The false eye business is removed.

This note, which reached the producers of Joe Orton's *Loot* in 1965 during what was meant to be a pre–West End tour of England, could be used verbatim as a poster for the show. (Oddly, the Lord Chamberlain took issue with a dead woman's eyeball popping out of her skull, but not with her dentures being used as castanets—by her own son!) Still, not even the juicy threat of censorship was enough to rescue what was, by all accounts, a disastrous first pass, marked with screaming matches, black eyes, and pages upon pages of new material.

It took a gut renovation two years later—with the help of a new director, American expatriate Charles Marowitz—to turn *Loot* into what it is today: the juiciest and, in its way, most subversive example of Orton's unique voice. "Ideally, it should be nearer *The Homecoming* than *I Love Lucy*," he wrote as a bit of guidance when the Marowitz staging triggered interest in a Broadway production. *Loot* has plenty of both, which is even harder to manage than it sounds. It also has introduced to the world an authority figure for

the ages in Truscott, a platitude-spouting psychopath in a police uniform. ("Have you never heard of Truscott? The man who tracked down the limbless girl killer? Or was that sensation before your time?")

Orton infused Oscar Wilde's drollery with a white-hot dose of anarchy, yet he obeyed the rules of structure with a faithfulness that would please the most rigid Aristotelian. He prided himself, meanwhile, on subject matter that would displease just about everyone—and he wrote a steady stream of scandalized letters to the editor about it, under false names like Edna Welthorpe.

When it finally reached New York in a new production, a year after a thirty-four-year-old Orton was bludgeoned to death by his lover, *Loot* met with mixed reviews and closed in less than three weeks. Its main claim to fame at the time was that it was the first Broadway box office to accept American Express cards as well as cash. But the *New York Times* review, an epic humblebrag by Clive Barnes, is worth quoting: "I liked it. But I do trust it's not for you, for you would be a far nicer person if it were not." Well, consider me a lot less nice than Barnes, because I love *Loot*.

OPPOSITE PAGE: William McAdam (a policeman) and Carole Shelley (Fay) in *Loot*, 1968.

BELOW: The 1986 revival of *Loot* (with, from left, Joseph Maher; Željko Ivanek, sneaking past with a corpse; Charles Keating; and Zoë Wanamaker) also starred Alec Baldwin in his Broadway debut.

A MAN FOR ALL SEASONS

BY ROBERT BOLT

From left, William Callan, Albert Dekker, William Redfield, Paul Scofield, Thomas Gomez (who replaced Leo McKern as Thomas Cromwell), and George Rose in the original Broadway production. Keith Baxter played Henry VIII.

For Sir Thomas More, the good old days ended twice: on July 6, 1535, and on April 30, 2009. The first of the two dates is when he was beheaded, a victim of Henry VIII's fickle tastes and of his own moral rectitude. The second was when Hilary Mantel's phenomenally popular book *Wolf Hall* came out, yanking More off his much-burnished pedestal and elevating his rival within Henry VIII's court, Thomas Cromwell.

Many people helped build that pedestal over the last few centuries—including, notably, Robert Bolt, whose play *A Man for All Seasons* is perhaps the preeminent

Scofield, Gomez, Dekker, and Callan. Noel Willman, a frequent collaborator of Robert Bolt, directed the 1961 production.

DATES:

November 22, 1961–June 1, 1963 at the ANTA Playhouse Theater (637 performances)

SYNOPSIS:

Henry VIII's wish to divorce Catherine of Aragon runs afoul of the Catholic Church and his Lord Chancellor, Sir Thomas More. Despite several opportunities to change his mind, More follows his principled stance all the way to the Tower of London.

AWARDS:

4 Tony Awards

NOTED REVIVALS AND ADAPTATIONS:

Broadway revival in 2008; movie version in 1966; TV version in 1988.

ORIGINAL STARS:

Paul Scofield, Leo McKern, Keith Baxter, George Rose

example of what could be called *Masterpiece Theatre* theater. This style of theater, traditionally catnip for both costume designers and actors with the stamina to spit out paragraphs of clever dialogue at a time, has fallen out of favor in recent years. But when it's done well—when the aphorisms fly and the moral dilemmas hover and the stentorian voices pound away—it can still make for a sinfully (if respectably) good time.

Thomas More was, as twentieth-century historian Hugh Trevor-Roper called him, "the first great Englishman whom we feel that we know." He wore a hairshirt. One of his shoulders rode a little higher than the other. He liked to sing in the church choir, though he had a terrible singing voice. He also burned books as well as heretics. But it was More's willingness to die for the sake of his conscience that attracted Bolt, who would later do time in jail for insisting on his right to protest nuclear proliferation. (*A Man for All Seasons* left out the part about burning the heretics.)

After the middling success of his 1957 play *The Flowering Cherry*, Bolt expanded an earlier radio play of his into *A Man for All Seasons*. The new version did well in London and even better on Broadway, and Scofield picked up a Tony Award, as well as an Oscar for his performance in the 1966 film version. Bolt died in February of 1995; a month later, the Vatican included *A Man for All Seasons* on its list of all-time great movies. Many of the writers in this book would have been horrified by such an honor. By all accounts, Bolt would not have been one of them.

MAN OF LA MANCHA

BY MITCH LEIGH, JOE DARION, AND DALE WASSERMAN

Once you eliminate the Bible, the Koran, and other religious tomes from the all-time bestseller list, Miguel de Cervantes' epic *Don Quixote de la Mancha* floats to the top. Playwright Dale Wasserman first jousted with its characters in his 1959 nonmusical teleplay *I, Don Quixote*, broadcast on CBS. Rather than attempt to depict the endless (mis)adventures of the man who would give the world the word "quixotic," he wisely chose to present a scant few hours in the life of Don Quixote's creator. Wasserman used the tale of Don Quixote as a storytelling device to help convince Cervantes' fellow prisoners why his life should be spared.

The subsequent musicalization had a bumpy path: poet W. H. Auden was removed as lyricist, no one wanted to produce it, and the intermission was cut, not for artistic reasons but to keep people from leaving halfway through. When Wasserman went to see

DATES:

November 22, 1965–June 26, 1971 at the ANTA Washington Square Theater, Martin Beck Theater, Eden Theater, and Mark Hellinger Theater (2,328 performances)

SYNOPSIS:

An imprisoned author spins tales of delusional knight errant Don Quixote, who is determined to rid the world of evil.

AWARDS:

5 Tony Awards

NOTED REVIVALS AND ADAPTATIONS:

Broadway revivals in 1972, 1977, 1992, and 2002; movie version in 1972

ORIGINAL STARS:

Richard Kiley, Joan Diener, Irving Jacobson

OPPOSITE PAGE: Joan Diener and Richard Kiley. Diener played serving girl (and sometime prostitute) Aldonza, whom Quixote believes to be his beloved Dulcinea. *Henry Groskinsky, The LIFE Picture Collection, Getty Images*

RIGHT: Richard Kiley won a second Tony for his performance in *Man of La Mancha* (after *Redhead*, 1959). Kiley performed the role again in the 1977 revival. In 1992, Raúl Juliá donned Quixote's armor, as did Brian Stokes Mitchell in the fourth Broadway revival a decade later.

a psychic at one point to ask if he should stay with the project, she assured him, "It will be extremely successful. In fact, it will overwhelm your life."

Man of La Mancha became a poster child for the burgeoning regional theater movement and, to a lesser extent, off-Broadway sensibilities. (A young Joseph Papp, who went on to be artistic director of the New York Shakespeare Festival and did as much as anyone to create off-Broadway as we know it, worked as a stage manager on *I, Don Quixote*.) *La Mancha*'s 1965 premiere at the Goodspeed Opera House in Connecticut marked the first time a regional theater was the progenitor of a successful commercial Broadway musical.

The show's odd journey continued with its transfer to Manhattan, where it took up residence not in Times Square but on West Fourth Street, downtown. The ANTA Washington Square Theater, a 1,150-seat thrust stage in the middle of Greenwich Village, was perfect for Howard Bay's no-frills unit set. Through the often-mystifying theatrical union rules, the ANTA was officially categorized as a Broadway house, which made any occupant eligible for a Tony Award.

Albert Marre's staging was so effective that major professional productions used it for more than thirty years, regardless of the theater configuration. The show moved uptown halfway through its six-year run, a stretch that saw Richard Kiley's star-making performance followed up by the likes of Hal Holbrook, Lloyd Bridges, and John Cullum.

The anthemic "The Impossible Dream" (originally titled "The Quest"), covered by legions of vocalists, did much to boost the show's image for years to come. It was a fitting sentiment for a musical that had beaten the odds, in a way that would do its windmill-tilting protagonist proud.

"MASTER HAROLD"... AND THE BOYS

BY ATHOL FUGARD

Zakes Mokae and Danny Glover in the 1982 Yale Repertory Theater production of *"Master Harold" . . . and the boys*, which transferred to Broadway that year.

Not long after winning a Tony Award for his performance as the dignified waiter Sam in Athol Fugard's *"Master Harold"... and the boys*, Zakes Mokae—who had been living in America since the late 1960s—went back to South Africa. Though a victory tour would have been understandable, Mokae was there on family business: he went back to try to prevent the death by hanging of his younger brother, for murders committed during a robbery. Mokae had learned of the death sentence the night of the Tony Awards. His brother's guilt was very much in question—he might not even have been there for the robbery—but Mokae's ministrations were unsuccessful. He reached Johannesburg in time to witness the hanging.

Fugard, also from South Africa, certainly has a sentimental streak as a playwright, but it's rooted in the

James Earl Jones, center, played the role of Sam alongside Delroy Lindo (Willie, right) following the original cast's departure. Charles Michael Wright (Hally, left) had been Lonny Price's standby.

brutal racial realities of his country's apartheid era. The oppression, the white guilt, the inability to communicate across races: Fugard and Mokae had explored these realities on stage as far back as 1960's *Blood Knot*. But nowhere did they play out as movingly as in "*Master Harold*," a coming-of-age play in which maturity—at least, for a white South African at the time—meant becoming a monster.

A young Fugard spit in the face of his family's longtime retainer, a black man; the act still burned in his memory decades later. "*Master Harold*" set this shocking image in the context of a heartfelt but all too breakable friendship among Hally, the playwright's surrogate; Sam; and Willie, a younger black man also in the employ of Hally's family. The piece offered crucial early roles for Danny Glover and, in the role of Hally, both Lonny Price and Matthew Broderick.

While Sam and Willie are practicing for a ballroom dancing competition, they demonstrate to Hally the beauty of "a world without collisions." Fugard's world has one devastating collision at its center, one that stands in for the countless bigger ones exploding all around him. But his depiction was, and is, beautiful. It certainly was to at least one American teenager, who was two or three years younger than Hally when a televised production of the play showed him just how unsparing—and how forgiving—the theater can be.

DATES:
May 4, 1982–February 26, 1983 at the Lyceum Theater (344 performances)

SYNOPSIS:
In 1950s South Africa, a white teenager's interaction with two black employees of his family comes to a vicious head when news arrives that the boy's father is being released from the hospital.

AWARDS:
1 Tony Award

NOTED REVIVALS AND ADAPTATIONS:
Broadway revival in 2003; movie version in 2010; TV version in 1985

ORIGINAL STARS:
Zakes Mokae, Lonny Price, Danny Glover

THE MERRY WIDOW

BY FRANZ LEHÁR, ADRIAN ROSS, VICTOR LEON, AND LEO STEIN

Grisettes (can-can dancers) from *The Merry Widow*, Vienna, 1906. The operetta premiered at Vienna's Theater an der Wien the previous year. *Ludwig Gutmann, Imagno, Getty Images*

Back before the New Amsterdam Theater had air conditioning, the summer months were unbearable. Runs were much shorter then, and most shows would simply close before the heat became an issue. But *The Merry Widow* opted to spend July and August of 1908 upstairs, at the theater's rooftop Aerial Gardens. That was pretty much the biggest problem the operetta's producers had, other than how to spend the tens of millions of dollars the show was making from sheet music and gramophone records alone, thanks to the popularity of songs such as "The Merry Widow Waltz" and "The Girls at Maxim's."

Franz Lehár's sparkling operetta, the quintessential example of the sturdy Viennese variety, quickly spawned road companies that crisscrossed the country. *Merry Widow* shoes, cigars, cocktails, dolls, hats, and, of course, corsets flooded the market, little if any of it authorized. (Just think how many corsets they could have sold if they had gone with the original German title, *Die Lustige Witwe*.)

Even less authorized—but nonetheless condoned— was *The Merry Widow Burlesque*, in which comedian

DATES:

October 21, 1907–October 17, 1908 at the
New Amsterdam Theater and Aerial Gardens
(416 performances)

SYNOPSIS:

The Eastern European duchy of Marsovia faces
bankruptcy if its wealthiest citizen, Sonia Sadoya,
marries a foreigner. The ambassador orders his
attaché, Prince Danilo Danilowitch, to make sure
that doesn't happen.

AWARDS:

None

NOTED REVIVALS AND ADAPTATIONS:

Broadway revivals in 1921, 1929, 1931, and 1943;
movie versions in 1918, 1925, 1934, 1952, and 1962;
TV version in 1955

ORIGINAL STARS:

Ethel Jackson, Donald Brian

Joe Weber had his way with the story. Rather than haul
Weber to court, Lehár and his producers gave him their
orchestrations and costume designs, guessing (correctly)
that the parody would generate additional attention for the
genuine article. *The Merry Widow* ran for a year and inspired
a batch of Viennese operettas with titles like *The Count of
Luxembourg* and *A Waltz Dream*.

But not even an era that inspires corsets and burlesques
can last forever. In one of those coincidences that would
raise the reader's eyebrows in a work of fiction, *The
Merry Widow* had its last gasp on Broadway in 1943, the
year Richard Rodgers and Oscar Hammerstein II wrote
their first musical (which also has a charity dance at its
center). Audiences soon shifted their affections from the
ballrooms of Vienna to the prairies of Oklahoma, and
operetta's days were officially numbered. Yet it had a very
long and very profitable run, and *The Merry Widow* was a
major reason why.

Joe Weber's *Merry Widow Burlesque* presented Franz Lehár's
melodies with a new book and lyrics. *Library of Congress*

METAMORPHOSES

BY MARY ZIMMERMAN

During one of his daily press conferences less than a week after the terrorist attacks of September 11, 2001, Mayor Rudy Giuliani made an odd request. He encouraged people to go see a Broadway show. "Maybe now you can get tickets to *The Producers*," he said.

The aftermath of 9/11 was devastating on so many levels, and it seems absurd to discuss it in the context of box office sales. But theater, one of New York City's primary industries, was reeling. Off-Broadway ticket sales were off by up to 80 percent the following week, and nearly a half-dozen Broadway shows posted closing notices. Many people have credited the success of *Mamma Mia!*, which opened in October of that year, with giving the city a much-needed lift, and I suspect they have a point. For me, though, the more welcome addition was a play rehearsing for an off-Broadway run at the time.

Mary Zimmerman had been developing *Metamorphoses* since 1996, eventually staging her adventurous takes on Ovid's myths in a thirty-foot-long swimming pool. The final result had its share of arch, even sophomoric commentary. Yet it also had images—King Midas' daughter unwittingly leaping into his arms, freezing in a mid-embrace rictus; an adoring couple asking the gods simply to "let me die the moment my love dies," and being rewarded with an eternity as two interwoven trees—that would be memorable under any circumstances. Given the context, they became unforgettable.

Its Broadway transfer pitted it against a strong group of plays, including Suzan Lori-Parks' *Topdog/Underdog* and Edward Albee's *The Goat, or Who Is Sylvia?* Albee won the Tony Award that year and Lori-Parks the Pulitzer Prize; sitting down with all three scripts shows those to be perfectly reasonable choices. But evenings at the theater are a very different thing. They happen in a room filled with people who breathe the same air as you, watch the same newscasts as you, fear at least some of the same things as you. *Metamorphoses* opened at a time when the air in New York City had only just begun to clear up again, when the newscasts and the fears were a daily, even hourly part of our lives.

Just about everything, and everyone, changes in *Metamorphoses*. In late 2001 and early 2002, in a pair of theaters with a pair of shimmering pools of water, change occurred on both sides of the footlights.

DATES:

March 4, 2002–February 16, 2003 at the Circle in the Square Theater (400 performances)

SYNOPSIS:

A series of vignettes explores the stories of King Midas, Orpheus and Eurydice, and several lesser-known tales from Ovid.

AWARDS:

1 Tony Award

NOTED REVIVALS AND ADAPTATIONS:

None

ORIGINAL STARS:

None

OPPOSITE PAGE: Doug Hara as Eros and Felicity Jones as Psyche. *Metamorphoses* took place in and around a pool, which played a key role in the play's striking imagery. Mary Zimmerman, a professor at Northwestern University (where the play premiered with the title *Six Myths*), wrote and directed. © *Joan Marcus*

BELOW: Phaeton (Hara), the son of Apollo, goes for a swim. He describes his issues with his father to a therapist, along with that time he drove too close to the sun. From left, Anjali Bhimani, Louise Lamson, and Mariann Mayberry. © *Joan Marcus*

THE MIRACLE WORKER

BY WILLIAM GIBSON

Anne Bancroft and Patty Duke in the original production of *The Miracle Worker*. Bancroft won a Tony (as did director Arthur Penn and the play itself), and both actresses won Oscars for their work in the 1962 film adaptation.

Child actors tend to work better in smaller doses. Rehearsals are tightly regulated, which puts a ceiling on just how much time they have to hone their parts. That, along with eight-show performance weeks and the limitations of even a gifted preteen performer, goes a long way toward explaining why characters like Tiny Tim and Cosette typically get just a few minutes of onstage time. Little Orphan Annie and Oliver Twist are the exceptions that prove the rule, although their fellow waifs have far less to do. Recent shows like *Billy Elliot* and *Matilda*, meanwhile, have skirted the problem by fielding a small platoon of young actors who can share the workload.

And then there's Patty Duke.

Duke was twelve years old when she began playing Helen Keller in *The Miracle Worker*, based on Keller's autobiography. Almost two years later, she was still playing her. By that point, she had received above-the-title billing alongside Anne Bancroft, who played her tough-love-dispensing teacher, Annie Sullivan. Two years after *that*, Duke

During the pivotal scene at the water pump, Helen Keller realizes that what Annie Sullivan is spelling in her hand—"w-a-t-e-r"— signifies the liquid she is touching. Keller (1880–1968) described the scene in her autobiography.

DATES:
October 15, 1959–July 1, 1961 at the Playhouse Theater (719 performances)

SYNOPSIS:
The Keller family is at its wits' end over tantrum-throwing Helen, who was rendered deaf, blind, and mute as an infant. Enter Annie Sullivan, a governess who requests just two weeks with the six-year-old wild child.

AWARDS:
4 Tony Awards

NOTED REVIVALS AND ADAPTATIONS:
Broadway revival in 2010; movie version in 1962; TV versions in 1979 and 2000

ORIGINAL STARS:
Anne Bancroft, Patty Duke

won an Academy Award for the film version. She flailed, lurched, and groaned in a way that had to seem out of control but was actually choreographed to the last inch. For the film version, she and Bancroft both wore padding during the protracted dining-room skirmish, but they didn't have that option on stage—or a second take if things went wrong.

Not every aspect of William Gibson's script, which he adapted from a 1957 teleplay that he also wrote, is as strong as these bruising confrontations. This and the incredible difficulty of the role of Keller might explain why a play as fondly remembered as *The Miracle Worker* is revived so infrequently. (Or is it the barrage of parodies over the years from the likes of *South Park* and *SCTV*?) A Broadway-bound production starring Hilary Swank never made it out of North Carolina in 2003. When the play did reach New York seven years later with a less glittery cast, it came and went within a month. But when the right Helen and the right Annie square off, as they did in 1959, words fail in more ways than one.

A MOON FOR THE MISBEGOTTEN

BY EUGENE O'NEILL

Cyril Cusack as Phil Hogan, Josie's father, in *A Moon for the Misbegotten*, 1957. Gjon Mills, *The LIFE Picture Collection*, Getty Images

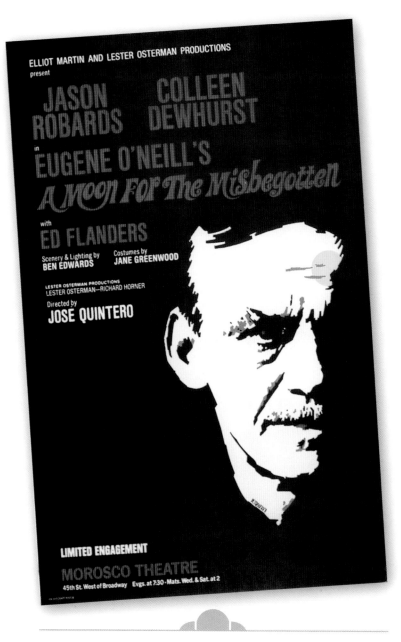

ELLIOT MARTIN AND LESTER OSTERMAN PRODUCTIONS
present

JASON ROBARDS   COLLEEN DEWHURST

in

EUGENE O'NEILL'S

A Moon For The Misbegotten

with

ED FLANDERS

Scenery & Lighting by
BEN EDWARDS

Costumes by
JANE GREENWOOD

LESTER OSTERMAN PRODUCTIONS
LESTER OSTERMAN—RICHARD HORNER

Directed by
JOSE QUINTERO

LIMITED ENGAGEMENT

MOROSCO THEATRE
45th St. West of Broadway   Evgs. at 7:30 · Mats. Wed. & Sat. at 2

Jason Robards played James Tyrone Jr. in the 1973 Broadway revival, opposite Colleen Dewhurst as Josie. The production ran for 313 performances. Quintero also directed the revival's cast for an ABC production of the play two years later.

DATES:
May 2–June 29, 1957 at the Bijou Theater
(68 performances)

SYNOPSIS:
Josie Hogan and her wily father conspire to get Josie married off to their landlord, the dissolute actor James Tyrone Jr. The would-be seduction takes up the bulk of a long night's journey into something close to redemption.

AWARDS:
None

NOTED REVIVALS AND ADAPTATIONS:
Broadway revivals in 1973, 1984, 2000, and 2007; TV version in 1975

ORIGINAL STARS:
Wendy Hiller, Franchot Tone, Cyril Cusack

Any actor knows the benefit of a delayed entrance. And James Tyrone Jr., last seen as the haunted older brother in Eugene O'Neill's *Long Day's Journey Into Night*, is an actor through and through—or would be, if he could ease up on the bourbon and the women and the crippling guilt. We spend the first two acts of O'Neill's *A Moon for the Misbegotten* anticipating his arrival. He does not disappoint when he finally does appear, staring at the ground, as Josie Hogan says, "like a dead man walking slow behind his own coffin."

Or at least, he doesn't disappoint us. The emotionally and physically sturdy Josie, onstage for every minute of the three-hour *Misbegotten*, is another matter. Josie is too good

for her dissipated soul mate, who has just buried his mother and is in the market for a replacement. Their asymmetrical, profane, desperate, exhausted, impossible relationship forms the basis of what is, to me—and I realize this is not universally held to be the case—one of the finest love stories of the twentieth century, in any medium. (It's also very funny: Josie and her reprobate father supply far more laughs than anything in *Ah, Wilderness!*, typically held up as O'Neill's only comedy.)

A 1947 tryout in Columbus, Ohio, was a bust, and *Misbegotten*'s Broadway debut a decade later made only a slightly bigger impact. As with O'Neill's *The Iceman Cometh*, it took an off-Broadway revival, this one in 1968, to make the case for his scouring genius. When the play was ready for Broadway again (or Broadway was ready for it again), in 1973, the *Iceman* tandem of Jason Robards and director José Quintero presented it with the formidable Colleen Dewhurst.

The possibility of city slicker James, who has seen "too goddamned many dawns creeping grayly over too many dirty windows," finding some level of solace and forgiveness in Josie's arms is so enticing, so potentially life-saving, that it will clearly never happen. It couldn't happen. O'Neill set *Misbegotten* in September 1923, just two months before his real-life older brother Jamie, practically blind from all the Prohibition-era rotgut he had drunk, entered an alcohol-induced coma and died. He had finally caught up to his own coffin. O'Neill gave him a marvelous send-off.

THE MOST HAPPY FELLA

BY FRANK LOESSER

Shorty Long (Herman) and Susan Johnson (Cleo) in *The Most Happy Fella*. The musical is based on the 1924 play *They Knew What They Wanted*, by Sidney Howard. *Yale Joel, The LIFE Picture Collection, Getty Images*

They don't come much bigger than *The Most Happy Fella*. When the characters in Frank Loesser's sprawling Napa Valley opera give voice to their deceptions and passions, their aching feet and breaking hearts, they sing songs like "Abbondanza" and "My Heart Is So Full of You." And when Columbia Records put those songs on vinyl, it did so in an unprecedented three-album set.

Loesser never quite signed on to the idea of *The Most Happy Fella* being an opera. He preferred to call it "a musical with music"—wonderful music, and lots of it, including pop hits ("Standing on the Corner," "Big D"), character numbers ("I Made a Fist"), charm songs ("Happy to Make Your Acquaintance"), choral stunners ("Song of a Summer Night"), and heavenly love songs ("Warm All Over," the aforementioned "My Heart Is So Full of You"). He also had the gumption to write his own libretto, adapting—and arguably improving upon—Sidney Howard's Pulitzer Prize–winning 1924 play *They Knew What They Wanted*.

Critics at the time seem to have been a bit bowled over by the sheer glut of musical styles, with nearly everyone praising some aspects but having misgivings about others. Audiences, however, didn't object: unlike such fellow operatic trailblazers as *Porgy and Bess* and *Street Scene*, *Fella* sold a ton of tickets, running for more than eighteen months.

Loesser's original description notwithstanding, the size of the voices required by Tony and Rosabella, the wonderfully mismatched central couple, and of the show itself gradually made *Fella* the almost-exclusive province of opera companies. A 1992 Broadway revival, which originated at Connecticut's jewel-box-size Goodspeed Opera House, took things in the opposite direction. Loesser had given his blessing to a reduction of his lush score to two pianos before his death, and that arrangement lent itself to a much smaller, more intimate staging. Some people missed the size of the original—musical theater historian Ken Mandelbaum compared the new version to an all-kazoo mounting of *La Traviata*—but even a slimmed-down *Fella* has more heft than a dozen spectacle-heavy pop operas. *Guys and Dolls* had put Loesser on a very small list of songwriters who could elicit belly laughs; with *The Most Happy Fella*, he joined the even smaller list of songwriters who could also milk a few tears.

The musical opens with Cleo and the other waitresses suffering from pained feet, endless messes, and unwanted advances. A letter offers Cleo hope that "somebody, somewhere wants me and needs me." *Yale Joel, The LIFE Picture Collection, Getty Images*

DATES:

May 3, 1956–December 14, 1957 at the Imperial Theater and Broadway Theater (676 performances)

SYNOPSIS:

After a four-month "mail-order love affair," Rosabella travels to Napa Valley to accept a marriage proposal from her correspondent, only to learn that the aging grape farmer Tony had sent her a picture of his hired hand Joe instead of himself. Unfortunately for all involved, Joe is still there when she arrives.

AWARDS:

None

NOTED REVIVALS AND ADAPTATIONS:

Broadway revivals in 1979 and 1992; TV version in 1980

ORIGINAL STARS:

Robert Weede, Jo Sullivan, Art Lund, Susan Johnson

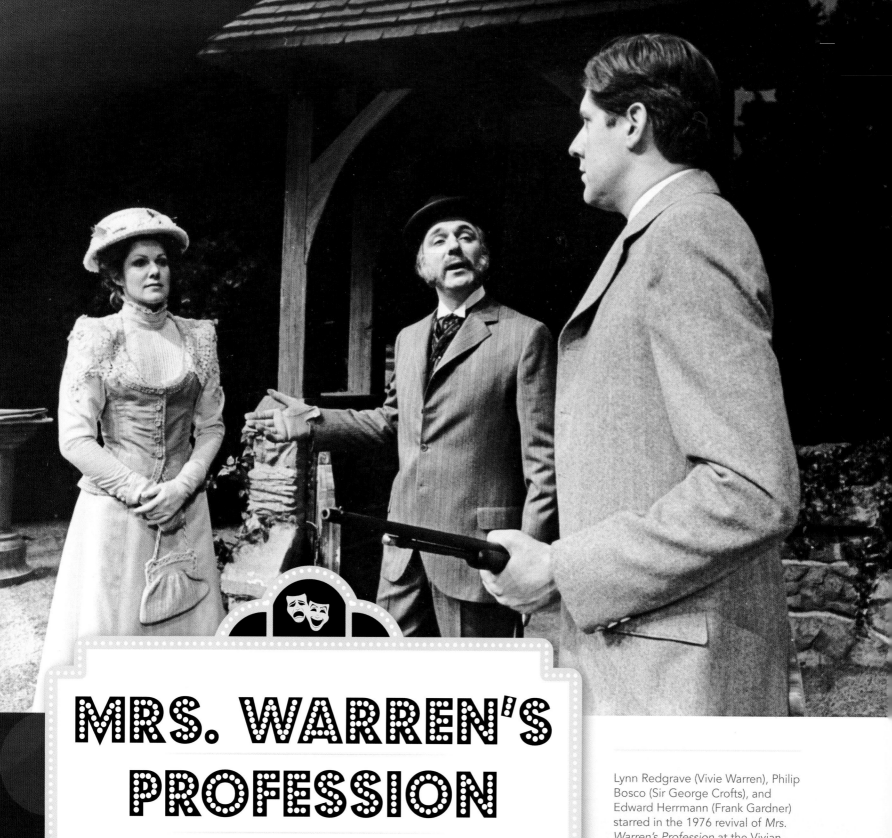

MRS. WARREN'S PROFESSION

BY GEORGE BERNARD SHAW

Lynn Redgrave (Vivie Warren), Philip Bosco (Sir George Crofts), and Edward Herrmann (Frank Gardner) starred in the 1976 revival of *Mrs. Warren's Profession* at the Vivian Beaumont Theater.

S end in the vice squad! That socialist vegetarian Irishman is at it again!

Tucked into a 1905 repertory Broadway engagement of six George Bernard Shaw plays was a little item called *Mrs. Warren's Profession*, which had only been produced earlier in a censor-skirting "private showing" at London's members-only New Lyric Club. New York City didn't have that option. It did, however, have one Anthony Comstock, secretary of the Society for the Suppression of Vice.

George Bernard Shaw, c. 1905. Shaw was a member of the socialist Fabian Society, an advocate for the reform of English spelling, and a theater critic for the *Saturday Review* in addition to being a Nobel Prize–winning playwright. *Photograph by Alvin Langdon Coburn, Library of Congress*

Comstock had been engaging in a war of words in the press with Arnold Daly, costar of the production, over whether *Mrs. Warren's Profession* was fit for public viewing. Daly invited Comstock to see a rehearsal. Comstock declined, but told the *New York Times* that the play was, compared with something called *Orange Blossoms*, "by far the more reprehensible" by reputation. Each then accused the other of seeking publicity. (Never mind that the *Times'* naming of Daly as "the principal member of the cast" in a show with two female leads says as much about the whole enterprise—and about Shaw's evisceration of Victorian hypocrisy—as any court transcripts would. But I'm getting ahead of myself.) Daly took the company up to New Haven, where police shut the production down after one performance.

So curiosity was high by the time Mrs. Warren made her scandalous way to the Garrick Theater for opening night on Monday, October 23—which also turned out to be closing night. William McAdoo, the city's police commissioner, arrested pretty much everyone involved with the play, calling it "revolting, indecent and nauseating where it was not boring." That line alone could have sold out the Garrick for months, but McAdoo canceled the remaining performances.

It wasn't until July 1906 that the cast and crew were cleared of all charges, albeit with the court citing the work's "repellent things" and "shock producers." (Something tells me Shaw would not disagree with those words, though court and author might differ on which bits qualified.) *Mrs. Warren's Profession* was back on Broadway by 1907, this time unimpeded, and it has been revived several times since. Now who's up for a revival of *Orange Blossoms*?

DATES:
October 23, 1905 at the Garrick Theater
(1 performance)

SYNOPSIS:
Hard-headed young Vivie Warren has a mathematics degree from Cambridge, a doting mother, and a dapper suitor. But everything threatens to come crashing down when she learns that her mom made her fortune as a prostitute and brothel owner.

AWARDS:
None

NOTED REVIVALS AND ADAPTATIONS:
Broadway revivals in 1907, 1918, 1922, 1976, and 2010; movie version in 1960; TV version in 1972

ORIGINAL STARS:
Mary Shaw, Chrystal Herne, Arnold Daly

THE MULLIGAN GUARDS' BALL

BY DAVID BRAHAM AND EDWARD HARRIGAN

An 1874 etching by Joseph Becker depicts a performance of one of the Mulligan Guards shows, at the Grand Duke Theater in the Five Points neighborhood of Manhattan. An 1887 *New York Times* article called the theater "a noted place in the days when the Five Points was the wickedest place on earth." The theater's "artists—there were no artistes—were among the most popular in the neighborhood." *Library of Congress*

In the 1870s, downtown Manhattan offered its own street theater in the form of inept weekend parades by neighborhood militias, whose members would imbibe absurd amounts of beer first. To commemorate these lurching bacchanals, former minstrel show performer Edward "Ned" Harrigan and his father-in-law, David Braham, wrote the song "Mulligan Guards' March." It was a massive hit for Harrigan and his stage partner, Tony Hart, and they decided to expand the shtick into a full evening. It was not unlike the inspiration to turn a *Saturday Night Live* skit into a movie.

A forty-minute minishow called *The Mulligan Guards' Picnic* gave way the next year to *The Mulligan Guards' Ball*.

Mulligan Guard Picnic

Composed arranged and Performed
BY

HARRIGAN AND HART

MUSIC BY

DAVE BRAHAM.

Nº 1. MULLIGAN GUARD PICNIC WALTZ .3¢   Nº 2. MULLIGAN GUARD PICNIC GALOP .3¢
Nº 3. MULLIGAN GUARD PICNIC QUADRILLE. 5

NEW-YORK
WM. A. POND & CO. 25 UNION SQUARE.

Chicago.
CHICAGO MUSIC CO. 152 STATE STREET.

Boston.   Philadelphia.   San Francisco.   Milwaukee.   New Orleans.
Carl Prufer.   W.H.Boner &Co.   M.Gray.   H.N.Hempsted.   L.Grunewald.

Copyright 1880 by Wm A.Pond&Co

The "Mulligan Guard Picnic" quadrille, 1880. *Library of Congress, Music Division*

DATES:
Opened January 13, 1879 at the Theater Comique
(138 performances)

SYNOPSIS:
Never mind the verboten love affair between
Dan Mulligan's son and a German girl. The Mulligan
Guards and a black militia have booked the same
ballroom at the same time!

AWARDS:
None

NOTED REVIVALS
AND ADAPTATIONS:
Various Broadway iterations in
subsequent years

ORIGINAL STARS:
Edward Harrigan, Tony Hart

Lower-class New Yorkers flocked to Harrigan's own Theater Comique, as did the vote-seeking politicians who had funded those militias in the first place. Decades before lyricists like Cole Porter and Ira Gershwin turned the use of slang and wayward grammar into an art form, Ned Harrigan gave the first taste of characters who sang more or less the same way his audiences spoke.

The show shared with its sketch-comedy successors a willingness to poke fun at everyone and everything: the Irish, black Americans, Germans, and anyone else in sight. Director/producer/lyricist/bookwriter Harrigan also played the saloon owner Dan Mulligan, while Hart took on roles ranging from Mulligan's son Tommy to an often-married African American servant named Rebecca Allup. (You can take the actor out of the minstrel show, but . . .)

Harrigan and Hart weren't above adding the "Mulligan Guards' March" and other bits into any show that needed a lift, so it's difficult to say which of the seventeen musicals they presented between 1878 and 1884 qualify as Mulligan Guards shows. The duo lasted only fourteen years—Hart struck out on his own, not long before dying of syphilis at the age of thirty-six—but their versatile bits of buffoonery played a massive role in establishing the ground rules for what we now think of as musical theater. They deserve a parade of their own—preferably one with a bit more polish, and a bit less beer, than the hapless *Mulligan Guards'* offerings.

THE MUSIC MAN

BY MEREDITH WILLSON

Philadelphia has its Rocky Balboa statue, and Seneca Falls, New York, lays claim to being the home of George Bailey and the rest of the *It's a Wonderful Life* crew. But if you want to see a town that really loves its cultural touchstone, take I-35 all the way to Mason City, Iowa.

There you'll find a pristine streetscape of what its thinly veiled fictional counterpart, River City, looked like circa 1912 in *The Music Man*. You can sit on Mrs. Paroo's cozy porch, see what sort of rapscallions are congregating around the pool hall, and wait to hear those seventy-six trombones rumble down the street. You'll be waiting a while, though; the band doesn't exist, just like in the effervescent show itself.

Mason City may feature a bronze statue of Meredith Willson as drum major (he frequently returned from California for the annual North Iowa

Band Festival), but Willson was essentially the opposite of Harold Hill, the would-be bandleader at the center of the show. Harold promises big and then hits the road before people realize how little he has to offer, whereas the inexperienced Willson—a former flautist for John Philip Sousa's band and the New York Philharmonic orchestra—spoke softly and created one of the most airtight pieces of wholesome entertainment Broadway had seen before, or has seen since. (Granted, it did take Willson eight years, thirty script revisions, more than twenty discarded songs, and the encouragement of mentor and fellow composer/lyricist/bookwriter Frank Loesser to get there. Loesser also contributed the lovely ballad "My White Knight," which Willson rather unchivalrously jettisoned for the movie version.)

From the rhythmic approximation of an Iowa-bound train in "Rock Island" to the canny mirroring of Harold's buoyant "Seventy-Six Trombones" and his love interest's "Goodnight, My Someone" to the artful counterpoint of "Pick-a-Little, Talk-a-Little" and "Good Night Ladies," Willson had some impressive tricks up his unassuming sleeve. And he had a bit of good luck when Bing Crosby and Ray Bolger both turned down the leading role, paving the way for the inimitable Robert Preston in his song-and-dance debut.

Some theater buffs will never forgive *The Music Man* for snagging the Tony Award for Best Musical over *West Side Story*. Hey, that's what Harold Hill does. He gets away with things—and earns a lot of good will in the process.

Both Barbara Cook (Marian the Librarian) and Preston won Tonys for their performances. "Till There Was You," their Act II duet, was performed later by Sonny Rollins, Peggy Lee, and the Beatles (among others).

DATES:
December 19, 1957–April 15, 1961 at the Majestic Theater and Broadway Theater (1,375 performances)

SYNOPSIS:
Harold Hill has just about everything he needs to bring the people of River City, Iowa, a cracker-jack marching band. He's got the patter and the charisma to warm even the heart of suspicious Marian the Librarian. Now all the town needs are those instruments . . .

AWARDS:
6 Tony Awards

NOTED REVIVALS AND ADAPTATIONS:
Broadway revival in 2000; movie version in 1962; TV version in 2003

ORIGINAL STARS:
Robert Preston, Barbara Cook, David Burns, Iggie Wolfington, Pert Kelton

MY FAIR LADY

BY FREDERICK LOEWE AND ALAN JAY LERNER

DATES:

March 15, 1956–September 29, 1962 at the Mark Hellinger Theater, Broadhurst Theater, and Broadway Theater (2,717 performances)

SYNOPSIS:

Esteemed phoneticist Henry Higgins takes a bet that he can transform a Cockney guttersnipe named Eliza Doolittle into a proper lady within six months.

AWARDS:

6 Tony Awards

NOTED REVIVALS AND ADAPTATIONS:

Broadway revivals in 1976, 1981, and 1993; movie version in 1964

ORIGINAL STARS:

Julie Andrews, Rex Harrison, Stanley Holloway, Robert Coote

Julie Andrews had made her Broadway debut (in *The Boy Friend*) just two years prior to turning Eliza Doolittle into a smash sensation.

The "Ascot Gavotte" scene satirized upper-class snobbery, with impeccable direction by Moss Hart and choreography by modern dancer/choreographer Hanya Holm.

Like so many Broadway successes (and more than a few failures), *My Fair Lady* should never have happened. George Bernard Shaw put out a blanket refusal on all musicalizations of his work in 1908, when *Arms and the Man* yielded the operetta *The Chocolate Soldier*. But Shaw's death in 1950 emboldened the team of Alan Jay Lerner and Frederick Loewe to approach his beloved *Pygmalion*, even after Oscar Hammerstein II and many others had written it off as unadaptable, with no love story and unsurpassable source material. Unfortunately, MGM wanted to have a go at *Pygmalion*, too. So Lerner and Loewe—and this is where aspiring musical theater writers who don't want to fritter away years of their lives might want to stop reading—forged ahead and spent half a year writing the show *without having the rights*. The gamble paid off.

So did casting twenty-year-old Julie Andrews as Eliza Doolittle, though only after director Moss Hart—and this is where directors who don't want a mutiny on their hands might want to stop reading—canceled rehearsals for two days to give her scene-by-scene, line-by-line instructions on how to play the part. Rex Harrison, who signed on as Henry Higgins after Noël Coward turned the role down, needed

no such remediation. But his, shall we say, inexperience in musical theater became clear on opening night in New Haven. According to Lerner, Harrison "announced that under no circumstances would he go on that night. He needed more time to rehearse with those thirty-two interlopers in the pit."

By the time it reached New York, words like "miraculous," "magic," and "masterpiece" were tossed around in the reviews, with an abandon that would have abso-bloomin'-lutely horrified Henry Higgins. Lerner and Loewe's previous musicals, *Brigadoon* and *Paint Your Wagon*, hadn't begun to prepare audiences for the verbal and musical sophistication of their newest show, which had such instant standards as "I Could Have Danced All Night," "On the Street Where You Live," and "Get Me to the Church on Time." The result would soon supplant *Oklahoma!* as Broadway's longest-running musical.

For an entire generation of impressionable young theater buffs, the image of God comes directly from the *My Fair Lady* album cover: Al Hirschfeld's caricature of a winged Shaw manipulating a marionette of Henry, who is in turn pulling Eliza's strings. Lerner, Loewe, and Hart were pious enough—or maybe just smart enough—to use entire verbatim chunks from *Pygmalion*. They, along with their (eventually) superb cast and a phenomenal design team that included Cecil Beaton and Oliver Smith, were more like acolytes, helping to create a joyful, witty, loverly noise.

NAUGHTY MARIETTA

BY VICTOR HERBERT AND RIDA JOHNSON YOUNG

It is New Orleans in 1780, the infamous Bras Priqué is on the loose, and an eerie melody is emanating from the town fountain. Is it coming from the ghost of one of the pirates' victims? Can the governor's son and a runaway contessa . . .

Let's stop there. Pirates, a quadroon ball, a cross-dressing heroine: if you were to look up "operetta" in the dictionary, *Naughty Marietta* would be a good candidate for the ultimate specimen. And in Victor Herbert, the United States had its first homegrown composer who could rival the likes of Offenbach and Léhar. Herbert, who was actually born in Ireland and trained in Germany, had lived in New York for nearly a decade before he wrote his first Broadway show in 1894.

The American setting is a deviation from the genre's love of far-flung locations, but then again, New Orleans *was* under foreign rule at the time. (Spanish rule, though, not French rule. *The New Moon*, another contender for the ultimate operetta, made the same mistake.) However, *Naughty Marietta* is noteworthy not so much for its American setting as for that song from the fountain, the inescapable "Ah! Sweet Mystery of Life." Its development and completion play a pivotal role in advancing the plot. All operettas live or die on the strength of their music; here, for arguably the first time, one actually moved forward *through* its music. Though *Naughty Marietta* is still a far cry from the integrated scores of *Oklahoma!* or even *Show Boat*, "Sweet Mystery" served notice that music could be used as a tool, not merely an ornament.

After the Archduke Franz Ferdinand was assassinated in 1914, and Europe played host to the unspeakable carnage of World War I, the travails of random Mitteleuropean royals suddenly didn't seem quite so important. Operetta moved to the periphery for several years, though the practical Herbert quickly adapted, writing songs for several editions of the *Ziegfeld Follies* and cofounding the American Society of Composers, Authors and Publishers (ASCAP).

The rights to *Naughty Marietta*, which would become one of the era's most popular and revived operettas, changed hands in the wake of another global upheaval, the stock market crash of 1929. Producer Arthur Hammerstein was forced to auction off thirty-one of his shows, including *Marietta*, *Rose-Marie*, and *Sweet Adeline*. The winning bidder—who also happened to be the only bidder—got the whole batch for $684. His name was Lee Shubert.

DATES:
November 7, 1910–March 4, 1911 at the New York Theater (136 performances)

SYNOPSIS:
See opposite page.

AWARDS:
None

NOTED REVIVALS AND ADAPTATIONS:
Broadway revivals in 1929 and 1931; movie version in 1935; TV version in 1955

ORIGINAL STARS:
Emma Trentini, Edward Martindel, Orville Harrold

OPPOSITE PAGE: Nelson Eddy (playing Captain Richard Warrington) and Jeannette MacDonald (Princess Marie de Namour de la Bonfain) in the 1935 movie adaptation of *Naughty Marietta*. © *MGM, courtesy Photofest*

BELOW: The Captain and Marietta in, from left, the 1910 Broadway production (Emma Trentini and Orville Harrold), the 1935 film (Eddy and MacDonald), and a 1955 TV production (Alfred Drake and Patrice Munsel). © *Bettmann/Corbis*

NO, NO, NANETTE

BY VINCENT YOUMANS, OTTO HARBACH, IRVING CAESAR, AND FRANK MANDEL

The original Broadway production of *No, No, Nanette*, 1925. The musical had already toured extensively, including a year-plus run in Chicago, by the time it reached Broadway.

No, *No, Nanette* opened on Broadway in September of 1925, but its history stretches well before that date and *well* after it. Arguably the two biggest dates in its history, in fact, are January 19, 1971, and October 27, 2004.

First, the early history: producer Harry Frazee sent the troubled show around the country (Chicago, Los Angeles) and even the world (London, Melbourne) before it reached Broadway. Along the way, he replaced the stars, booted the director, revamped the script, junked half of the lyrics, and had his songwriting team write two new songs, "Tea for Two" and "I Want to Be Happy," which became by far the show's biggest hits. Middling reviews from the critics—who might have been put out by *Nanette*'s healthy earlier life far from New York—didn't stop it from running on Broadway for nine months.

Flash forward to the flashy revival in 1971, one of the first cases of an all-but-forgotten hit being revived in the true sense of the word. The book once again received a complete overhaul, this time from Burt Shevelove, who had excavated an even older text (from 191 BCE) for *A Funny Thing Happened on the Way to the Forum*. Although legendary choreographer Busby Berkeley's name was plastered all over the revival's posters, his contributions were virtually nonexistent. Still, plenty of old-timers did contribute, among them the performers Ruby Keeler, Helen Gallagher, and Jack Gilford. The production ran for two years.

Other shows' revivals have since run even longer, notably those of *Chicago* and *Cabaret*, but the audiences flocking to *Chicago* productions today aren't exactly nostalgic for the post-Watergate cynicism of the mid-1970s. In fact, as New York City was becoming more dangerous and many Broadway musicals were copying the youthful sounds of *Hair*, that very cynicism is what made the Charlestons and flirtations of *No, No, Nanette* so irresistible to many theatergoers.

The last major event took place in St. Louis, when Edgar Rentería dribbled a ground ball toward the pitcher's mound in Game 4 of the 2004 World Series. That mound was inhabited by a Boston Red Sox player whose subsequent toss to first base officially ended the eighty-six-year "Curse of the Bambino." The curse, which stemmed from a blend of misinformation and anti-Semitism, allegedly began when Red Sox owner Harry Frazee sold Babe Ruth to the New York Yankees in order to back the original *Nanette*. While it is true that Frazee dabbled in Broadway producing and that he sometimes used funds from one venture to subsidize the other, *Nanette* premiered a full four years after the trade.

Still, the legend has some basis in fact. The musical actually started life as a play called *My Lady Friends*, which Frazee produced just a month before the Ruth trade was finalized. So, one way or another, *No, No, Nanette* has the Bambino's fingerprints on it. No matter: the curse is over, and now there's no reason for anyone not to enjoy *Nanette*'s good old-fashioned charms.

Ruby Keeler (Sue Smith) and Bobby Van (Billy Early) in the 1971 Broadway revival, which ran for 861 performances at the 46th Street Theater. Susan Watson played Nanette.

DATES:
September 16, 1925–June 19, 1926 at the Globe Theater (321 performances)

SYNOPSIS:
Who will cause the most trouble for Bible publisher Jimmy Smith: his impulsive ward Nanette, eager to live a little before tying the knot; his three (platonic) lady friends, who are hatching a blackmail scheme; or his pious wife, Sue, once she finds out about the other women?

AWARDS:
None

NOTED REVIVALS AND ADAPTATIONS:
Broadway revival in 1971; movie versions in 1930 and 1940

ORIGINAL STARS:
Louise Groody, Charles Winninger, Georgia O'Ramey, Jack Barker, Eleanor Dawn

NOISES OFF

BY MICHAEL FRAYN

Backstage comedies are nothing new to Broadway. From *A Midsummer Night's Dream* to *Present Laughter* to *The Real Thing*, theater folk typically love nothing more than to play theater folk (usually theater folk less talented than themselves).

Noises Off took that idea and vaulted it into a whole other comic stratosphere. If it's as hard as everyone says it is to be good at being bad, then Michael Frayn's depiction of onstage entropy is one of the finest comedies of the twentieth century. Scratch that: *Noises Off* is, without qualification, one of the finest comedies of the twentieth century.

Shakespeare's rude mechanicals in *Midsummer* are plenty funny, but their *Pyramus and Thisbe* has got nothing on *Nothing On*. That's the name of the ghastly sex farce being rehearsed (poorly) a few hours before opening night in the first act of Frayn's ingeniously constructed play. Then, in Act II, the stage set, with its plates of sardines and its doors galore, spins around 180 degrees to give us a stagehand's-eye view of a subsequent performance. As bad as things seemed to be early on, they have gotten worse. But they aren't as bad as they'll get for the third act, when the perspective shifts again and we are in the audience for the final performance of *Nothing On*—or whatever simulacrum of *Nothing On* the company is capable of presenting at this point.

The biggest sticking point for American theatergoers rests at the center of the play. For the most part, Broadway has been spared the sorts of door-slamming sex farces that London theatergoers have propped up for years at a time. As a result, the shudders of recognition elicited by *Noises Off* have less to do with the play being depicted than with the parallel love triangles among its cast and crew.

Frayn has tempted fate with a series of rewrites over the years. (A hideous film version, as bad in its own way as any production of *Nothing On*, demonstrates the risks involved in tampering with the final product.) Frank Rich of the *New York Times* famously called *Noises Off* "the funniest play written in my lifetime" in 1983. Now that we're an additional three decades into that lifetime, it is hard to imagine him modifying that statement.

OPPOSITE PAGE: From left, Amy Wright, Dorothy Loudon, Brian Murray, Paxton Whitehead, and Linda Thorson, with Victor Garber above, in *Noises Off*, 1983.

BELOW: The 2001 revival at the Brooks Atkinson Theater starred, from left, Peter Gallagher, Faith Prince, Robin Weigert, Katie Finneran, Richard Easton, Patti LuPone, Edward Hibbert (front), Thomas McCarthy, and T. R. Knight. © *Joan Marcus*

DATES:

December 11, 1983–April 6, 1985 at the Brooks Atkinson Theater (553 performances)

SYNOPSIS:

Under the best of circumstances, the sex farce *Nothing On* appears to be tough going for the audience. Three different performances of the show—well, of Act I—show it being performed under just about the worst of circumstances.

AWARDS:

None

NOTED REVIVALS AND ADAPTATIONS:

Broadway revival in 2001; movie version in 1992

ORIGINAL STARS:

Brian Murray, Dorothy Loudon, Douglas Seale, Deborah Rush, Victor Garber

THE ODD COUPLE

BY NEIL SIMON

"What have you got?"
"I got brown sandwiches and green
    sandwiches. Well, what do you say?"
"What's the green?"
"It's either very new cheese or very old meat."
"I'll take the brown."

Outside of Shakespeare and maybe David Mamet, is any playwright as easily recognizable with as few words? For more than three decades, Bronx-born Neil Simon was virtually synonymous with Broadway comedies, musical comedies, and somewhat serious comedies. He had as many as four shows running simultaneously, not even counting the many he helped "doctor" anonymously during previews, including *A Chorus Line*. And in 1983 he became the only living playwright ever to have a Broadway theater named after him. (August Wilson would have been the second, but he died just two weeks before the Virginia Theater renaming ceremony.)

Comedy is constantly given short shrift, as any comedian will tell you. Critical consensus about Simon's greatness grew as he began to tackle weightier material in the late 1970s (*Chapter Two*) and 1980s (particularly his "Eugene trilogy," which began with *Brighton Beach Memoirs*), culminating in a Pulitzer Prize for *Lost in Yonkers* in 1991. Still, for an example of American boulevard comedy at its finest—exaggerated but recognizable characters muddling through ludicrous but not exactly implausible situations, demonstrating a suspicious but satisfying knack for *le mot juste*—*The Odd Couple* is hard to beat.

Whether they're hurling linguine (*not* spaghetti) against the wall or honking their sinuses clear at two in the morning or making a botch of a double date with the Pigeon sisters, Felix and Oscar have become the American stage's most enduring duo. They've even survived a gender swap in 1985, when Simon rejiggered the show for Sally Struthers and Rita Moreno (as Florence Ungar and Olive Madison), as well as a 2005 revival that amounted to a victory lap for Nathan Lane and Matthew Broderick after their success in *The Producers*.

That durability comes from the sort of rigor that is too often obscured by all the belly laughs. "He rewrote and rewrote and rewrote because he wanted to," said Mike Nichols, the original production's director, in an interview with *New Yorker* writer John Lahr. "We had so many endings I don't remember how the play ends. Walter [Matthau, the original Oscar] kept saying, 'What do you care? It's gonna run for years anyway.' It was that he knew he could do better."

OPPOSITE PAGE: Art Carney, Walter Matthau, Monica Evans, and Carole Shelley in the original Broadway production of *The Odd Couple*.

BELOW: Felix and Oscar face off. *Mark Kauffman, The LIFE Images Collection, Getty Images*

DATES:
March 10, 1965–July 2, 1967 at the Plymouth Theater and Eugene O'Neill Theater (964 performances)

SYNOPSIS:
When Felix Ungar gets thrown out by his wife, the neurotic neatnik lands on the Upper West Side doorstep of his slovenly pal Oscar Madison. The new arrangement doesn't go well.

AWARDS:
4 Tony Awards

NOTED REVIVALS AND ADAPTATIONS:
Broadway revival in 2005, plus the distaff adaptation of 1985; movie version in 1968 and sequel in 1998; TV series in 1970, 1975, 1982, and 2015

ORIGINAL STARS:
Art Carney, Walter Matthau

OF THEE I SING

BY GEORGE GERSHWIN, IRA GERSHWIN, GEORGE S. KAUFMAN, AND MORRIE RYSKIND

Of Thee I Sing satirized political shenanigans, and as such will forever be topical. One running joke was the powerlessness of the vice president, Alexander Throttlebottom, played by Victor Moore. Gaxton and Moore went on to work together on numerous musicals and several films.

In December 1931, an increasingly demoralized America was getting ready to participate in its first presidential election since the Great Depression had begun, two years earlier. Politics was in the air, and George and Ira Gershwin—who had previously written a war-skewering musical, *Strike Up the Band*, that had been heavily defanged on its way to Broadway—were ready to take another stab at tweaking democracy. This time they collaborated with the guy who did the defanging (Morrie Ryskind) as well as the guy whose script got junked (George S. Kaufman). The four of them wound up writing *Of Thee I Sing*, the first musical to employ satire from beginning to end.

Kaufman, who also directed, wasn't convinced. In fact, his famous quote, "Satire is what closes on Saturday night," was coined in reference to *Of Thee I Sing*, which tempted fate by opening on a Saturday. It didn't close until fifty-four Saturdays later.

Despite a deep interweaving of book and score—complete with several extended Gilbert-and-Sullivan-style passages—numbers like "Who Cares?" and the title song emerged as hits. (The title song, with its saucy appending of "baby" to the end of that

Lois Moran (Mary Turner) and William Gaxton (John P. Wintergreen) in *Of Thee I Sing*. Wintergreen falls in love with Mary, a pageant coordinator, because of her irresistible corn muffins.

DATES:

December 26, 1931–January 14, 1933 at the Music Box Theater and 46th Street Theater (441 performances)

SYNOPSIS:

John P. Wintergreen's presidential campaign, founded on a platform of love, runs aground when he reneges on a promise to marry the winner of a beauty pageant. The ensuing diplomatic crisis (the spurned pageant winner is French) requires the intervention of the Supreme Court.

AWARDS:

Pulitzer Prize

NOTED REVIVALS AND ADAPTATIONS:

Broadway revival in 1952; TV version in 1972

ORIGINAL STARS:

William Gaxton, Victor Moore, Lois Moran, Grace Brinkley

familiar patriotic phrase, generated a bit of controversy during rehearsals.) The pairing of William Gaxton and Victor Moore as running mates proved to be a fruitful one; they went on to costar in several films and six other Broadway musicals, including an unsuccessful sequel to *Of Thee I Sing* by the same writers, called *Let 'Em Eat Cake*.

It was enough to make *Of Thee I Sing* the first musical ever to win the Pulitzer Prize for Drama, an honor that has only been given out seven other times in the intervening eighty-plus years. But just like the show's frequently forgotten vice presidential candidate, Alexander Throttlebottom, George Gershwin was left out in the cold: the Pulitzer committee thought of the prize as a literary award, and they honored the entire writing team except for the composer. (A new committee reconsidered in 1998, sixty-two years after George's death, and awarded him a posthumous Pulitzer.) He had to content himself with having written his biggest hit during his lifetime.

Kaufman may have been one of the unassailable theater geniuses of his or any age, but even a beautifully made clock can be wrong a few times a day.

TILL THE CLOVDS ROLL BY

COMSTOCK – ELLIOTT CO.

PRESENTS

THE NEW MVSICAL COMEDY

OH BOY!

BOOK & LYRICS BY

GVY BOLTON AND
P. G. WODEHOUSE

MUSIC BY

JEROME KERN

T. B. HARMS
COMPANY
NEW YORK

1917

OH, BOY!

EROME KERN, GUY BOLTON,
AND P. G. WODEHOUSE

At 299 seats, the Princess Theater, on West 39th Street, was half the size of even the smallest Broadway theater today. Finding out how to turn a profit in such a small space in the 1910s was tricky. After a dramatic repertory company failed to make the Princess work, the idea of presenting intimately scaled (and budgeted) musicals was introduced, as a sort of counterprogramming to the Florenz Ziegfelds and Victor Herberts of the world.

The team entrusted with this task wasn't exactly made up of newcomers: a thirty-year-old Jerome Kern had already written songs for nearly fifty (!) Broadway shows, and lyricist P. G. Wodehouse signed on for the third "Princess Theater musical," as they became called, after parlaying his early success as a novelist in England into a gig at the brand-new *Vanity Fair* magazine. Only librettist Guy Bolton, who had recently abandoned his vocation as an architect, was a relative tyro.

The first Princess musical, by Kern and Bolton, was a rewrite of a British musical; it came and went without much incident in 1915. Their next one, *Very Good Eddie*, was a hit that same year, though. The addition of Wodehouse to the team in 1917 paid off in dividends with *Oh, Boy!*

You wouldn't necessarily know it from a plot synopsis, with its flappers emerging out of nowhere and an Act II number called "Flubby Dub, the Cave-Man," but *Oh, Boy!*—and the Princess Theater musicals in general—represented a major leap forward in terms of sophistication and unforced charm. Interpolated bits of vaudeville were

---

"Till the Clouds Roll By" was later used as the title of a 1946 fictionalized film biography of Jerome Kern, with an astonishingly starry cast that included Judy Garland, Angela Lansbury, Frank Sinatra, Lena Horne, Cyd Charisse, Dinah Shore, Gower Champion, Esther Williams, June Allyson, and Kathryn Grayson. *Sheet music.*

DATES:
February 20, 1917–March 30, 1918 at the Princess Theater and Casino Theater (463 performances)

SYNOPSIS:
A college girl on the run from the law takes refuge in a nice young man's apartment. This doesn't go over so well when the nice young man's wife comes home. And what will his Quaker aunt say?

AWARDS:
None

NOTED REVIVALS AND ADAPTATIONS:
Movie version in 1919

ORIGINAL STARS:
Anna Wheaton, Tom Powers, Hal Forde, Edna May Oliver

---

out; songs usually flowed logically from the scenes that preceded them. Even within this less freewheeling setting, the sublime "Till the Clouds Roll By" became one of Kern's biggest hits. The show sold well enough to transfer to the far larger Casino Theater, and it went on to a successful run in London, which was all but unheard of then. (Having two transplanted Brits in Wodehouse and Bolton probably helped on that score.)

The heyday of the Princess Theater musicals was a brief one: arguments over money prompted Kern's departure in 1918, and the other two members limped along with one final musical, *Oh, My Dear!*, before closing up shop. But in just four years, this potent trio had hacked away at many of the excesses and indulgences that plagued the form (and that have never vanished for good). The American musical emerged smaller, and better, as a result of their efforts.

OKLAHOMA!

BY RICHARD RODGERS AND OSCAR HAMMERSTEIN II

ABOVE: *Oklahoma!* was Agnes de Mille's first time choreographing a Broadway musical. Her work changed the way dance and plot connected to each other on the stage, and keenly illuminated characters' inner struggles. It was also great fun, as in the square dance "The Farmer and the Cowman."

OPPOSITE PAGE: From left, Betty Garde (Aunt Eller), Joan Roberts (Laurey), Alfred Drake (Curly), Lee Dixon (Will Parker), and Celeste Holm (Ado Annie) in the original Broadway cast.

Who needs legs or jokes when you have the most influential musical of all time?

To be fair, *Oklahoma!*—which received the infamous dismissal "No legs, no jokes, no chance" from producer Mike Todd during its out-of-town tryout in New Haven—has a few jokes, courtesy of the wacky Persian peddler Ali Hakim and the take-no-guff Aunt Eller. (Imagine how many more it would have had if Richard Rodgers, Oscar Hammerstein II, and director Rouben Mamoulian had taken one producer's advice and cast Groucho Marx as Ali Hakim.) And a few legs do get flashed during Agnes de Mille's pioneering "dream ballet" of Act II, although Todd wouldn't have known about that. He left *Away We Go!*, as it was then called, at intermission.

As easy as it is to mock Todd's myopia, *Oklahoma!* must have seemed willfully, almost suicidally daring in 1943. The curtain opens on a lone guy singing about a "bright golden

DATES:

March 31, 1943–May 29, 1948 at the St. James Theater (2,212 performances)

SYNOPSIS:

The farmers and the cowmen in turn-of-the-century Oklahoma tend not to be friends, and Curly McLain and Jud Fry are no exception. Each seeks the hand of Laurey for the box social, with violent consequences. True love runs only slightly smoother for Will Parker and his wayward fiancée, Ado Annie.

AWARDS:

1 Tony Award (fifty years after the fact); a "special" Pulitzer Prize

NOTED REVIVALS AND ADAPTATIONS:

Broadway revivals in 1951, 1979, and 2002; movie version in 1955

ORIGINAL STARS:

Alfred Drake, Joan Roberts, Celeste Holm, Lee Dixon, Howard Da Silva

haze on the meadow"—miles away from the flashy, chorus-heavy openings upon which Todd and so many others had relied for years.

Rodgers and Hammerstein had separately blazed trails within the world of musical theater in the past. The history of Broadway musicals, however, almost instantly divided between what came before *Oklahoma!* and what came after it. Was this because Rodgers could finally work from a completed song lyric, something his previous collaborator, Lorenz Hart, had been unable to provide? Was it the foresight the show's team demonstrated by having the original Broadway performers make a cast recording, the first of any American musical? Was it the sheer American-ness of the show in the middle of World War II? Or was it simply the alchemic ability of Rodgers, Hammerstein, Mamoulian, and de Mille to make every note, every dance step, every transition, and every word amplify one another in a way that had never been done

before? Many historians feel that *Show Boat* was just as pioneering as *Oklahoma!*, and they raise good points. But plenty of post–*Show Boat* musicals look just like the ones that preceded that show. The same cannot really be said for *Oklahoma!*

Over the decades, everyone from Fred Allen to Holly Golightly to the Kinks to Fozzie Bear has paid tribute to the show. It ran six nights a week for almost thirty-five years at a theater outside of Tulsa, and the title song (which had not yet been written when Mike Todd saw the production in New Haven) is now Oklahoma's official state song. Boy, does *Oklahoma!* have legs. And that's no joke.

ON THE TOWN

BY LEONARD BERNSTEIN, BETTY COMDEN, AND ADOLPH GREEN

Set designer Oliver Smith, who also designed the *Fancy Free* set, created an electrifying rendering of Times Square. Smith was nominated for twenty-five Tony Awards during his career; he won ten.

DATES:
December 28, 1944–February 2, 1946 at the Adelphi Theater, 44th Street Theater, and Martin Beck Theater (462 performances)

SYNOPSIS:
Three sailors on a twenty-four-hour furlough during World War II seek love (and maybe a trip to the Hippodrome) as they make their way from Carnegie Hall to the Congacabana to Coney Island.

AWARDS:
None

NOTED REVIVALS AND ADAPTATIONS:
Broadway revivals in 1971, 1998, and 2014; movie version in 1945

ORIGINAL STARS:
Betty Comden, Adolph Green, Cris Alexander, John Battles, Nancy Walker, Sono Osato

If you don't know the rules, you don't know when you're breaking them. Such was the case when choreographer Jerome Robbins and his pals Leonard Bernstein, Betty Comden, and Adolph Green—all shy of their thirtieth birthdays—partnered for an endeavor completely unconnected to the Broadway establishment.

On the Town, with its five ambitious ballets nestled in among the goofy bits of sketch comedy, has always defied categorization. Part revue, part book musical, and part ballet, it sits uneasily on the boundary separating the then-brand-new Rodgers and Hammerstein standard from the no-holds-barred revues and musical comedies that preceded it.

The idea for *On the Town* began as an expansion of the 1944 Robbins-Bernstein ballet *Fancy Free*, in which three lusty sailors vie for the attention of the only two available girls at a New York bar. Not even a fragment of *Fancy Free*'s storyline or score made it into *On the Town*, although the idiosyncratic rhythms and angular melodies of both are instantly recognizable as Bernstein's. Comden and Green created roles for themselves, as they had done during their cabaret days.

The whole thing promised to be a hodgepodge by a bunch of people who didn't really know the first thing about making a Broadway musical, and several established directors turned it down, including Elia Kazan. It was the venerable George Abbott who ultimately chose to come to the rescue of the four neophytes. He did not, however, choose ballerina Sono Osato, a Robbins favorite who had never sung or spoken a line of dialogue onstage, to play the elusive dream girl "Miss Turnstiles." In fact, two days before the opening, Abbott told her, "Now, Sono, you would not be *my* choice for this role." Nonetheless, casting a Japanese-American woman as a Broadway lead was a bold choice, at a time when others with her features were being shipped to internment camps. To the credit of the press, not one major review mentioned her ethnicity.

The show's open attitude to casual sexual relations was tempered by the deep melancholy depicted; there was, *On the Town* made clear, so little time in the face of an extremely uncertain future. It spoke to war-weary audiences the same way *Oklahoma!* had a year earlier—only this time the servicemen were on both sides of the footlights. When two of the sailors' voices dropped a full octave between the first two words as they sang "Oh well, we'll catch up some other time," the gap undoubtedly felt very, very wide.

OUR TOWN

BY THORNTON WILDER

"An archaeologist's eyes combine the view of the telescope and the view of the microscope. He reconstructs the very distant with the help of the very small. It was something of this method that I brought to a New Hampshire village."

When Thornton Wilder wrote these words in his preface to *Our Town* in 1938, the dawn of the twentieth century was a lot less distant than it is today. By looking with incredible, at times heart-ravaging specificity into Grover's Corners, right down to its latitude and longitude (which would actually put the town in Massachusetts, but never mind), Wilder reconstructed a smallish, happyish place that has seen its share of misery.

The play's blend of homespun charm and raw emotion, culminating in a young woman being permitted to have one last look back from the grave, has prompted many to quibble over whether *Our Town* is a tragedy. The best response seems to be that it isn't, except when it is. Predicting when it won't be is very difficult—just as in life. Or, as the Stage Manager and play's narrator puts it, "The cottage, the go-cart, the Sunday-afternoon drives in the Ford, the first rheumatism, the grandchildren, the second rheumatism, the deathbed, the reading of the will. Once in a thousand times it's interesting."

OPPOSITE PAGE: The Stage Manager (Frank Craven) narrates the goings-on of Grover's Corners, New Hampshire. The town's residents include Mrs. Gibbs (Evelyn Varden, center), Emily Webb (Martha Scott, in white), and George Gibbs (John Craven, Frank's son, face down).

BELOW: David Cromer's 2009 off-Broadway production of *Our Town*, with James McMenamin as George, Jason Butler Harner (center, background) as the Stage Manager, and Jennifer Grace as Emily. © *Carol Rosegg*

DATES:

February 4–November 19, 1938 at Henry Miller's Theater and the Morosco Theater (336 performances)

SYNOPSIS:

"Well, I'd better show you how our town lies." So says the Stage Manager about Grover's Corners, New Hampshire. And he does.

AWARDS:

Pulitzer Prize

NOTED REVIVALS AND ADAPTATIONS:

Broadway revivals in 1969, 1988, and 2002; movie version in 1940; TV versions in 1977, 1989, and 2003

ORIGINAL STARS:

Frank Craven, John Craven, Martha Scott

Wilder fought bitterly throughout rehearsals with director/producer Jed Harris, who seemed far more interested in the play's young lovers than in its metatheatrical metaphysics. But Harris did honor Wilder's stage directions—"No curtain. No scenery."—and created a teeming village through the simplest of visuals. When that young couple, for instance, spoke from their respective bedrooms, they climbed up a pair of onstage ladders. This minimalist approach led to plenty of audience walkouts in Boston, so Harris cut the tryout short and headed to New York, where the reception was much warmer.

More than thirty years passed before *Our Town* made it back to Broadway, during which time it became entrenched as an essential text, and maybe America's best-loved glimpse into its own increasingly hazy past. (David Cromer's revelatory off-Broadway revival another forty years later, in 2009, was the longest-running production in the play's long history. It unearthed entire new veins from *Our Town*'s seemingly strip-mined text, right down to a tipsy and surprisingly angry choir director weaving his sad way home.)

That glimpse can take a toll, something *New York Times* critic Walter Kerr alluded to in 1969. "We bring a curious intensity to our visits to *Our Town* these days, going to each successive revival in a strangely mixed hope and fear that the work will at last seem tarnished," he wrote. "I think we hope it will tarnish so that it will stop affecting us." No such luck.

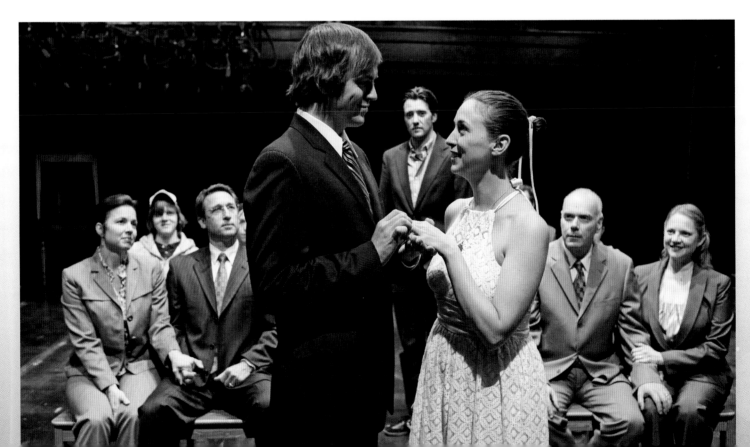

PAL JOEY

BY RICHARD RODGERS, LORENZ HART, AND JOHN O'HARA

ABOVE: Gene Kelly's stardom was solidified in *Pal Joey*, two years after his Broadway debut in Cole Porter's *Leave It to Me!* and a year after his breakthrough in *The Time of Your Life*.

OPPOSITE PAGE: Harold Lang played Joey Evans in the 1952 revival, which ran for 540 performances at the Broadhurst Theater. Vivienne Segal (front, center) costarred, and Helen Gallagher and Elaine Stritch were also in the cast.

From the original reviews of *Pal Joey*, you would think the critics had never met a protagonist with clay feet before. Never mind the huge popularity of sullen, hard-drinking private eyes like Sam Spade or Philip Marlowe in the 1930s. Or that the biggest movie of the previous year featured a vain, conniving gal by the name of Scarlett O'Hara. Those characters were from books and movies. Joey Evans, on the other hand, was in a *musical*, and the Broadway confectioners of the time were not in the habit of handing their big song-and-dance numbers to two-bit gigolos.

But that's what Joey was in John O'Hara's astringent *New Yorker* short stories, and that's what he remained when O'Hara teamed up with Richard Rodgers and Lorenz Hart (and, via a healthy dose of uncredited rewrites, director George Abbott) to bring him to life. They knew they needed a likeable leading man to give Joey a chance with audiences; Gene Kelly, who took his *Pal Joey* momentum straight to Hollywood, certainly fit the bill.

Though the nightclub-heavy setting allowed Rodgers and Hart to fit a bunch of juicy extraneous numbers into the score, they also delivered some of their

strongest character-driven work with "I Could Write a Book" and "Bewitched (Bothered and Bewildered)." But a contract dispute with ASCAP kept those songs off the radio for almost a year, starting just six days after *Pal Joey* opened.

The biggest hitch, however, was the mix of begrudging respect and outright revulsion from the critics. Brooks Atkinson's famous question in his *New York Times* review—"Can you draw sweet water from a foul well?"—is the most obvious example. But he was hardly alone in grumbling about the very existence of a leading man who would say things like the following (to the married socialite who has been paying his bills):

> Vera: I have a temper, Beauty, and I want to say a few things before I lose it.
> Joey: Lose it. It's all you got left to lose.

Critics were more open to the idea of a front-and-center cad by the time *Pal Joey* was revived in 1952, in a production that became the longest-running musical revival until that point. (Bob Fosse understudied the title role in it—and has there ever been a better match of performer and character?) Hart's viability as a functioning collaborator was nearing its end by 1940, and it's entirely possible that those intervening twelve years might have seen Rodgers and a less self-destructive Hart build on the leap they had made in narrative ambition. Rodgers would have to follow that path with Oscar Hammerstein II instead. But *Pal Joey* pointed the way.

DATES:
December 25, 1940–November 29, 1941 at the Ethel Barrymore Theater, Shubert Theater, and St. James Theater (374 performances)

SYNOPSIS:
Joey Evans, a charming but amoral nightclub hoofer, tries to juggle two lady friends, the naïve stenographer Linda English and the seen-it-all socialite Vera Simpson.

AWARDS:
None

NOTED REVIVALS AND ADAPTATIONS:
Broadway revivals in 1952, 1976, and 2008; movie version in 1957

ORIGINAL STARS:
Gene Kelly, Vivienne Segal, Leila Ernst, June Havoc, Jean Casto

THE PERSECUTION AND ASSASSINATION OF JEAN-PAUL MARAT AS PERFORMED BY THE INMATES OF THE ASYLUM OF CHARENTON UNDER THE DIRECTION OF THE MARQUIS DE SADE

BY PETER WEISS

DATES:

December 27, 1965–April 30, 1966 at the Martin Beck Theater (145 performances)

SYNOPSIS:

The title essentially is a synopsis. The Marquis de Sade really did write plays for his fellow inmates in the beginning of the nineteenth century, and they might well have looked like this one.

AWARDS:

4 Tony Awards

NOTED REVIVALS AND ADAPTATIONS:

Broadway revival in 1967; movie version in 1967

ORIGINAL STARS:

Ian Richardson, Patrick Magee, Glenda Jackson

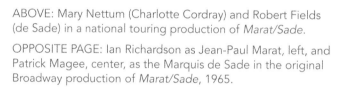

ABOVE: Mary Nettum (Charlotte Cordray) and Robert Fields (de Sade) in a national touring production of *Marat/Sade*.

OPPOSITE PAGE: Ian Richardson as Jean-Paul Marat, left, and Patrick Magee, center, as the Marquis de Sade in the original Broadway production of *Marat/Sade*, 1965.

It's two days after Christmas in 1965. The curbs of Manhattan are just starting to fill up with discarded trees, and the visiting relatives are starting to get on one another's nerves. Hey, there's a new Broadway play opening! What better way to get everyone out of the house, even if the top ticket prices have crept all the way up to $7.50? Hmmm, this title is really long. . . .

A similar idea occurs to the director of the titular asylum in *The Persecution and Assassination of Jean-Paul Marat as Performed by the Inmates of the Asylum of Charenton Under the Direction of the Marquis de Sade*, henceforth known as *Marat/Sade*. He brings his wife and daughter to the performance in question, which turns out to be about as good an idea as bringing your family to Peter Weiss' scabrous drama. What is on display for us is a fairly typical play within a play, but with one crucial difference: the parts in de Sade's play are all being performed by the insane.

Marat/Sade features a man listed in the program as "Mad Animal," who says at one point, "The earth is spread thick with squashed human guts." Judging by what awaited audiences, he wasn't too far off the mark. In 1964, director Peter Brook had helped the Royal Shakespeare Company assemble what he called a "Theater of Cruelty" season, made up of works that expanded upon the precepts of

Antonin Artaud's famously unstageable movement of the same name. *Marat/Sade* was the runaway success of the season, a visceral gauntlet thrown at the feet of theatergoers. Nudity, violence, effluvia: this was going to be a very different theatergoing experience, both in London and during the subsequent RSC mounting in New York.

Much of what Weiss and Brook created had been seen in the more experimental corners of the theater world by the mid-1960s, but the sight of it at the Royal Shakespeare Company served notice. Richard Peaslee's abrasive incidental music became an unlikely hit, even turning up as a medley on a Judy Collins album, and playwrights from Mike Leigh to David Hare have cited *Marat/Sade* as a major influence. The stages of both New York and London would soon be spread thick with the guts of the old ways.

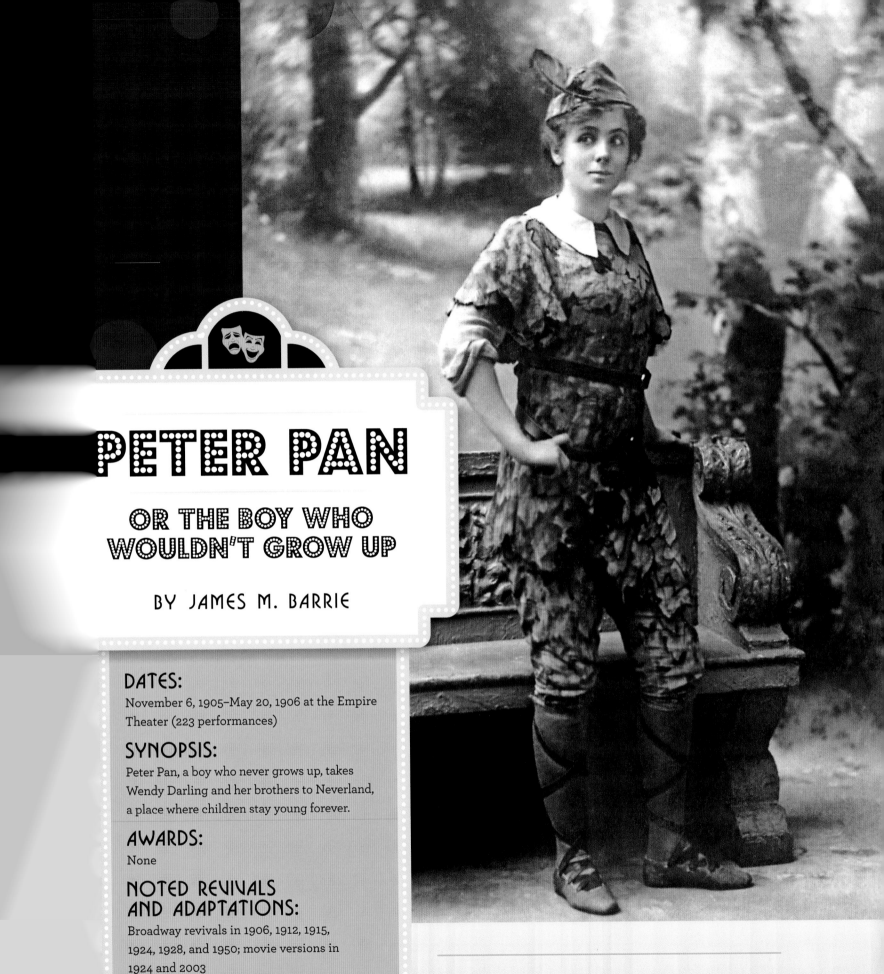

PETER PAN

OR THE BOY WHO WOULDN'T GROW UP

BY JAMES M. BARRIE

DATES:

November 6, 1905–May 20, 1906 at the Empire
Theater (223 performances)

SYNOPSIS:

Peter Pan, a boy who never grows up, takes
Wendy Darling and her brothers to Neverland,
a place where children stay young forever.

AWARDS:

None

**NOTED REVIVALS
AND ADAPTATIONS:**

Broadway revivals in 1906, 1912, 1915,
1924, 1928, and 1950; movie versions in
1924 and 2003

ORIGINAL STARS:

Maude Adams, Ernest Lawford, Mildred Morris

Maude Adams, born Maude Kiskadden in 1872, was one of the
highest-paid performers of her time. © *Glasshouse Images, Alamy*

Before there were Mary Martin on wires and Robin Williams in green shorts, rides at Disney World and racy comic books, there was Maude Adams.

To be fair, before there was Maude Adams, there was Nina Boucicault, who first donned Peter Pan's feathered cap in London in 1904. But Adams, who, unlike the character she played, really did grow up on the stage—she was first carried onstage by her actress mother when she was nine months old—turned Peter Pan into *the* iconic stage character for children.

Broadway producer Charles Frohman discovered a teenage Adams in 1889. He had been trying to cajole James M. Barrie into adapting his book *The Little Minister* into a play; Barrie relented after seeing Adams perform in another of Frohman's shows. The result was a huge success for all three, who would go on to collaborate repeatedly.

After an emergency appendectomy almost knocked her out of the production, Adams opened in the title role of *Peter Pan, or the Boy Who Wouldn't Grow Up*. (The title had said "Couldn't Grow Up," but Frohman changed it.) The rounded white collar that she helped design for her costume was a hit—it's known as a Peter Pan collar to this day—and so was the show. Adams appeared in return engagements for the next decade, earning as much as $1 million a year. When she played Peter for the final time in 1915, she was forty-three.

Major stage performers like Marilyn Miller and Eva Le Gallienne took on the role in the 1920s. Despite all of the adaptations that popped up in its wake, Barrie's original script hasn't been seen on Broadway since 1950. Leonard Bernstein wrote five songs for that production, which starred Jean Arthur and, in the role of Captain Hook, Boris Karloff.

One person who wasn't around to experience these iterations was Frohman; he was aboard the *Lusitania* ocean liner when a U-boat torpedo struck it in 1915. (Jerome Kern had booked passage on the ship but overslept.) Frohman attached lifejackets to baskets holding sleeping infants as the boat sank, and just before being swept away, he was heard asking, "Why fear death? It is the most beautiful adventure in life." The line is from *Peter Pan*.

Marilyn Miller played Peter Pan in a 1924 Broadway revival, after starring in the *Ziegfeld Follies of 1919*. The beloved star died tragically at age thirty-seven.

PETER PAN

BY MOOSE CHARLAP, CAROLYN LEIGH, AND JAMES M. BARRIE, WITH ADDITIONAL MUSIC BY JULE STYNE AND LYRICS BY BETTY COMDEN AND ADOLPH GREEN

Just 152 performances for the beloved Mary Martin as the even-more-beloved Peter Pan? With singing material by that virtual songwriters' hall of fame listed at right? As it happens, the producers of the musical *Peter Pan* had bigger and better things planned for it.

Martin was known for not missing many performances. Still, she would have had to do eight shows a week at the Winter Garden for just over 104 *years* to reach the 65 million people who reportedly watched *Peter Pan* live on NBC on March 7, 1955. The *Producers' Showcase* presentation, the first full Broadway production to be shown on color television, was the most watched show in TV history at the time.

Are 65 million people ever wrong? Of course, all the time. But they weren't this time. Jerome Robbins—who had bailed out of a 1950 *Peter Pan* "play with songs" that briefly morphed into a full-fledged Leonard Bernstein musical, before Bernstein himself jumped ship—did some salvage work on the piece during a West Coast tryout, bringing in Jule Styne, Betty

ABOVE: Peter (Mary Martin) and Captain Hook (Cyril Ritchard) face off in the original Broadway production.

OPPOSITE PAGE: Mary Martin as Peter Pan in a 1960 TV version. Martin starred in the original Broadway production of *Peter Pan* after originating the role of Nellie Forbush in *South Pacific*, and before originating the role of Maria Von Trapp in *The Sound of Music*. She won Tony Awards for all three roles. © NBC, courtesy Photofest

Comden, and Adolph Green to add "Never Never Land," the underrated "Captain Hook's Waltz," and other music. Certain foolproof aspects were there from the beginning, however: the audience being asked to clap to bring Tinker Bell back to life and, with the help of stage effects pioneer Peter Foy and his brand-new "Inter-Related Pendulum" system, the still-miraculous "I'm Flying" sequence.

Years later, first Sandy Duncan and then Cathy Rigby made second careers out of the titular role on Broadway, on the road, and (in Rigby's case) on television again. The production tends to get an additional nip and tuck these days. The "Ugg-a-Wugg" musical number, featuring Peter's offer to "come and save the brave noble redskin," is typically among the first to go.

DATES:
October 20, 1954–February 26, 1955 at the Winter Garden Theater (152 performances)

SYNOPSIS:
See previous show.

AWARDS:
3 Tony Awards

NOTED REVIVALS AND ADAPTATIONS:
Broadway revivals in 1979, 1990, 1991, 1998, and 1999; TV versions in 1955, 1956, 1960, and 2014

ORIGINAL STARS:
Mary Martin, Cyril Ritchard

If you're concerned that kids today are too jaded, do what I did and take a three-year-old to see *Peter Pan*. And then take a look at his red palms after he has clapped Tinker Bell back to life.

THE PHANTOM OF THE OPERA

BY ANDREW LLOYD WEBBER, CHARLES HART, AND RICHARD STILGOE

By 1984, Andrew Lloyd Webber had written five hit musicals—with nothing really resembling romance in any of them. Mary Magdalene didn't know how to love Jesus, Eva and Juan Perón had more of a marriage of convenience, and T. S. Eliot never got around to writing any feline love songs.

Lloyd Webber and super-producer Cameron Mackintosh changed that in a big way when they settled on Gaston Leroux's novel *The Phantom of the Opera* for their project, with the leading role of Christine tailored to Lloyd Webber's wife at the time, Sarah Brightman. His original plan was to rely on existing opera music; luckily for him and his accountant, that plan changed. The original cast recording alone has sold more than forty million copies worldwide.

Although theater is no longer the prevailing form of entertainment, *The Phantom of the Opera* spent more than a decade as the most successful piece of entertainment in any medium, surpassing even the films *Avatar* and *Titanic*. *The Lion King* has since eclipsed it financially, but there's no competition from the standpoint of longevity. *Phantom* has a nine-year head start over its closest challenger, the revival of *Chicago*.

Why has it stuck around so long? Are there that many fans of George Lee Andrews, who made the *Guinness Book of World Records* by playing the opera manager Monsieur André more than 9,300 times? More likely candidates for such fandom include the crashing chandelier at the end of Act I and Michael Crawford, with his remarkably convincing transformation from gawky ingénue circa *Hello, Dolly!* to man of mystery. Director Harold Prince's peerless eye for complicated stage pictures helped, too, as did his zeal for keeping standards high: a YouTube montage of a few dozen chandelier crashes shows an incredible, almost spooky consistency over the decades and around the world.

And of course, there is Lloyd Webber's score, a zestful mix of Puccini and pop that promises a new sweeping melody every few minutes. The less admirable lyrics were written by committee, with a group that included Alan Jay Lerner of *My Fair Lady* fame and *Starlight Express*' Richard Stilgoe.

Love Never Dies, Lloyd Webber's 2010 attempt to replicate *Phantom*'s success with a sequel set in Coney Island, has been only slightly more successful than such previous stage follow-ups as *Bring Back Birdie* and *Annie 2: Miss Hannigan's Revenge*. But while *Love Never Dies* died a relatively quick death in London and never made it to New York, the love for its predecessor really does appear to be immortal.

OPPOSITE PAGE: "Masquerade," at the beginning of Act II, showcased the lavishness of *Phantom*'s costumes and sets (both by Maria Björnson). © *Joan Marcus*

RIGHT: Michael Crawford, the original Phantom of the Opera. Crawford performed the role more than 1,300 times.

DATES:
Opened January 26, 1988 at the Majestic Theater (11,239 performances as of February 1, 2015)

SYNOPSIS:
Christine Daaé unexpectedly ascends the ranks of the Paris Opera House in 1881 with the help of her mysterious voice teacher, a disfigured phantom who falls in love with his protégée.

AWARDS:
7 Tony Awards

NOTED REVIVALS AND ADAPTATIONS:
Movie version in 2004

ORIGINAL STARS:
Michael Crawford, Sarah Brightman, Steve Barton, Judy Kaye

THE PHILADELPHIA STORY

BY PHILIP BARRY

Dan Tobin (Alexander Lord) and Katharine Hepburn (socialite Tracy Lord) in *The Philadelphia Story*, 1939.

When David Ogden Stewart received the Best Adapted Screenplay Academy Award in 1940 for the film version of *The Philadelphia Story*, he simply said, "I have no one to thank but myself!" He really needn't have been so brief—the awards show wasn't televised, so it's not like he had to worry about the orchestra cutting him off.

Following are a few suggestions of people Stewart might have thanked:

★George Pierce Baker, who taught the famous playwriting course known as 47 Workshop at Harvard to Philip Barry, along with Eugene O'Neill, George Abbott, S. N. Behrman, and Thomas Wolfe. (Yes, the author of *Look Homeward, Angel* started out as a budding playwright and was a classmate of Barry's—and a rather envious one, at that.)

Van Heflin (reporter Macaulay Connor), Shirley Booth (photographer Elizabeth Imbrie), and Hepburn.

DATES:

March 28, 1939–March 30, 1940 at the Shubert Theater (417 performances)

SYNOPSIS:

Among the attendees of the socially prominent Tracy Lord's wedding are a fast-talking tabloid newspaper reporter and Tracy's first husband. What could possibly go wrong?

AWARDS:

None

NOTED REVIVALS AND ADAPTATIONS:

Broadway revival in 1980; movie version in 1940; TV version in 1954

ORIGINAL STARS:

Katharine Hepburn, Joseph Cotten, Van Heflin, Shirley Booth

★ Helen Hope Montgomery Scott, "the unofficial queen of Philadelphia's WASP oligarchy," who danced with Josephine Baker in Paris and talked Edward VIII into standing on his head.

★ Ellen Barry, Philip's wife, who convinced him to write a comedy of manners about the Main Line social elite of Philadelphia, centering on a "virgin goddess" who learns to become a free spirit—one not unlike Ms. Scott. (Scott's husband and Philip were old Harvard chums.)

★ Katharine Hepburn, who convinced Barry to write the part in said play for her shortly after being branded "box office poison" in Hollywood, and who even footed the bill for the production herself.

★ Howard Hughes, who had a fling with Hepburn and subsequently bought her the film rights to the play, which she then sold to MGM at a reduced rate, provided she could have approval of her costars and director. She also got to pick the screenwriter and chose . . . Barry's old friend David Ogden Stewart, the one who purportedly made it to the big screen all by himself. To quote Cole Porter, who tried adding tunes to the story (unnecessarily) for the 1956 film *High Society*, "Well, did you evah?"

★ Oh, and Stewart might have mentioned Barry himself, who may have written better plays than *The Philadelphia Story* over the course of a surprisingly diverse career (*Holiday*, for one), but who never matched the success of this effervescent charmer.

PICNIC

BY WILLIAM INGE

William Inge spent more than a quarter of a century thinking about *Picnic*—or, as it was called at various times, *Summer Brave*, *Front Porch*, *The Man in Boots*, and *Women in Summer*. It is this last title that speaks most decisively to Inge's empathic gifts: though *Picnic* may be remembered as the play that (eventually) vaulted Paul Newman into stardom, it is really about the women who exist in an uneasy orbit around Hal Carter, the handsome diving champion who floats in and out of their sleepy Kansas town. And with apologies to Edward Albee and to Inge's early champion Tennessee Williams, Inge may have written better roles for women than any other male playwright.

Better, but not always happier. Every woman in *Picnic* is lonely. Tomboyish Millie Owens doesn't have a date to the neighborhood picnic; her beautiful sister, Madge, tolerates her well-heeled boyfriend but desires Hal; their widowed mother, Flo, ran away with a man like Hal in her youth and lived to regret it. And then there's Rosemary, their alcoholic spinster—she prefers the word "independent"—of a boarder.

Despite winning Inge a Pulitzer Prize and spawning a hit 1955 film, *Picnic* never quite sat right with its author. Director Joshua Logan had pushed a fair number of changes during the original production, notably by having Madge chase hunky Hal out of town. Inge went back to his original text and created something rare for Broadway: a do-over of something that didn't need to be redone. *Summer Brave* opened on Broadway in 1975, two years after Inge's death, and closed fourteen performances later.

While Inge was conspiring to keep his protagonists apart, the understudies were forging their own connection. Paul Newman lobbied hard for the role of Hal, but Logan didn't think he was tall enough. So Ralph Meeker got the part, and Newman began his *Picnic* life as first the newspaper boy Bomber and then Madge's level-headed boyfriend Alan before finally becoming Meeker's understudy. Along the way, he met Janice Rule's understudy for the role of Madge—Joanne Woodward. It was another five years before Newman and Woodward got together for good, but that time they stayed together for fifty years.

DATES:
February 19, 1953–April 10, 1954 at the Music Box Theater (477 performances)

SYNOPSIS:
A handsome stranger rocks a small Kansas town— and particularly a handful of its women—over Labor Day weekend.

AWARDS:
2 Tony Awards

NOTED REVIVALS AND ADAPTATIONS:
Broadway revivals in 1994 and 2013; movie version in 1955; TV versions in 1986 and 2000

ORIGINAL STARS:
Ralph Meeker, Janice Rule, Kim Stanley, Peggy Conklin, Paul Newman

PIPPIN

BY STEPHEN SCHWARTZ AND ROGER O. HIRSON

ABOVE: John Rubinstein originated the role of Pippin, who is surrounded by a troupe of players with questionable scruples.

OPPOSITE PAGE: Ben Vereen as the Leading Player in the original Broadway production. Vereen won a Tony for his performance; the role also earned Patina Miller a Tony for the 2013 Broadway revival.

NEXT PAGE: The 2013 revival, with Miller front, hands raised, was directed by Diane Paulus and choreographed by Chet Walker. It honored the original Fosse choreography while bringing in circus elements, from trapezes to handwalking. © Joan Marcus

DATES:

October 23, 1972–March 15, 1977 at the Imperial Theater and Minskoff Theater (1,944 performances)

SYNOPSIS:

War, sex, power, domestic life: nothing seems to give Pippin, son of Charlemagne, the contentment he seeks. The Leading Player and the performing troupe under his command have a suggestion, though . . .

AWARDS:

5 Tony Awards

NOTED REVIVALS AND ADAPTATIONS:

Broadway revival in 2013; TV version in 1981

ORIGINAL STARS:

Ben Vereen, John Rubinstein, Jill Clayburgh, Leland Palmer, Irene Ryan

Most of us would consider it a good year if we won both a Tony Award and an Academy Award. Or maybe an Emmy Award instead of one of the others. You know what? Just one would be perfectly fine.

Bob Fosse may have been a glass-half-empty kind of guy, but even he couldn't have been too displeased with winning all three awards in 1973. *Pippin* opened on the heels of two collaborations with John Kander, Fred Ebb, and Liza Minnelli, the film version of *Cabaret* and the TV special *Liza With a Z*; Fosse's new proficiency with the camera would come in handy for *Pippin*.

Along with composer/lyricist Stephen Schwartz, who was just coming off his own smash success with the off-Broadway musical *Godspell*, Fosse found ways to turn the rather arch material—an abandoned student musical from Schwartz's college days—into a sinuous, ironic picaresque, a *Candide* for the Me Generation. He also drove the twenty-four-year-old Schwartz crazy in the process, as was his wont. Coproducer Motown Records must have softened the blow a bit by getting some of Schwartz's charming tunes, including "Morning Glow" and "I Guess I'll Miss the Man," into the hands of the Jackson 5 and the Supremes.

When a chunk of the show's funding fell through, Fosse reconceived the entire evening as a spare, story-theater-style production, anchored by Jules Fisher's alluring lighting. He sent Ben Vereen to study Bill "Bojangles" Robinson and Jimmy Slyde clips while he figured out what to do with the Leading Player, ultimately turning him into a Mephisphelean tour guide with immolation on his mind.

The team did spend money on one thing, though: television. Commercials for Broadway shows with actual footage were unheard of in 1972, and the sixty-second clip of Vereen, Candy Brown, and Pamela Sousa performing the "Manson Trio" sequence from the song "Glory" was just the latest in Fosse's innovations for the stage. "You can see the other 119 minutes of *Pippin* live at the Imperial Theater . . . without commercial interruption," intoned the announcer. Audiences took him up on the offer for almost five years.

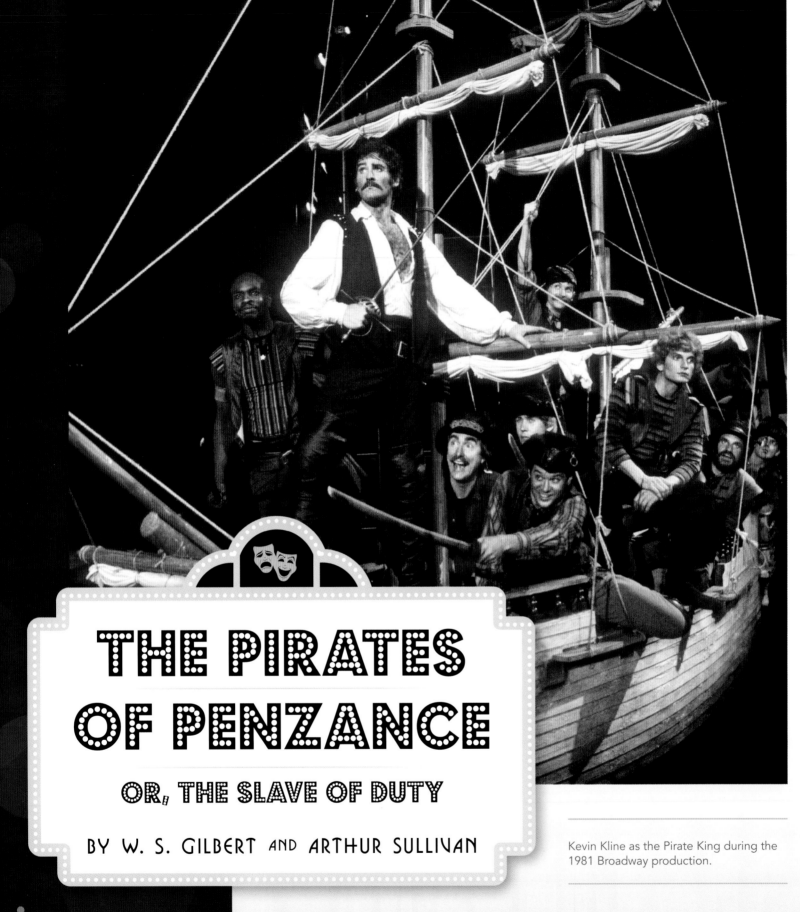

THE PIRATES OF PENZANCE

OR, THE SLAVE OF DUTY

BY W. S. GILBERT AND ARTHUR SULLIVAN

Kevin Kline as the Pirate King during the 1981 Broadway production.

"If you must steal," according to the old theater adage, "steal from the best." W. S. Gilbert and Arthur Sullivan were unquestionably the best of their (or any) era at writing witty operettas, and roughly 150 unauthorized productions of their wildly popular *H.M.S. Pinafore* dotted the United States immediately following its London premiere. While not illegal (copyright laws between America and Great Britain were extremely inconsistent), these pilfered *Pinafore*s denied Gilbert and Sullivan a fortune in lost royalties; they were also often complete travesties of the duo's work.

DATES:

Opened December 31, 1879 at the Fifth Avenue Theater (number of performances unknown)

SYNOPSIS:

Wide-eyed young Frederic instantly falls in love with Mabel, the Major-General's daughter. But there's the issue of his February 29 birthday, which extends his apprenticeship to a tender-hearted group of pirates by a few decades.

AWARDS:

None

NOTED REVIVALS AND ADAPTATIONS:

More than two dozen Broadway revivals, most recently in 1981; movie version in 1983; several TV versions

ORIGINAL STARS:

J. H. Ryley, Hugh Talbot, Signor Brocolini, Blanche Roosevelt, Alice Barnett

Signor Brocolini, who originated the role of the Pirate King, is said to have changed his name from John Clark in honor of his beloved Brooklyn. *TSC1.3651, Harvard Theatre Collection, Houghton Library, Harvard University*

Determined to defeat these authorial brigands, Gilbert and Sullivan and their producer, Richard D'Oyly Carte, hatched a plan to premiere their next work simultaneously in both countries. New Year's Eve, 1879, saw a glossy New York premiere of *The Pirates of Penzance*, which had made a more modest English debut the previous afternoon in the sleepy coastal village of Paignton, two hundred miles from London.

The plan hit a few snags: Sullivan, en route to conduct the US production, realized he had forgotten to pack a goodly portion of the score. He was forced to reconstruct much of it from memory during his voyage across the Atlantic. Meanwhile, without the authors present and with a grand total of one rehearsal, the Paignton "production" was a glorified staged reading, with actors in mufti clutching their scripts. But at least the multinational copyright was secured.

Although Gilbert's domineering personality often threatened to divide the pair, his exacting attention to the clothing, the setting, the props, and everything else resulted in unusually satisfying satires. He also insisted that his lyrics never be a slave to the music, as was the case in most operettas. Arguably for the first time, the words were equal, and possibly even superior, to the melodies,

yielding a true collaboration of music and theater. Gilbert and Sullivan's combined work would influence everyone from Ira Gershwin to Stephen Sondheim; it also introduced the term "patter song" into the vernacular.

For most of the twentieth century, *Pirates* was revived under the dauntingly long shadow of the D'Oyly Carte Company, whose manner of staging was considered sacrosanct. That changed in 1980, when Joseph Papp's New York Shakespeare Festival had the audacity to leave the text intact but toss the dusty traditions overboard. The boisterous Central Park revival, featuring Kevin Kline as a swashbuckling Pirate King, transferred to Broadway and ran for almost two years. Producers have gleefully stolen from it ever since.

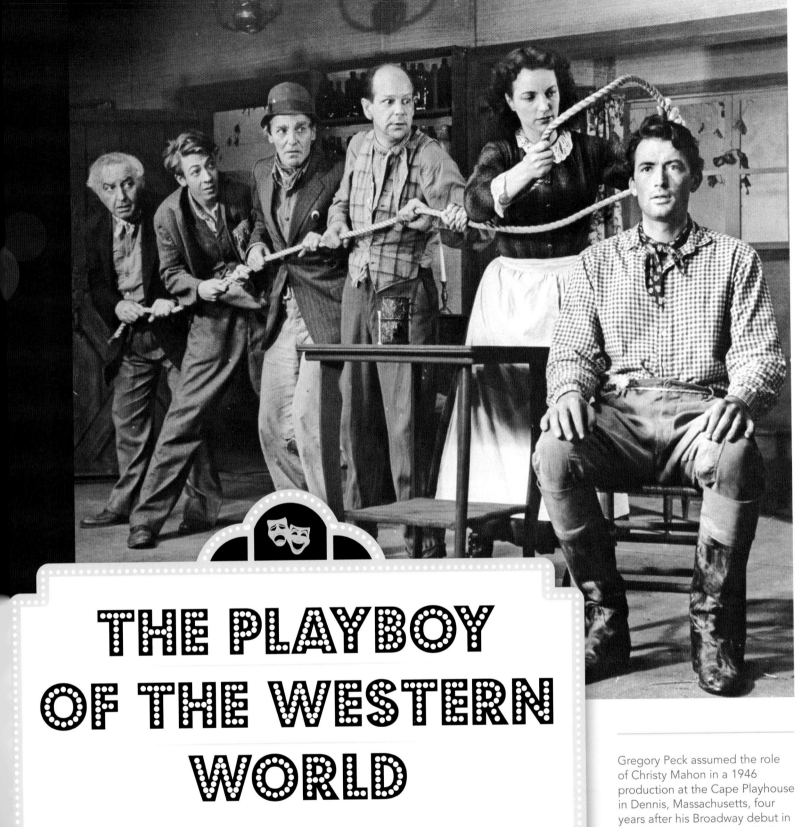

THE PLAYBOY OF THE WESTERN WORLD

BY JOHN MILLINGTON SYNGE

Gregory Peck assumed the role of Christy Mahon in a 1946 production at the Cape Playhouse in Dennis, Massachusetts, four years after his Broadway debut in *The Morning Star*. Eileen Darby, *The LIFE Images Collection,* *Getty Images*

Four years had elapsed since the Dublin premiere of *The Playboy of the Western World* by the time the Abbey Players left Ireland for a US tour, yet time had done little to soothe the crowds. John Millington Synge's fanciful black comedy had generated riots when it opened in 1907; a reference to "a drift of Mayo girls standing in their shifts" was cited as a reason, but the bigger issue was his central character. Christy Mahon, who boasts of killing his own dad—and can't even succeed at that—fell far short of the heroic image the

The 1946 Broadway revival of *Playboy of the Western World* starred, from left, Barry Macollum, Eithne Dunne, Dennis King Jr., Burgess Meredith (as Christy), J. M. Kerrigan, and J. C. Nugent.

Irish nationalists of the era wanted to present to the world. Sympathetic newspapers like the *Gaelic American* did their bit to urge stateside readers to "drive the vile thing from the stage"—and to remind them that Synge was a Protestant.

By the time *Playboy* reached New York, in repertory with more than a dozen other plays by such fellow politically suspect sorts as Lady Gregory and W. B. Yeats, the audiences had their vegetables, stink bombs, and fists at the ready. Though arrests (on the grounds that the performance was immoral) didn't come until the players headed to Philadelphia, Synge's play struck a nerve in each city.

It still does, which may be why playwrights have tried adapting *Playboy* by setting it in a variety of times and places, including Appalachia in the 1930s and Trinidad in the 1950s. As engrossing as these reworked versions can be, the thick, peaty language that Synge gave his County Mayo characters is as crucial to his work as it is to that of such fellow Irishmen as Samuel Beckett and Martin McDonagh (who knows a thing or two about seemingly dead characters returning to the stage).

Unlike those two figures, Synge found and cultivated a sense of delight in his characters' foibles. "On the stage one must have *reality* and one must have *joy*," he once wrote, going on to describe "the rich joy found only in what is superb and wild in reality." Christy Mahon's tale of patricide certainly qualifies as both wild and superb; the awestruck townspeople he encounters would agree. That the reality is a good bit less bloody doesn't make it any less joyful.

DATES:
Opened November 20, 1911 at Maxine Elliott's Theater (number of performances unknown)

SYNOPSIS:
Flaherty's sleepy tavern in County Mayo, Ireland, gets a welcome dose of scandal when Christy Mahon stumbles in after killing his father. The news makes Christy an unlikely celebrity—until the old codger shows up with little more than a bad headache.

AWARDS:
None

NOTED REVIVALS AND ADAPTATIONS:
Broadway revivals in 1913, 1921, 1930, 1934, 1937, 1946, and 1971; movie version in 1962; TV version in 1994

ORIGINAL STARS:
Molly Allgood, Arthur Sinclair, J. M. Kerrigan

PORGY AND BESS

BY GEORGE GERSHWIN, IRA GERSHWIN, AND DuBOSE HEYWARD

George Gershwin could write a song in an hour or two, but he took his time with his "American folk opera" *Porgy and Bess*. The idea of adapting DuBose Heyward's novel *Porgy* had been on Gershwin's mind as far back as 1926, just after the book's publication, but it was years before he could secure the rights. (At one point, it looked like Jerome Kern and Oscar Hammerstein II would get to it first—as a vehicle for Al Jolson!) Gershwin then spent the better part of two years composing and orchestrating the piece, even joining Heyward on a research expedition to one of the islands off Charleston, South Carolina. His brother Ira, who collaborated with Heyward on the lyrics, stayed in New York.

The result, with its precedent-setting cast of classically trained African American singers, was George's last major theater composition. When the production closed at a complete financial loss, he headed west to compose for Hollywood. *Porgy and Bess* was also, upon his sudden death at age thirty-eight two years later, appraised as Gershwin's least valuable composition: it was determined to be worth $250, less than one-eightieth what "Rhapsody in Blue" was worth at the time.

ABOVE: *Porgy and Bess*, 1935. The show premiered in Boston before its Broadway run, then toured to Philadelphia, Pittsburgh, Chicago, and Washington, D.C. *Library of Congress*

OPPOSITE PAGE: Todd Duncan and Anne Brown as Porgy and Bess. Duncan became the first African American singer to perform with a major US opera company in 1945, when he played Tonio in *Pagliacci* at the New York City Opera.

DATES:
October 10, 1935–January 25, 1936 at the Alvin Theater (124 performances)

SYNOPSIS:
The South Carolina town of Catfish Row is beset by hurricanes as well as the abusive Crown and the local drug dealer Sportin' Life. Both men are interested in the self-destructive Bess. So is a decent but crippled beggar named Porgy.

AWARDS:
None

NOTED REVIVALS AND ADAPTATIONS:
Broadway revivals in 1942, 1943, 1953, 1976, 1983, and 2011; movie version in 1959; TV versions in 1993 and 2002

ORIGINAL STARS:
Todd Duncan, Anne Brown, John W. Bubbles, Ruby Elzy, Warren Coleman

Since then, *Porgy and Bess* has become enshrined as possibly America's greatest opera, although its ascent into, and ultimately to the top of, the canon was a remarkably choppy one. Black intellectuals were initially wary of it, then begrudgingly accepting of it, and then incensed about it. (Notably immune to this wariness was the jazz world, where everyone from Sidney Bechet to Billie Holiday to Ella Fitzgerald to Miles Davis has dived fruitfully into Gershwin's blend of blues, folk, overheard Charleston street chants, and Jewish liturgical music.)

The show's fortunes didn't really pick up until producer Cheryl Crawford chopped out Gershwin's operatic recitatives for a well-received 1942 revival, for which Todd Duncan and Anne Brown reprised their original roles as Porgy and Bess. Decades later, for a 2011 revival, director Diane Paulus and her collaborators suggested their own modifications, prompting Stephen Sondheim to weigh in via a furious public letter.

Sondheim, as it happens, has repeatedly talked up the efforts of Heyward as a lyricist—at the expense of Ira Gershwin, whose *Porgy* contributions he finds "easily distinguishable by their firmly traditional, generalized stance." According to Gershwin historian Robert Kimball, though, that ain't necessarily so. Heyward needed a certain number of credits to qualify for membership in the songwriters union ASCAP, Kimball has said, and so Ira gave Heyward the credit for several lyrics that he himself had written. Such generosity permeates every note of *Porgy and Bess*, which serves both as a painful reminder of the Gershwin scores we never got to hear and as a brass ring. Broadway composers have been grabbing for it ever since.

PRIVATE LIVES

BY NOËL COWARD

Noël Coward and Gertrude Lawrence (as Elyot Chase and Amanda Prynne) in *Private Lives*, 1931. Lawrence had starred in Coward's musical revue *London Calling!* in London in 1923, and in 1936 they costarred in his *Tonight at 8:30*.

With 150 plays and musicals in this book, some titles are bound to be more beloved than others. I respect *The Most Happy Fella* enormously, but I adore *Guys and Dolls*. *Long Day's Journey Into Night* and *The Iceman Cometh* rightly earned Eugene O'Neill his spot in the pantheon of American playwrights, but it's *A Moon for the Misbegotten* that invariably moves me to tears. *The Black Crook*'s (debatable) status as the very first example of American musical theater goes a *long* way toward explaining its inclusion here.

And then there's Noël Coward.

There are any number of theater lovers who find "Don't quibble, Sibyl"—the male lead's dismissal of his new, and soon to be former, wife in *Private Lives*—to

DATES:
January 27–September 1931 at the Times Square Theater (256 performances)

SYNOPSIS:
Five years after getting divorced, Elyot and Amanda find themselves honeymooning with their new, younger spouses in the same Deauville, France, hotel—in adjoining rooms.

AWARDS:
None

NOTED REVIVALS AND ADAPTATIONS:
Broadway revivals in 1948, 1969, 1975, 1983, 1992, 2002, and 2011; movie version in 1931; TV versions in 1959 and 1976

ORIGINAL STARS:
Noël Coward, Gertrude Lawrence, Laurence Olivier, Jill Esmond

---

In one of the play's seven Broadway revivals (2002), Alan Rickman and Lindsay Duncan played the sparring exes.

---

be at or very near the apex of wit. I don't happen to be one of those people. At the risk of channeling Coward's self-satisfied, aphorism-happy style, my admiration of him knows bounds.

So why is *Private Lives* included here? For starters, look at that original cast. Directing yourself in a leading role that you wrote for yourself is one thing. Casting Laurence Olivier and his real-life wife, Jill Esmond, as the two temporary spouses—parts described by Coward himself as "extra puppets, lightly wooden ninepins"—is another thing entirely.

Also, notwithstanding Coward's self-positioning as the Quintessential Englishman, *Private Lives* was actually more successful in New York than it was in London. Only one decade (the 1950s) has elapsed since then that has not featured a revival on Broadway, allowing everyone from Richard Burton (teamed up with his own on-again-off-again spouse, Elizabeth Taylor) to Maggie Smith to Alan Rickman to Tammy Grimes to savor the roles that Coward and Gertrude Lawrence memorized together in a villa in southeastern France.

Coward said of the initial response to his play, "The critics described *Private Lives* variously as 'tenuous, thin, brittle, gossamer, iridescent, and delightfully daring.'" I would say that this is one time when the critics got it right. Yet this admittedly glib cocktail has been popular enough to ensnare theatergoers consistently ever since. When caught in the right mood, I could be one of those people.

THE PRODUCERS

BY MEL BROOKS AND THOMAS MEEHAN

Hit musicals can be hard to predict sometimes. Just ask the creative team behind *Springtime for Hitler*, the intentionally horrible Nazi toe-tapper whose unexpected success means jail for the titular scammers of *The Producers*. Occasionally, though, one will have "smash" written all over it from the beginning.

Nathan Lane had long been considered the heir apparent to Zero Mostel, the original star of Mel Brooks' 1967 smash comedy film *The Producers*, and Matthew Broderick was an ideal substitute for Mostel's costar Gene Wilder. (The two former *Lion King* voice actors would go on to score big in Broadway revivals of *The Odd Couple* and *It's Only a Play*.) Director/choreographer Susan Stroman's seemingly bottomless bag of staging tricks was a perfect match for Brooks' anything-goes style of humor, and she surrounded the leads with an irresistible batch of comic character actors.

Sure enough, *The Producers* broke *Hello, Dolly!*'s thirty-seven-year record by winning twelve Tony Awards; the only ones it lost were given to cast members in the same category. (Sorry, Matthew Broderick!) Amid all the hubbub, *The Producers* also mastered the fledgling practice of dynamic pricing. Just as the TKTS booth offered deals on seats that would otherwise go unfilled, box offices started offering really good seats at a massive markup.

In one crucial way, though, *The Producers* was a victim of its success—a fact that the producers (the real ones) quickly took into account. Lane and Broderick's faces were plastered everywhere, and when their contracts were up, the show reeled from a lack of marquee-worthy names to play Bialystock and Bloom. Henry Goodman is a gifted musical theater actor, but he didn't sell tickets, and so he was shown the door a month after being hired to replace Lane. It took a much-ballyhooed (and extremely well-compensated) return by the two leads near the end of the run to goose ticket sales.

DATES:

April 19, 2001–April 22, 2007 at the St. James Theater (2,502 performances)

SYNOPSIS:

The conniving Broadway producer Max Bialystock and his lily-livered accountant, Leo Bloom, hatch a can't-miss scheme: sell 25,000 percent of the rights to a guaranteed flop, then pocket the "losses."

AWARDS:

12 Tony Awards

NOTED REVIVALS AND ADAPTATIONS:

Movie version in 2005

ORIGINAL STARS:

Nathan Lane, Matthew Broderick, Gary Beach, Cady Huffman, Roger Bart, Brad Oscar

Take a peek at the posters of the hit musicals to reach Broadway since then: *Wicked, Monty Python's Spamalot, Jersey Boys, The Book of Mormon, Aladdin.* Recognize any familiar faces? Nope. Every one of those shows won at least one acting Tony Award, but you never saw Sara Ramirez or James Monroe Inglehart on the posters. That green makeup and that Mormon suit are a lot easier to replace. Bialystock and Bloom may not have known how to make a flop, but they taught a lot of people how to make a hit.

PROMISES, PROMISES

BY BURT BACHARACH, HAL DAVID, AND NEIL SIMON

From left, Dick O'Neill, Henry Sutton, Jerry Orbach (Chuck Baxter), Ronn Carroll, and Paul Reed in the original Broadway production. Orbach originated the roles of El Gallo in *The Fantasticks* (off-Broadway), Billy Flynn in *Chicago*, and Julian Marsh in *42nd Street*.

DATES:
December 1, 1968–January 1, 1972 at the Shubert Theater (1,281 performances)

SYNOPSIS:
If turning his apartment into a love nest for various lecherous higher-ups is what it takes to get Chuck Baxter that promotion, so be it. The plan hits a snag, though, when he falls in love with one of those bosses' conquests.

AWARDS:
2 Tony Awards

NOTED REVIVALS AND ADAPTATIONS:
Broadway revival in 2010

ORIGINAL STARS:
Jerry Orbach, Jill O'Hara, Marian Mercer, A. Larry Haines, Edward Winter

CONSOLIDATED LIFE

Broadway has traditionally been less than hospitable for pop songwriters. Producers are more than happy to ransack an old song catalog and assemble a *Mamma Mia!* or a *Movin' Out* or a *Beautiful*, with or without the original songwriter's help. But with the exception of Elton John, who has both rejiggered preexisting music (*The Lion King*) and written new shows (*Aida, Billy Elliot*), the stages of New York are littered with the equivalent of one-hit— or one-flop—wonders.

Paul Simon wrote one, and only one, musical (*The Capeman*). Same with Boy George (the autobiographical *Taboo*). The travails of *Spider-Man: Turn Off the Dark* would have been enough to put Cole Porter off Broadway for good, let alone U2's Bono and The Edge. Randy Newman has been trying to get his delightful *Faust* to Broadway for twenty years. While it's too soon to know whether Sting (*The Last Ship*) or Cyndi Lauper (*Kinky Boots*) or Trey Anastasio (*Hands on a Hardbody*) will make it back for seconds, history would tell us not to hold our breath.

Anyone who did so while waiting for Burt Bacharach and Hal David to follow up on *Promises, Promises* would have expired some time ago. Their glistening adaptation of the 1960 Billy Wilder film *The Apartment*, complete with a very strong book by Neil Simon, made Broadway seem like a completely natural home for their rhythmically enticing, melodically daring grown-up pop. Importing the songwriting duo was producer David Merrick's idea; a no less important hire was first-time orchestrator Jonathan Tunick, who was tasked with making Bacharach's studio-friendly sound work on the stage.

Jerry Orbach delivered Simon's blue-chip jokes directly to the audience; choreographer Michael Bennett sent legions of dancers to the chiropractor with his riotous "Turkey Lurkey Time"; a quartet of female vocalists ooohed and waaahed from the pit; Marian Mercer walked away with the show as a bibulous would-be one-night stand; and Bacharach got two songs from the show—the title song and "I'll Never Fall in Love Again"—onto the pop charts, with the help of frequent collaborator Dionne Warwick.

Bennett and Tunick would soon join Stephen Sondheim on *Company*, in the process becoming arguably the two preeminent figures in their respective fields. Simon was already at the top of his, but the famously exacting Bacharach had no intention of joining them. To this day, he recalls hearing from producer David Merrick two weeks after *Promises, Promises* had opened—Rodgers had attended a matinee, and Merrick informed Bacharach that that performance's orchestra had five substitute players in it. Bacharach had had his fill of Broadway. The feeling was not, and is not, mutual.

PYGMALION

BY GEORGE BERNARD SHAW

Even Siri, the iPhone's disembodied personal assistant, recognizes a superior intellect when she hears one. Go ahead and ask her whether she would have voted for Barack Obama or Mitt Romney. She'll tell you, "I can't vote. But if I did, I would vote for ELIZA. She knows all."

She's referring to a pioneering computer program invented in the mid-1960s, which took its name from Eliza Doolittle, the "deliciously low" flower girl in George Bernard Shaw's *Pygmalion*. Shaw, in turn, got that name from Eliza Armstrong, a thirteen-year-old girl who was purchased for £5 in 1885 in a sex-trafficking sting operation, which was in fact a bizarre conflation of high-minded civic responsibility and bottom-feeding tabloid journalism.

Shaw's Eliza is herself the subject of a £5 wager, and while that transaction is a good bit less nefarious than her namesake's, it speaks volumes to the author's views on class, privilege, and presumption. *Pygmalion* may be Shaw's most accessible play, owing only in part to the incredible success of its musical adaptation, *My Fair Lady*; its popularity doesn't diminish Shaw's contempt toward a class-bound society in which how you sound matters more than who you are. No wonder he took his script and premiered *Pygmalion* in Vienna

ABOVE: Lynn Fontanne as Eliza Doolittle in the 1926 Broadway revival, directed by Dudley Digges and costarring Reginald Mason as Henry Higgins. Henry Travers played Eliza's father, Alfred Doolittle.

OPPOSITE PAGE: Mrs. Patrick Campbell played Eliza (alongside Edmund Gurney, center, as Alfred and Sir Herbert Beerbohm Tree, right, as Henry) in both London (shown) and New York in 1914, following *Pygmalion*'s Vienna debut. *Hulton Archive, Getty Images*

Shaw's insistence that Eliza not end up with her purchaser/professor/mentor Henry Higgins by the final curtain. The leads' coupling was a temptation from the very beginning: Shaw returned to the original London production after a few months to find that his Higgins, Sir Herbert Beerbohm Tree, was throwing his leading lady a bouquet of flowers at the end. "My ending makes money," Tree grumbled in protest. "You ought to be grateful." Shaw wasn't.

One line in particular did need to be updated, though. "Mrs. Pat," as Campbell was known, caused a sensation in 1914 in both New York and, especially, London, when Eliza gave away her humble origins by using her newly acquired linguistic skills to say, "Not bloody likely." By 1956, that phrase was not bloody likely to have the same reaction, and so her transgression was upgraded to "Move yer bloomin' arse!" This Eliza, it appears, still had plenty to learn.

rather than his usual London home. (A mild nervous breakdown suffered by Mrs. Patrick Campbell, for whom Shaw wrote the part of Eliza despite her being forty-nine years old at the time, also had something to do with the *way*-out-of-town production.)

The creators of *My Fair Lady* were wise enough to leave large portions of *Pygmalion* intact. And they honored

RAGTIME

STEPHEN FLAHERTY, LYNN AHRENS, AND TERRENCE MCNALLY

DATES:
January 18, 1998–January 16, 2000 at the Ford Center for the Performing Arts (834 performances)

SYNOPSIS:
Where to begin? *Ragtime* features as much of early-twentieth-century America as possible, including assimilation, trips to the North Pole, racial prejudice, and abandoned babies. Harry Houdini and anarchist Emma Goldman are thrown into the mix, too.

AWARDS:
4 Tony Awards

NOTED REVIVALS AND ADAPTATIONS:
Broadway revival in 2009

ORIGINAL STARS:
Brian Stokes Mitchell, Peter Friedman, Marin Mazzie, Audra McDonald, Marc Jacoby, Steven Sutcliffe

During the 1980s and most of the 1990s, Broadway preferred to import its spectacles. Pop operas like *Les Misérables* and *Phantom of the Opera* were still going strong, with American characters confined to a handful of G.I.s in *Miss Saigon* and a bratty grandmaster in the short-lived *Chess*. It took Garth Drabinsky, a flamboyant Canadian with deep pockets, to give America its own lush musical epic.

Everything about *Ragtime* was big: the twenty-eight musicians in the pit, the cavalcade of characters famous and not, the new theater Drabinsky built for it out of two older ones. (Broadway purists griped about the precedent of naming the Ford Center for the Performing Arts after its corporate sponsor. The presence of a full-size Model T on the stage didn't do much to allay those concerns, even if Henry Ford *was* a major character in the show.)

Composer Stephen Flaherty and lyricist Lynn Ahrens were one of eight songwriting teams to audition for the gig by writing four songs on spec; this also ruffled some feathers within the theater community. Flaherty and Ahrens had repeatedly shown a gift for charming, character-driven material in smaller shows like *Once on This Island* and *Lucky Stiff*, and Flaherty's rich melodies adapted well to the immeasurably larger setting. Three of

their spec songs ended up in the show, including an Act I finale, "Till We Reach That Day," that I like to think got them hired on the spot.

Terrence McNally, meanwhile, did yeoman's work condensing E. L. Doctorow's sprawling 1975 novel into a workable script, although the three main plot threads didn't always sit comfortably alongside the J. P. Morgans and Booker T. Washingtons interwoven throughout.

And the cast! Brian Stokes Mitchell, Audra McDonald, Marin Mazzie, and Peter Friedman had all done wonderful, even Tony Award–winning work before, but *Ragtime* elevated everyone's game. (Mitchell and Mazzie, who deserved a bit of fun after this rather serious show, headlined a boisterous *Kiss Me, Kate* revival the following year.) Many feel that *Ragtime* might still be running today if not for (1) the attention-grabbing opening two months earlier of *The Lion King* across the street, and (2) the abrupt bankruptcy of Drabinsky's company, Livent. His swan song opened big, closed big, and still lives large in a lot of theater lovers' minds.

OPPOSITE PAGE: Brian Stokes Mitchell and Audra McDonald played Coalhouse Walker Jr. and Sarah in the original Broadway production. McDonald won her third of a record-setting six Tony Awards for her performance. © *Catherine Ashmore*

BELOW: Lea Michele (the Little Girl) and Peter Friedman (Tateh). © *Catherine Ashmore*

A RAISIN IN THE SUN

BY LORRAINE HANSBERRY

"**N**ever before, in the entire history of the American theater, had so much of the truth of black people's lives been seen on stage."

This was how James Baldwin described the impact of Lorraine Hansberry's *A Raisin in the Sun* in 1959. Historians tend to focus on how the twenty-nine-year-old Hansberry (who died of pancreatic cancer just six years later) was the first black woman to write a Broadway play, and how Lloyd Richards was the first black man to direct one. But arguably the bigger impact was seen and felt on the stage as opposed to off it, for the very reason that Baldwin described.

To appreciate this, it is necessary first to dispel an extremely tenacious misconception about *A Raisin in the Sun*. A *New York Times* article from April 1959 paraphrased Hansberry as having called *Raisin* not a "Negro" play but rather "a play about honest-to-God, believable, many-sided people who happen to be Negroes." This was a mistake—

ABOVE: From left, Sidney Poitier, Claudia McNeil (Lena, Walter's mother), Ruby Dee, Glynn Turman (the Youngers' son, Travis), and Diana Sands (Beneatha, Walter's sister).

OPPOSITE PAGE: Poitier and Dee as Walter Lee Younger and his wife Ruth. Walter dreams of wealth; Ruth tries to keep him grounded.

Now, this may seem like semantic squabbling a half century later. But it does speak to a basic fact that the era's overwhelmingly white ranks of newspaper critics and tastemakers had trouble grasping. They loved the play, with its warm familial humor that gives way to first bruising tragedy and then battle-scarred resilience. And they knew very, very little about black life as lived by black people. Therefore, something that seemed familiar—that seemed knowable—must not really be about black life at all.

Luckily, *A Raisin in the Sun* survived this strain of well-meaning paternalism. In an era when many protagonists were wrenching themselves away from their families, *Raisin* showed the comforts, and even the necessity, of pulling together. (This is something that *Clybourne Park*, Bruce Norris' unofficial sequel, also conveys in its own astringent way; *see the entry on* Clybourne Park.) The people being depicted are the Youngers. The woman depicting them was Lorraine Hansberry. And that is more than sufficient.

Hansberry's scrapbook had the clipping with a note next to it saying "Never said NO SUCH THING"—but nonetheless it was repeated a month later in another *Times* article. Soon it had been embellished to have her refer to herself as not a Negro writer but a writer who, etc., etc. Hansberry's widower didn't help matters by turning the original paraphrase into a direct quote, which has since been cited repeatedly—incorrectly.

RENT

BY JONATHAN LARSON

It's hard to remember now, with *Frozen* and *Wicked* and *Glee* having reclaimed musicals as at least relatively acceptable for young people, but "the musical for people who hate musicals" was considered a legitimate tagline for a hit Broadway show in the mid-1990s.

That unfortunate slogan was used for the *La Bohème*-in-Alphabet City rock opera *Rent*, and it's one the show's creator, Jonathan Larson, would have despised. Larson, who died of an aortic dissection the morning of the show's first preview off-Broadway, was an unabashed lover of musicals—he laced his scores with *Sunday in the Park With George* references and spent seven years adapting George Orwell's *1984* into a musical. (Stephen Sondheim saw a workshop of that project and was a big behind-the-scenes supporter of Larson's work.) Yes, he also loved rock music, and his stated goal with *Rent* was to "blast people out with a grisly, messy show." He had originally wanted to put a full Broadway orchestra on one side of the stage and a rock band on the other. But when's the last time you saw a poster promising "a rock concert for people who hate rock concerts"?

It was impossible to separate the tragedy of the thirty-five-year-old dying from the media maelstrom that ensued: the magazine covers, the Stevie Wonder cover of "Seasons of Love," the Pulitzer Prize for Drama (only the seventh one ever given to a musical), the "Rentheads" who saw the show dozens and even hundreds of times. To some degree, it is still impossible.

ABOVE: Daphne Rubin-Vega as Mimi Marquez in the original Broadway production. *Rent* was Rubin-Vega's Broadway debut, as it was for Idina Menzel and Adam Pascal. © *Joan Marcus*

OPPOSITE PAGE: The cast, with Anthony Rapp (Mark Cohen) front, celebrates "La Vie Bohème." © *Joan Marcus*

DATES:
April 29, 1996–September 7, 2008 at the Nederlander Theater (5,123 performances)

SYNOPSIS:
A motley crew of East Village squatters, anarchists, drag queens, and documentarians struggles to find love, support, inspiration, and warmth under the specter of AIDS.

AWARDS:
4 Tony Awards; Pulitzer Prize

NOTED REVIVALS AND ADAPTATIONS:
Movie version in 2005

ORIGINAL STARS:
Adam Pascal, Anthony Rapp, Daphne Rubin-Vega, Idina Menzel, Taye Diggs, Jesse L. Martin, Wilson Jermaine Heredia

Whereas previews are where a lot of the heavy lifting on a show really happens, the decision was made to leave *Rent* just as Larson had left it. Would it have become even better during a normal preview process? Or would the magic somehow have dissipated? We'll never know. But for a very large number of people, this genre-skipping, full-throttle examination of love in the time of AIDS was just fine as it was.

By the time *Rent* closed in 2008, rehearsals had begun for a new Fox TV show that hoped to appeal to those same young audiences, by bringing together a similar melding of pop and Broadway. At William McKinley High School, where *Glee* is set, the only person who hates musicals is the villainous cheerleading coach. When the show suffered its own untimely loss in 2013, the cast commemorated the death of one of its costars by singing "Seasons of Love" along with the Pretenders and Bruce Springsteen. I suspect Jonathan Larson, who would have been only fifty-three at the time, would have liked that very much.

ROSENCRANTZ AND GUILDENSTERN ARE DEAD

BY TOM STOPPARD

"We do on stage the things that are supposed to happen off. Which is a kind of integrity, if you look on every exit being an entrance somewhere else."
—Player, *Rosencrantz and Guildenstern Are Dead*

Tom Stoppard has said that he takes screenwriting assignments for the likes of *Shakespeare in Love* and even *Indiana Jones and the Last Crusade* as a way of refueling while waiting for a new idea to come his way. Though his erudition and philosophical playfulness give him the impression of someone for whom things come easily, subject matter apparently doesn't. So it makes sense that *Rosencrantz and Guildenstern Are Dead*, the mind-scramblingly original play that put Stoppard on the map, was content to lurk in the nooks and crannies of a preexisting work. Or, rather, *the* preexisting work, at least from the viewpoint of Western theater: *Hamlet*.

Shakespeare may have bumped off Hamlet's two sycophantic school friends in the original, but Stoppard—who got his title from an Act V declaration—set about revivifying these doomed nonentities. What are they up to, he wondered, while the royal family is lurking, stabbing, brooding, and dueling? Well, they flip coins a lot. They play a boisterous game of "question tennis." They philosophize their way into a sort of paralysis, in marked contrast to Hamlet's equally well-reasoned spur to action. And in their eternal bafflement, they vindicate modern-day audience members who, whether they admit it or not, can be baffled at times by Shakespeare's language.

An earlier version of the play was called *Rosencrantz and Guildenstern in the Court of King Lear*, but the action was confined to *Hamlet* by the time a group of Oxford undergraduates brought the twenty-nine-year-old Stoppard's play to the sprawling Edinburgh Fringe Festival. Critic Kenneth Tynan soon caught wind of it and alerted Laurence Olivier to its existence, culminating in one of the more unlikely successes first in London and then New York.

OPPOSITE PAGE: John Wood (Guildenstern), Paul Hecht (the Player), and Brian Murray (Rosencrantz) in the original Broadway production.

RIGHT: Tom Stoppard in 1967, the year *Rosencrantz and Guildenstern Are Dead* premiered on Broadway. Stoppard was born in Czechoslovakia in 1937 and moved to Britain in 1946. He was knighted in 1997.

Stoppard has referred to Rosencrantz and Guildenstern as "the most expendable people of all time." That status changed the minute he depicted them flipping their coins and asking their questions and sailing into oblivion—"the endless time of never coming back"—without ever quite knowing why.

DATES:
October 16, 1967–October 19, 1968 at the Alvin Theater and Eugene O'Neill Theater (420 performances)

SYNOPSIS:
Two amiable but somewhat confused guys link up with an old school chum in Denmark. They watch a play their friend puts on, and then they join him on a boat to England.

AWARDS:
4 Tony Awards

NOTED REVIVALS AND ADAPTATIONS:
Movie version in 1990

ORIGINAL STARS:
Brian Murray, John Wood, Paul Hecht

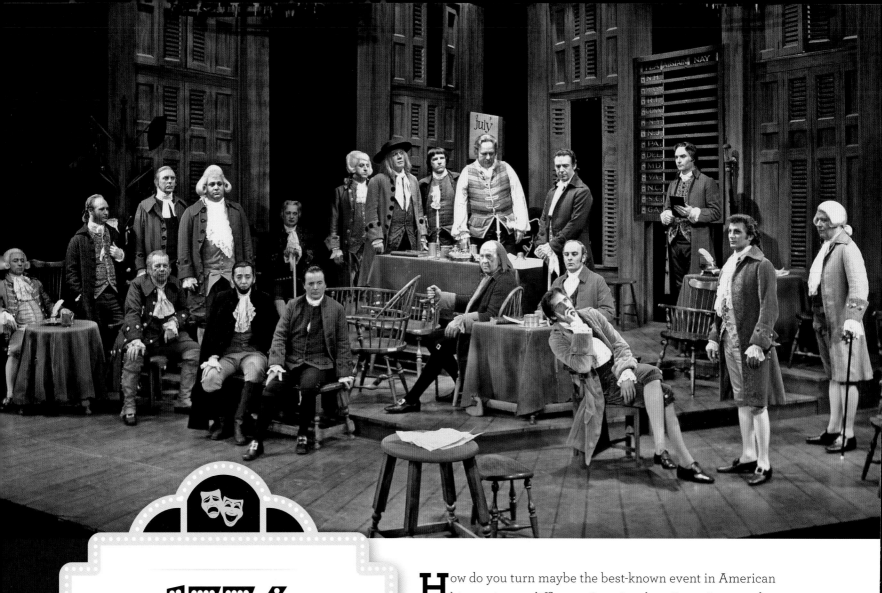

1776

BY SHERMAN EDWARDS AND PETER STONE

How do you turn maybe the best-known event in American history into a cliffhanger? *1776* authors Peter Stone and Sherman Edwards somehow squeezed every ounce of suspense from a foregone conclusion, with characters reverently or furiously tearing away daily calendar pages as July 4 draws nearer and nearer.

Edwards, a former history teacher, was working at New York's famous Brill Building and writing tunes for the likes of Elvis Presley and Johnny Mathis when the idea of a musical about the birth of America struck him. He researched, wrote, and composed the project for ten years before producer Stuart Ostrow convinced a reluctant Edwards that he needed a collaborator.

Stone's libretto is given an unusual, even unprecedented amount of room to shine: its third scene holds the record for the longest segment in a Broadway musical without a single note of music. (I spent time with the pit orchestras of several Broadway musicals in 1997 while researching an article, and some of the *1776* musicians actually ran errands during this stretch.) Stone later stated that *1776* would have made an excellent play without music but that the humanity of the characters would have been lessened.

Never didactic, always entertaining, *1776* appeared at a time when seventh-grade history taught all of the mythic qualities of the founding fathers and none of their frailties. The musical's Ben Franklin, on the other hand, was as witty and avuncular as we might imagine, yet his weakness for prostitutes was more than hinted at. Legendary firebrand John Adams and his wife, Abigail, had a surprisingly modern and tender relationship. Historical inaccuracies are plentiful throughout *1776*—the authors would be the first to point them out—but none was glaring enough to tarnish its reputation, then or now.

DATES:

March 16, 1969–February 13, 1972 at the 46th Street Theater, St. James Theater, and Majestic Theater (1,217 performances)

SYNOPSIS:

Perpetual squeaky wheel John Adams goads a do-nothing Congress to debate and ultimately declare independence from England—until a rift with the Southern delegates over slavery threatens to derail everything.

AWARDS:

3 Tony Awards

NOTED REVIVALS AND ADAPTATIONS:

Broadway revival in 1997; movie version in 1972

ORIGINAL STARS:

William Daniels, Howard Da Silva, Clifford David, Virginia Vestoff, Ken Howard, Paul Hecht, Betty Buckley

Through a byzantine and even litigious set of circumstances, the rock musical *Hair* had had to sit out the previous year's Tony Awards, and when the 1970 prizes were handed out, many carped that it lost to its cantankerous forefathers. But who were the real rebels here? When *1776* came to the silver screen three years later (complete with many Broadway cast members), the producers cut the conservative-baiting song "Cool, Cool, Considerate Men," arguably after being pressured by President Nixon himself. The draft-dodging rabble-rousers of *Hair* could only dream of that kind of reaction.

SHE LOVES ME

BY JERRY BOCK, SHELDON HARNICK, AND JOE MASTEROFF

Daniel Massey and Barbara Cook costarred as Georg Nowack, the manager of Maraczek's Parfumerie, and Amalia Balash, the shop's newest employee, in *She Loves Me*.

Can a show be too good for its own good? *She Loves Me* finds itself on virtually every musical theater lover's short list of criminally underrated shows. The original underperformed in both New York and London, as did a charming 1993 revival that marked the Broadway directing debut of the versatile Scott Ellis. So why does everyone love this show except for the audience?

For one thing, Jerry Bock's score—a series of musical jewel boxes for more than a half-dozen exquisitely drawn characters—veers close to classical operetta, befitting its Mitteleuropean setting of 1934 Budapest. Also, it opened in the same season as *Hello, Dolly!* and *Funny Girl*, shows that make no apologies for wanting your love and standing ovations. *She Loves Me* didn't use its chorus or its choreographer much, and its final moments are given over to two people singing in the snow on Christmas Eve. (A woman next to me at the 1993 revival was an absolute puddle during that scene.) Barbara Cook gave her single best performance as the lovelorn Amalia, but

DATES:

April 23, 1963–January 11, 1964 at the Eugene O'Neill Theater (301 performances)

SYNOPSIS:

Georg Nowack and Amalia Balash, coworkers at a Budapest parfumerie, can barely stand each other. One catch: unbeknownst to either of them, they are also adoring (and anonymous) pen pals.

AWARDS:

1 Tony Award

NOTED REVIVALS AND ADAPTATIONS:

Broadway revival in 1993; TV version in 1978

ORIGINAL STARS:

Barbara Cook, Daniel Massey, Barbara Baxley, Jack Cassidy

only Jack Cassidy, who played the resident cad—and who had introduced Bock to lyricist Sheldon Harnick at a party seven years earlier—was recognized when awards time came around.

And so in-the-know theater fans content themselves with cast recordings and memories of songs like "Ice Cream," "A Trip to the Library" (with uncharacteristically show-offy lyrics from Harnick), "Will He Like Me?," "Ilona," and others. Bock, Harnick, and producer Harold Prince seem to have taken *She Loves Me*'s status as a *succès d'estime* in stride. Soon after opening night, Prince started raising some much-needed money for the songwriting team's new show, which seemed even less saleable. It was set in Anatevka, Russia, and was about a guy named Tevye.

The head waiter at Café Imperiale attempts to maintain a "Romantic Atmosphere," but mayhem gets in the way. Carol Haney, who won a Tony for her performance in 1954's *The Pajama Game*, choreographed.

SHOW BOAT

BY JEROME KERN AND OSCAR HAMMERSTEIN II

Show Boat, 1927. Oscar Hammerstein II staged the production himself, with Ziegfeld alum Zeke Colvan. Joseph Urban, also a longtime Ziegfeld collaborator (and designer of the Ziegfeld Theater), did the scenic design.

Today we would never dream of a trendy novel popping up on stage before Hollywood has had its way with it. In 1927, Edna Ferber's sprawling yarn *Show Boat* was one of the biggest prizes up for adaptation. Miscegenation, unhappy marriages, gambling addiction: rarely had so many hot-button issues been tackled in any theatrical work, let alone a musical. Was *Show Boat* a serious operetta, seemingly a contradiction in terms? It certainly wasn't musical comedy.

In an era when most shows were written in six weeks, composer Jerome Kern and lyricist and bookwriter (and de facto director) Oscar Hammerstein II devoted a year to *Show Boat.* Hammerstein had his moral compass pointing in the right direction throughout, especially in the scene where Julie is "discovered" to be of mixed race. Kern's phenomenally lush blend of Negro spirituals and operetta yielded a still-unsurpassed six standards, including "Why Do I Love You?" and "Bill" (which had been cut from two earlier shows), while "Ol' Man River" was so convincing as a folk song that many believed the two had plunked an authentic nineteenth-century spiritual into their score.

Black and white choruses appeared on stage together for the first time, and the number of African American principals was considerable—with one notable omission and one notable exception. Hammerstein and Kern wrote the part of the stevedore Joe for Paul Robeson, but a production

TOP: Paul Robeson as Joe in the 1932 Broadway production. Robeson also played the role in 1928 in London, in the 1936 film adaptation (alongside Irene Dunne, Allan Jones, Hattie McDaniel, and Helen Morgan), and in 1940 in Los Angeles.

BOTTOM: Buddy Ebsen and Collette Lyons as show boat performers Ellie and Frank in the 1946 revival at the Ziegfeld Theater. Helen Tamiris, a modern dance innovator, choreographed.
Archive Photos, Getty Images

DATES:

December 27, 1927–May 4, 1929 at the Ziegfeld Theater (572 performances)

SYNOPSIS:

Cap'n Andy's floating theater runs afoul of Southern law when it is revealed that two performers of different races are married. The captain's distraught daughter Magnolia, after leaving her show business family, struggles to survive her ne'er-do-well husband Gaylord's indulgences.

AWARDS:

None

NOTED REVIVALS AND ADAPTATIONS:

Broadway revivals in 1932, 1946, 1983, and 1994; movie versions in 1936 and 1951; TV version in 1989

ORIGINAL STARS:

Charles Winninger, Helen Morgan, Norma Terris, Jules Bledsoe, Aunt Jemima, Edna May Oliver, Howard Marsh

delay prevented him from originating the role. (He would later play Joe on four separate occasions.) Meanwhile, the "colored mammy" Queenie was played by Tess Gardella, an Italian American in blackface who used the stage name from her vaudeville days: Aunt Jemima.

Producer Florenz Ziegfeld stepped into the world of book musicals for the first time, underwriting the leisurely writing pace as well as his usual massive physical production. The Ziegfeld Theater was built specifically for *Show Boat*, which opened not with Ziegfeld's usual phalanx of semi-clad showgirls but with a burly group of stevedores. The curtain went down on opening night to almost complete silence. Ziegfeld feared that the biggest gamble of his life had also been his biggest mistake. However, the rapturous reviews the next morning showed that the silence had not been a sign of rejection. It had been something closer to disbelief—astonishment at the sight of the most influential show of its generation.

THE SHOW-OFF

BY GEORGE KELLY

ABOVE: Joe E. Brown and Helen Chandler in a 1941 production of *The Show-Off* in San Francisco, directed by Russell Fillmore.

OPPOSITE PAGE: Helen Hayes played Mrs. Fisher opposite Clayton Corzatte (Aubrey Piper) in the 1967 revival at the Lyceum Theater. Hayes, the "First Lady of the American Theater," received the Presidential Medal of Freedom and was the second person to win an Emmy, Grammy, Oscar, *and* Tony (EGOT). (The first was Richard Rodgers.)

The 1920s and 1930s were an unbelievably fertile time for American playwrights. Everyone from Eugene O'Neill to Maxwell Anderson to Elmer Rice got their feet wet on realism, then turned their ears to the exciting trends washing over from Europe. Narrative, aesthetics, chronology: it was all up for grabs.

And then there was Pennsylvanian playwright George Kelly, a former vaudevillian who hit gold in 1922 (just a few months before Rice's Expressionist masterpiece *The Adding Machine* premiered) with a barbed send-up of experimental theater folk called *The Torch Bearers*. He never looked back—or, that is to say, never looked forward. Kelly spent the next thirty years going back to the well of the well-made play long after it had gone dry; the last two decades of his playwriting career were marked by one resolutely realistic flop after the next.

Kelly won the Pulitzer Prize in 1926 for his rather stern drama *Craig's Wife*, but many feel the award was a compensation for the previous year, when Columbia University officials overrode the Pulitzer jury and passed over Kelly's delectable satire *The Show-Off*. Time has validated the jury's original selection, as *The Show-Off*—an expanded version of one of Kelly's earlier vaudeville sketches—continues to show an ebullience and technical confidence that most playwrights today would kill for.

The play has particularly choice parts in the carnation-wearing, effervescently annoying Aubrey and his withering mother-in-law, Mrs. Fisher. (No less than Helen Hayes played the latter part in one of the piece's many Broadway revivals.) If there's a more succinctly character-defining stage description than this one, of Aubrey, I don't know it: "He gives the table a double tap with his knuckles, then laughs." Those twelve words paint a marvelously vivid picture both of the character and of any number of real-life Aubreys you might have the misfortune of knowing. Eugene O'Neill's stage directions, in their excavations of the unknowable depths of his characters, could sometimes be ten times longer than that. The surface suited George Kelly just fine.

DATES:
February 5, 1924–June 1925 at the Playhouse Theater (571 performances)

SYNOPSIS:
Aubrey Piper's opinion of himself as "the pride of old West Philly" is not shared by many, least of all the family of his sweetheart, Amy. His shiny toupee and constant white lies don't help his case. Neither does hitting a policeman while in a borrowed car.

AWARDS:
None

NOTED REVIVALS AND ADAPTATIONS:
Broadway revivals in 1932, 1937, 1950, 1967, and 1992; movie versions in 1926, 1934, and 1946

ORIGINAL STARS:
Louis John Bartels, Helen Lowell, Regina Wallace

SHUFFLE ALONG

BY EUBIE BLAKE, NOBLE SISSLE, FLOURNOY MILLER, AND AUBREY LYLES

For all the tremendous African American talent on the vaudeville circuit in the 1910s and early 1920s, the top acts didn't have much exposure to one another's work. This wasn't because of competitive pique; it was because the presenters would book one, and only one, black act at a time. The only exception was the all-black Theater Owners Booking Association (TOBA) circuit, which paid far less and was nicknamed "Tough on Black Asses."

DATES:
May 23, 1921–July 15, 1922 at the 63rd Street Music Hall (484 performances)

SYNOPSIS:
Two grocery store co-owners become dueling candidates for the mayorship of Jimtown, leading to fistfights, accusations of corruption, and, eventually, the introduction of a reform candidate named Harry.

AWARDS:
None

NOTED REVIVALS AND ADAPTATIONS:
Broadway revivals in 1932 and 1952

ORIGINAL STARS:
Aubrey Lyles, F. E. Miller, Roger Matthews, Lottie Gee

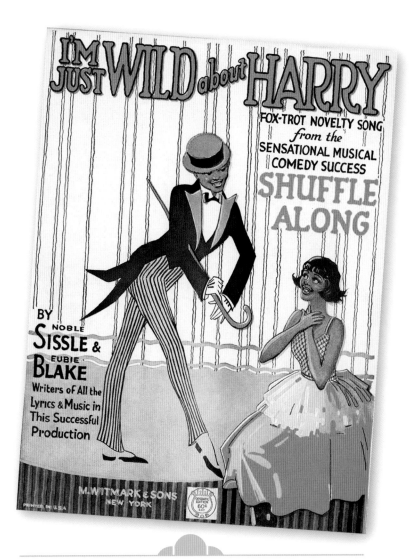

ABOVE: "I'm Just Wild About Harry" was originally a waltz, but Eubie Blake turned it into a fox trot—and a national smash hit. *Sheet music*

OPPOSITE PAGE: Flournoy E. Miller (left) and Aubrey Lyles (right) in *Shuffle Along*. The duo worked together for several years following their hit show.

It took an NAACP benefit in Philadelphia in 1920 to bring four of the leading vaudevillians into the same room at the same time. Talk quickly turned to collaborating on a musical comedy, which would let them all be in the same theater at the same time.

The lanky Flournoy "F. E." Miller and diminutive Aubrey Lyles had written themselves a popular vaudeville sketch called *The Mayor of Dixie*, while composer Eubie Blake and lyricist Noble Sissle toured as the Dixie Duo. The four changed Dixie to "Jimtown, USA" for the pioneering *Shuffle Along*, which fielded a glittery cast even after turning away a fifteen-year-old Josephine Baker. (The show ran long enough for Baker to have a birthday and then join the cast. Paul Robeson also sang in the chorus before the run was over.)

Shuffle Along may not have been the first Broadway production written and performed by African American actors, and its origins in the less-enlightened precincts of vaudeville were apparent in songs like "Sing Me to Sleep, Dear Mammy (With a Hush-a-Bye Pickaninny Tune)." But it did have the first legitimate romantic plot between two black characters, and it played a major role in desegregating Broadway theaters. Langston Hughes even credited the show's success with black audiences way up on 63rd Street as being a major force behind the Harlem Renaissance. Shows like *Lucky Sambo* and the *Blackbirds*

revues soon followed in its wake, demonstrating to Broadway audiences just how much underrecognized black talent was out there.

Revivals of *Shuffle Along* in 1932 and 1952 ran a mere twenty-one performances combined (a fate that a proposed 2016 demi-revival featuring the likes of Audra McDonald and Savion Glover hopes to avoid). Still, at least one aspect of the show went on to have a healthy afterlife. After the subject of one adoring song was switched from the mayor of Jimtown to the sitting vice president of the United States, "I'm Just Wild About Harry" became the campaign song for Harry S. Truman in 1948.

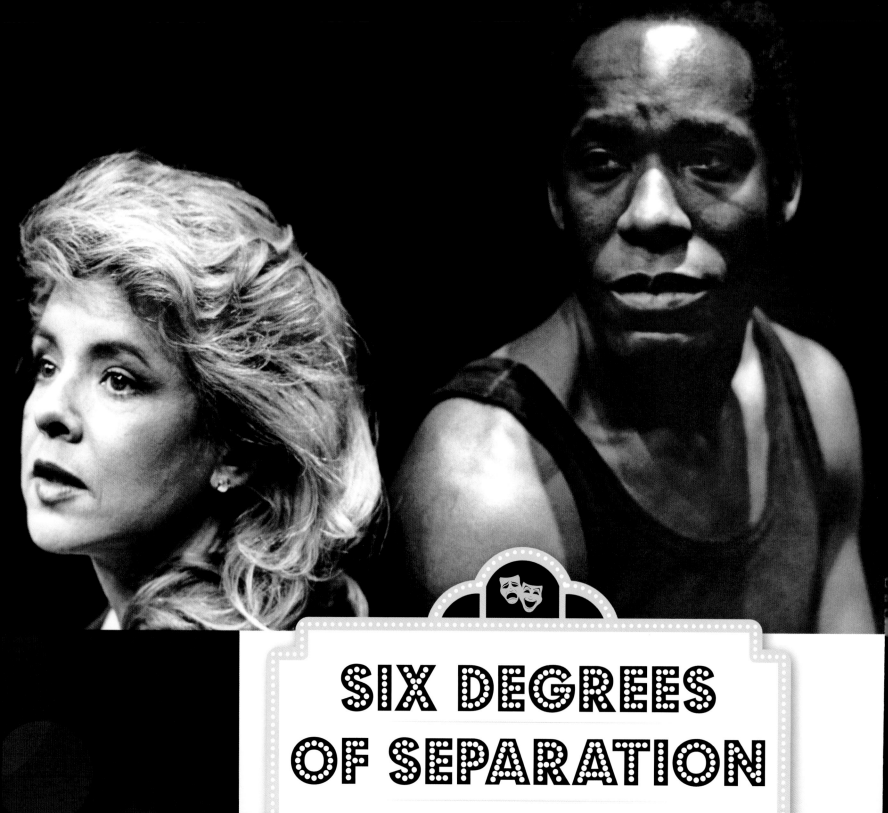

SIX DEGREES OF SEPARATION

BY JOHN GUARE

Back in 1997, when Facebook founder Mark Zuckerberg was still a preteen, the social network SixDegrees.com promised to shrink the world. Its title was a riff on the notion that only six mutual connections separate each human being from every other person on the planet. That notion had been circulating for decades, but it took John Guare's exquisite snapshot of moneyed New York City to sear it into the popular consciousness. It was an idea that was both comforting and unsettling.

In *Six Degrees of Separation*, Paul, a well-spoken young black man—later iterations of racial condescension would classify him as "articulate"—ingratiates himself with various

DATES:

November 8, 1990–January 5, 1992 at the Vivian Beaumont Theater (485 performances)

SYNOPSIS:

Sidney Poitier's brilliant son winds up at the Upper East Side doorstep of Ouisa and Flan Kitteredge, promising mystery, cachet, and maybe even small parts in the movie version of *Cats*. His unmasking as a fraud leads Ouisa and her peers to question Paul's—and, by extension, their—true identity.

AWARDS:

1 Tony Award

NOTED REVIVALS AND ADAPTATIONS:

Movie version in 1993

ORIGINAL STARS:

Stockard Channing, Courtney B. Vance, John Cunningham

OPPOSITE PAGE: Stockard Channing and James McDaniel (a replacement for Courtney B. Vance) in the original production of *Six Degrees of Separation*.

RIGHT: David Hampton presented himself as the son of Sidney Poitier in real life as part of a money-making con. *Kimberly Butler, The LIFE Images Collection, Getty Images*

affluent New York families and . . . what, exactly? He doesn't steal anything or hurt anybody, at least not consciously. He just sort of floats and mingles and absorbs. It is this non-mercenary tendency that seems to rattle the characters as much as the scam itself.

The plot device is as old as the Greeks: low-born trickster finagles his way into the rarefied precincts of the wealthy, exposing their hypocrisies and weaknesses in the process. But Guare infused the idea with an aggressively modern litany of cultural references, from Donald Barthelme to *Starlight Express*. (Many shows in this book pay homage to other plays or musicals, but none as wickedly as *Six Degrees* does with *Cats*.) The play's torn-from-the-society-page-headlines immediacy ended up generating its own headlines. Guare, who wrote the play

after reading about a real-life Paul type, became embroiled in a legal dispute when the actual scammer wanted a cut of the *Six Degrees* profits.

Six Degrees has earned a reputation as the theatrical corollary to *The Bonfire of the Vanities*, Tom Wolfe's gimlet-eyed 1987 look at race and resentment in 1980s New York. Yet Guare takes a far more empathic, even loving approach. His characters want more out of life, and for all of their ethical and interpersonal blind spots, they deserve it. (Well, maybe not the victims' hilariously loathsome children.) The only way they'll be able to achieve this, it seems, is by connecting. SixDegrees.com and its successors have made it both much easier and much harder to do so, a paradox that Guare almost appears to have anticipated. The smartest play of its generation turned out to be the wisest one, too.

THE SKIN OF OUR TEETH

BY THORNTON WILDER

Thornton Wilder's reputation as a master of cozy, fine-boned naturalism, the Norman Rockwell of the stage, evaporates if you take just a cursory glance at his work. Even *Our Town*, his paean to lives, loves, and laments in New Hampshire, has far sharper teeth than people seem to remember. But Wilder never got any wilder than he did in 1942, when he plunked the millennia-spanning Antrobus family, their saucy maid, and their pet dinosaurs into Excelsior, New Jersey. Until *Angels in America* came along fifty years later, *The Skin of Our Teeth* was the loopiest play to win the Pulitzer Prize, and it's debatable whether even *Angels* out-weirds it. *Time* magazine came as close as anyone ever has by calling the play "a sort of *Hellzapoppin'* with brains." Yet that description—*Hellzapoppin'* was a famously free-wheeling revue from the 1930s—only hints at the metatheatrical games Wilder set out to play. The oblique nods to James Joyce's *Finnegans Wake*, the Biblical allusions (Wilder originally gave Mr. Antrobus, the brother-murdering inventor of the wheel and the alphabet, the name Cain), the "actors" taking ill mid-performance and being replaced by philosophy-quoting "civilians": each of these could fill a book of its own, let alone two pages of this book. So let's confine our attentions to some theater gossip instead.

Tallulah Bankhead, who created the role of the maid/temptress/narrator Sabina, had it written into her contract that she was not to have an understudy; that way, the show couldn't go on without her, giving her leverage. The show's producer broke the contract, however, and hired a twenty-year-old actress named Elizabeth Scott to play "Girl"—and to understudy Sabina. Bankhead reacted as you'd expect, but she never missed a performance. Elizabeth Scott ultimately ditched both *Skin* and the first letter of her name, and Lizabeth Scott went on to become a husky-voiced favorite of film noir directors.

I bring this up mostly because the Bankhead-Scott dynamic is one of two examples cited as inspirations for Hollywood's legendary love/hate letter to Broadway, 1950's *All About Eve*. I saw that film at far too young an age, maybe ten or eleven, and was instantly taken with the character of the acidulous theater critic, Addison DeWitt. His drawn-out bass voice was familiar to me (the actor, George Sanders, had also voiced the tiger Shere Khan in *The Jungle Book*), and his vocation of seeing plays for a living struck me as almost criminally pleasant. So I might never have become a theater critic if Elizabeth Scott hadn't been hired for *The Skin of Our Teeth*. There are other, far worthier reasons to cherish this play, which is a virtual sandbox for any inventive director. But I'm out of room.

ABOVE: Fredric March (George Antrobus), Florence Eldridge (Maggie Antrobus), and Tallulah Bankhead (Sabina). Act II takes place on the boardwalk of Atlantic City, New Jersey, but resembles the story of Noah's Ark.

OPPOSITE PAGE: March and Frances Heflin, framed by a dinosaur and a mammoth (Remo Bufano and Stanley Prager, respectively). Elia Kazan directed the original production of *The Skin of Our Teeth*.

DATES:
November 18, 1942–September 25, 1943 at the Plymouth Theater (359 performances)

SYNOPSIS:
Sabina, the Antrobus family's maid, says in the play's opening speech that *The Skin of Our Teeth* is "all about the troubles the human race has gone through." With an Ice Age, a Great Flood, and a Miss America pageant on display, she's not too far off.

AWARDS:
Pulitzer Prize

NOTED REVIVALS AND ADAPTATIONS:
Broadway revivals in 1955 and 1975; TV version in 1983

ORIGINAL STARS:
Tallulah Bankhead, Fredric March, Florence Eldridge, Montgomery Clift, Frances Heflin, Florence Reed

SLEUTH

BY ANTHONY SHAFFER

ABOVE: Anthony Quayle played writer Andrew Wyke in the original production. Laurence Olivier and Michael Caine played the role in the 1972 and 2007 films, respectively.

OPPOSITE PAGE: Milo Tindle (Keith Baxter) and Andrew Wyke (Quayle) face off.

What is it with Broadway and stage thrillers these days? Horror abounds on television, on movie screens, in video games, in haunted houses—and in practically every community and regional theater in America. Rarely does more than a season go by in a regional theater without a whodunit or a *Wait Until Dark* popping up. Agatha Christie's *The Mousetrap*, meanwhile, has been running in London for more than sixty years, the longest-running play in West End history; *The Woman in Black* is in a distant, but still respectable, second place.

New York City long ago conceded its mystery niche to off-Broadway's *Perfect Crime*, which has been chugging along in various theaters since 1987. This is a major shift from the 1970s—

for much of that decade, two twisty thrillers about malevolent mystery writers riveted audiences. Ira Levin's *Deathtrap* (1978) had a longer run, in part because it hired name actors like Stacy Keach and Farley Granger as replacement cast members. (One cast member who needed no such substitution was the irreplaceable Marian Seldes, who never missed a single one of the show's 1,793 performances.)

Deathtrap has its own sadistic charms, but it owes a substantial debt to *Sleuth*, which began its life in the land of *The Mousetrap*. "The mystery needed a new coat of paint," said the playwright and practicing barrister Anthony Shaffer, who set out to dismantle the class-bound tropes of the genre.

For the sake of clarification, Shaffer never used *Who's Afraid of Stephen Sondheim?* as an alternate title for the play, although (a) it is common knowledge that Shaffer used the puzzle-loving Sondheim as a template for the role of Andrew Wyke, and (b) Sondheim did receive a copy of the manuscript with that title. (Producer Morton Gottlieb has since been fingered as the likely culprit.) Not long after Laurence Olivier starred in the 1972 film version of *Sleuth*, he met the composer and told him, "I've been playing you." Sondheim thought Olivier meant he had been playing his records. He responded, "Which show?"

The shocks and reversals of *Sleuth* are in many ways impossible to replicate today. TV shows and movies have so absorbed the twists-within-twists approach to mystery writing that audiences are now habituated to accepting every triple-cross as a mere setup for a quadruple-cross. But as *New York Times* critic Clive Barnes wrote, "Mr. Shaffer is one of the rare, rare murder writers it is even a pleasure to see through." Rarer than even Barnes realized: with the exception of *Deathtrap*, Broadway has yet to see a successful new whodunit in the decades since.

DATES:
November 12, 1970–October 13, 1973 at the Music Box Theater (1,222 performances)

SYNOPSIS:
Acclaimed mystery writer Andrew Wyke summons his wife's lover, Milo Tindle, to his home. A fake robbery is hatched. Crimes are committed. Inquiries are made. Tables are turned.

AWARDS:
1 Tony Award

NOTED REVIVALS AND ADAPTATIONS:
Movie versions in 1972 and 2007

ORIGINAL STARS:
Anthony Quayle, Keith Baxter

THE SOUND OF MUSIC

BY RICHARD RODGERS, OSCAR HAMMERSTEIN II, HOWARD LINDSAY, AND RUSSEL CROUSE

Had Richard Rodgers' older brother never introduced him to fraternity brother Oscar Hammerstein II at Columbia, each would be remembered individually for such rich, effortlessly melodic works as *Show Boat*, *Pal Joey*, *On Your Toes*, and *Very Warm for May*. The two are instead linked forever in the public imagination, owing to a seventeen-year partnership that ended in 1959 with *The Sound of Music*.

As odd as it is to imagine now, the duo's initial involvement in *The Sound of Music* was negligible. It was originally conceived as a play for Mary Martin, with some material from the real

Trapp Family Singers added. But then producers Richard Halliday—who also happened to be Martin's husband—and Leland Hayward asked Rodgers and Hammerstein about maybe contributing a new song or two. They responded by writing one of the most hit-packed scores ever. Howard Lindsay and Russel Crouse took the already exciting story of the Von Trapp family and gave it a ton of charm, along with a few considerable gooses. (That flight over the Swiss Alps by foot? They actually took a train.)

The show was never a hit with critics, who considered it treacly and sentimental, but it certainly resonated with the public. The original cast recording spent more than five years on the *Billboard* charts, and everyone from John Coltrane to the Carpenters to Christina Aguilera to Alvin and the Chipmunks has had his or her way with songs like "My Favorite Things" and "Climb Ev'ry Mountain."

Ironically, the tandem that did so much to revolutionize musical theater with *Oklahoma!* in 1943 reverted to an older template for their final effort. Those absurdly green Alps hills are alive with the sound of something very close to operetta, a form that had long since gone out of vogue by 1959. Songs like "Edelweiss" and "Do-Re-Mi" are commonly thought to go back even farther. Theodore Bikel, who created the role of Baron Von Trapp and first sang "Edelweiss," described how Austrians would come up to him after performances and say what a thrill it was to hear that old folk song again.

"Edelweiss" was, sadly, the last song Rodgers wrote with Hammerstein, who had emergency surgery for stomach cancer during *Sound of Music* rehearsals. Rodgers had worked with a sick collaborator before—he once rented the hospital room next to Lorenz Hart's so they could continue writing during Hart's alcohol-binge-fueled stays. Hammerstein's decline was much quicker. Nine months after the show's opening (and well before the phenomenal success of the 1965 film, which remains one of the most popular movies ever made), he was dead. Rodgers kept at it with another five scores over the next fourteen years, and *No Strings* and *Do I Hear a Waltz?* have their moments. Still, the five of them combined did not run as long as *The Sound of Music.*

ABOVE LEFT: Mary Martin with the children of *The Sound of Music,* 1959. *Toni Frissell Collection, Library of Congress*

ABOVE RIGHT: Julie Andrews in the 1965 film adaptation. *© Twentieth Century Fox Film Corp., courtesy Photofest*

OPPOSITE PAGE: *The Sound of Music* tied for top Tony Award honors with *Fiorello!* Mary Martin is with, from left, William Snowden, Joseph Stewart, Mary Susan Locke, Marilyn Rogers, Lauri Peters, Kathy Dunn, and Evanna Lien.

DATES:
November 16, 1959–June 15, 1963 at the Lunt-Fontanne Theater and Mark Hellinger Theater (1,443 performances)

SYNOPSIS:
Maria, a high-spirited postulant at Nonnberg Abbey, is sent to be governess to the seven rambunctious children of a severe-but-soft-underneath-it-all naval captain, just as the Nazi threat begins to loom over Austria.

AWARDS:
5 Tony Awards

NOTED REVIVALS AND ADAPTATIONS:
Broadway revival in 1998; movie version in 1965; TV version in 2013

ORIGINAL STARS:
Mary Martin, Theodore Bikel, Patricia Neway

SOUTH PACIFIC

BY RICHARD RODGERS, OSCAR HAMMERSTEIN II, AND JOSHUA LOGAN

DATES:
April 7, 1949–January 16, 1954 at the Majestic Theater and Broadway Theater (1,925 performances)

SYNOPSIS:
World War II nurse Nellie Forbush confronts her own prejudices when she discovers that her lover, the French planter Emile de Becque, has biracial children from a former relationship.

AWARDS:
10 Tony Awards; Pulitzer Prize

NOTED REVIVALS AND ADAPTATIONS:
Broadway revivals in 1955 and 2008; movie version in 1958; TV version in 2001

ORIGINAL STARS:
Mary Martin, Ezio Pinza, William Tabbert, Betta St. John, Juanita Hall, Myron McCormick

South Pacific, like virtually every other show by Richard Rodgers and Oscar Hammerstein II, works its magic with a seeming indifference to the conventions of musical theater. The two romantic leads, Emile de Becque and Nellie Forbush, hardly sing together at all, and Emile sings for less than fifteen minutes the whole night. (This was actually stipulated in the contract of noted operatic bass Ezio Pinza, who had amortized over eight performances the vocal equivalent of two opera performances a week, the usual workload at the time.) The team that had given the world *Oklahoma!* and *Carousel* would have no dream ballets in *South Pacific*, their most realistic work. In fact, they didn't even have a choreographer, having soured on the legendary Agnes de Mille after her direction of the problematic *Allegro* (1947).

By 1949, Hammerstein had forgotten more about theater than most writers would learn in their lifetimes. Military life, on the other hand, was a bit out of his comfort zone; additionally, one of the James Michener short stories that inspired *South Pacific* was a little too close to *Madame Butterfly* for his and Rodgers' tastes. Joshua Logan, a former Army captain who had cowritten and directed the successful naval play *Mister Roberts* the previous year, signed on for identical duties here. He played a crucial role in fleshing out the script, then directed the production as a stripped-down "musical staging."

The result ran for almost five years, spawned *South Pacific* lipstick and hairbrushes, and earned scalpers a then-staggering $100 a ticket. It was—and still is—the only musical to sweep all four acting Tony Awards. Its Pulitzer

Prize was noteworthy because, for the first time, the composer was acknowledged as part of the collaborative team. (George Gershwin had been omitted for *Of Thee I Sing* in 1932.) Apparently a list of melodies that included "Some Enchanted Evening," "Younger Than Springtime," "There Is Nothing Like a Dame," and "Bali Ha'i" simply couldn't be ignored.

Mary Martin's ebullience helped endear Nellie to theatergoers, despite the character's deeply rooted streak of prejudice. Along those lines, the authors ignored repeated pleas to remove the antiracism song "You've Got to Be Carefully Taught," which spurred a pair of Georgia legislators to threaten banning musicals with "an underlying philosophy inspired by Moscow." One advantage of producing and financing your own show, as Rodgers and Hammerstein had done, is that you are not held captive to investors or grandstanding politicians.

OPPOSITE PAGE: Ezio Pinza (Emile), Barbara Luna (Ngana), Michael De Leon (Jerome), and Mary Martin (Nellie) in the original Broadway production.

RIGHT: Nellie washes that man right out of her hair. Martin came up with the idea for a song performed while she shampoos her hair on stage.

BELOW: "There Is Nothing Like a Dame," the sailors proclaim. Joshua Logan's staging of the song, with the men pacing back and forth, heightened the sense of aggravated waiting that comes with inaction during war.

South Pacific is also noteworthy for what it didn't say. Despite appearing just four years after the end of World War II and featuring several veterans in the cast, it almost never named the Japanese as the enemy. Here the antagonist was not a specific character or army, or even a specific race. Instead, it was racism, something Hammerstein believed could live in all of us, if and when we're taught it.

SPRING AWAKENING

BY DUNCAN SHEIK AND STEVEN SATER

Jonathan Groff (Melchior), John Gallagher Jr. (Moritz, upside down center), and the restless teenagers of *Spring Awakening*. The musical's Tony wins included Best Musical, Best Original Score (Duncan Sheik and Steven Sater), Best Direction (Michael Mayer), and Best Choreography (Bill T. Jones). © *Joan Marcus*

Suicide, abortion, sadomasochism, rape, sexual torment: if the Germans hadn't invented the phrase "sturm und drang" in the eighteenth century, Frank Wedekind would have forced the issue a century later with his scandalous 1891 play *Spring Awakening*. When the play finally reached New York in 1915, it took a court injunction for just one matinee performance to be permitted.

Duncan Sheik and Steven Sater could have coasted on the piece's inherent shock value for their musical adaptation, but instead they did something a lot trickier. Sheik, a 1990s one-hit wonder ("Barely Breathing"), and Sater managed to turn *Spring Awakening* into a period piece with microphones and neon lights.

Patricia Cohen of the *New York Times* has convincingly argued that the idea of adolescence as a developmental stage came into existence during Wedekind's time, and that the Germany of his youth played a big part in cementing the idea. Cohen quotes *Adolescence*, G. Stanley Hall's definitive 1904 treatise on the subject: "Youth awakes to a

DATES:

December 10, 2006–January 18, 2009 at the
Eugene O'Neill Theater (859 performances)

SYNOPSIS:

German schoolchildren explore their sexuality in
various forms, with decidedly unhealthy results.

AWARDS:

8 Tony Awards

**NOTED REVIVALS
AND ADAPTATIONS:**

None

ORIGINAL STARS:

Lea Michele, Jonathan Groff, John Gallagher Jr.

Lea Michele (Wendla), Groff, and a number of their cast mates
were future stage and screen stars. © Joan Marcus

new world and understands neither it nor himself." Sheik
and Sater's anachronistic treatment of Wedekind serves as
an explanation and also an update: "I go up to my room, turn
the stereo on, / Shoot up some you in the You of some song."

You might notice that not a single syllable from that lyric
could plausibly be set in 1891. A crucial part of the show's
success came from director Michael Mayer's decision to
have the musical numbers—and only the musical numbers—
vault out of the period and into jangly folk-pop. Also
helping to bridge the gap were both Bill T. Jones' cryptic
dances, filled with hypnotic arm movements and utterly
unlike typical Broadway choreography, and a future who's
who of telegenic performers, all of whom were twenty-four
or younger (and a few of whom disrobed within feet of
onstage audience members).

Most people can count on one hand the number of
Broadway musicals that "get" what it's like to be young.
(Costar Lea Michele, who was twenty when the show
opened on Broadway, had spent the previous *seven years*
workshopping it.) At times, I myself would modify that
statement to "count on one finger." Either way, *Spring
Awakening* qualifies.

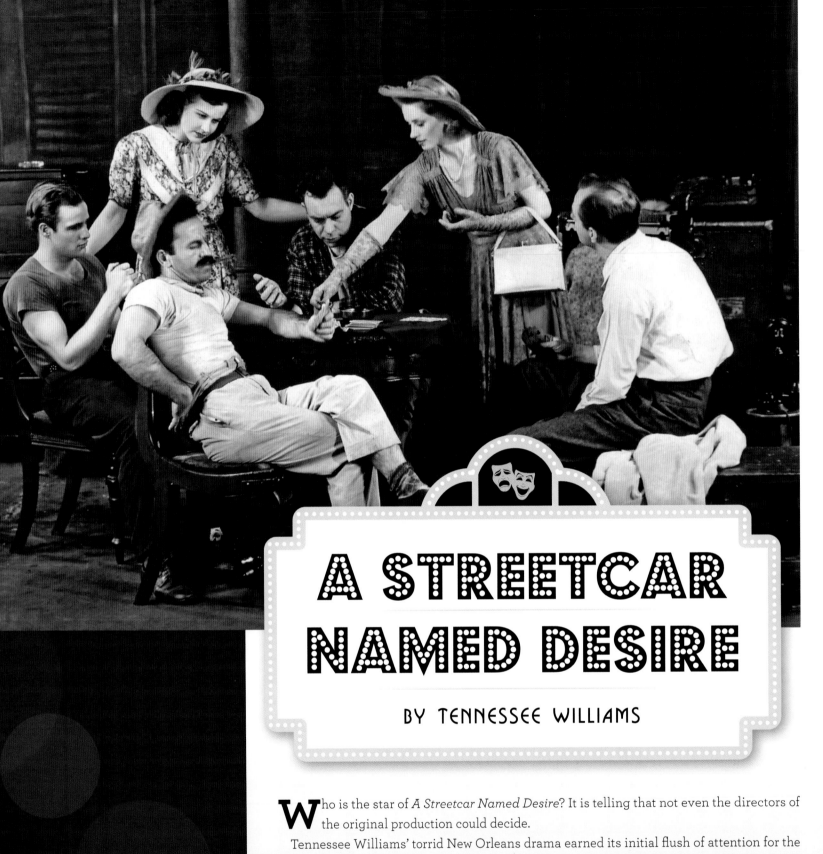

A STREETCAR NAMED DESIRE

BY TENNESSEE WILLIAMS

Who is the star of *A Streetcar Named Desire*? It is telling that not even the directors of the original production could decide.

Tennessee Williams' torrid New Orleans drama earned its initial flush of attention for the sweaty subject matter (noted critic George Jean Nathan called it *"The Glands Menagerie,"* riffing on Williams' hit play of two years earlier)—and for Marlon Brando, the twenty-three-year-old actor playing Stanley Kowalski. This had a lot to do with director Elia Kazan's conception of the character, a feral, preening man capable of domestic violence and worse.

Not so fast, though. Williams created fluttering, damaged Blanche DuBois ("I don't want realism. I want magic!") with his sister Rose in mind, just as he had with Laura in *The Glass Menagerie*. But Brando's sheer magnetism, along with the play's discomfitingly heartfelt delineation of Stanley's frame of mind, inspired critic and director Harold Clurman to bemoan how *Streetcar* became "the triumph of Stanley Kowalski with the collusion of the audience." Oddly for a critic, albeit one who had directed the premieres of *Awake and Sing!* and *Waiting for Lefty*, Clurman got a chance to practice what he preached when he helmed the national *Streetcar* tour, with Uta Hagen as Blanche. Realism had had its turn. It was time for magic to take the spotlight. To this day, the balance can sway in either direction.

Jessica Tandy made a strong impression as the original Blanche. (Incredibly, in the six separate productions to reach Broadway so far, Tandy won the only Tony Award that *Streetcar* has ever received in any category. And she had to share it with Judith Anderson and Katharine Cornell!) It wasn't strong enough, however, to keep Vivien Leigh from landing the role in the 1951 film version, for which Kazan was able to keep just about everyone else from the Broadway company.

The movie had one other key difference from the play: the ending. In order to keep Stanley's rape of Blanche, Williams appeased the censors by having a pregnant Stella leave the big lug, ostensibly to protect her child. While it's easy to scoff at the scandalized prudes of the past, the Kowalskis' deeply dysfunctional—and incredibly sexy—marriage was, and is, among the more disconcerting of the American stage. What was too shocking for moviegoers in 1951 has scarcely lost its punch even today.

DATES:
December 3, 1947–December 17, 1949 at the Ethel Barrymore Theater (855 performances)

SYNOPSIS:
Blanche DuBois, a flamboyantly fading Southern belle, begrudgingly moves in with her sister, Stella, and brother-in-law, Stanley Kowalski. She quickly and irreparably overstays her welcome in their New Orleans apartment.

AWARDS:
1 Tony Award; Pulitzer Prize

NOTED REVIVALS AND ADAPTATIONS:
Broadway revivals in 1973, 1988, 1992, 2005, and 2012; movie version in 1951; TV versions in 1984 and 1995

ORIGINAL STARS:
Marlon Brando, Jessica Tandy, Kim Hunter, Karl Malden

ABOVE: Jessica Tandy and Marlon Brando as Blanche DuBois and Stanley Kowalski.

OPPOSITE PAGE: Brando, Kim Hunter, Nick Dennis, Rudy Bond, Tandy, and Karl Malden in *A Streetcar Named Desire*.

THE STUDENT PRINCE IN HEIDELBERG

BY SIGMUND ROMBERG AND DOROTHY DONNELLY

ABOVE: *The Student Prince in Heidelberg* original Broadway production, 1924. J. C. Huffman directed the massive cast, led by Howard Marsh, right, as Prince Karl Franz.

OPPOSITE PAGE: Poster for Philadelphia tour stop.

DATES:

December 2, 1924–May 18, 1926 at Jolson's 59th Street Theater (608 performances)

SYNOPSIS:

Unbeknownst to his university classmates at Heidelberg, Karl Franz is actually the prince of Karlsberg. His romance with beer-garden waitress Kathie is imperiled when he must return to Karlsberg and become king.

AWARDS:

None

NOTED REVIVALS AND ADAPTATIONS:

Broadway revivals in 1931 and 1943; movie versions in 1927 and 1954

ORIGINAL STARS:

Howard Marsh, Ilse Marvenga, Roberta Beatty, Greek Evans

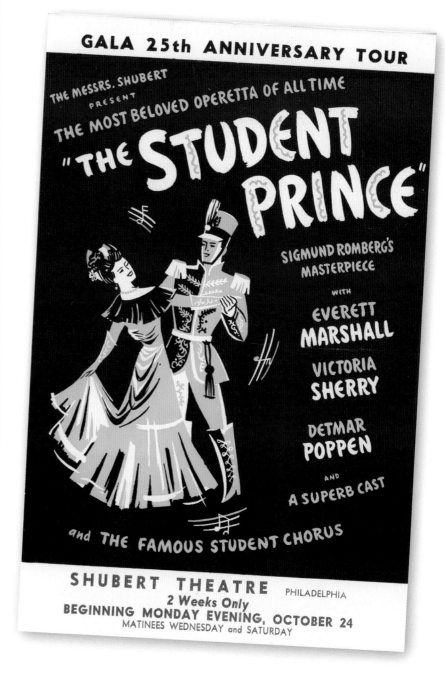

It's no secret that Broadway producers often try to do more with less. Live animals can be expensive, so they'll use a stuffed dog or a puppet instead. "Chamber-size" revivals of musicals generally employ a fraction of the musicians, and the backstage wings of any costume drama are littered with enough fake wigs, beauty marks, and facial hair to help supporting performers double, triple, and quintuple up.

Flash back to 1924, when producers Lee and J. J. Shubert flooded the stage of Jolson's 59th Street Theater with 150 performers. This horde was performing in the premiere of what would become the most popular show of the 1920s, *The Student Prince in Heidelberg*, known by one and all without the "in Heidelberg."

Sigmund Romberg wrote more than fifty musicals in forty years (he was technically an employee of the Shubert brothers, who clearly got their money's worth), and so audiences might have assumed they knew what they would be getting this time around—from both him and his underrated collaborator, the former stage actress Dorothy Donnelly. But *The Student Prince* took a different tone. Not exactly a calmer one—the Act I "Drinking Song," with its ringing chorus of "Drink! Drink! Drink!," was a favorite in a country that was four years into Prohibition—but certainly a more somber one. Star-crossed romances are a dime a dozen in operetta, yet these stars never get uncrossed: love

does not find a way to bridge the class differences between Prince Karl Franz and the lowly waitress Kathie. Their Act IV reunion culminates in nothing more than a parting of the ways and a tearful reprise of "Deep in My Heart, Dear."

Downbeat endings, though still rare, are much more common in musicals today. In 1924, the ending was so daring that J. J. Shubert panicked and started tinkering with the piece himself, eventually barring an apoplectic (but, let's remember, salaried) Romberg from the building. Cooler heads ultimately prevailed—albeit after Romberg sued Shubert—and the bittersweet ending proved to be the right one. The wiser Shuberts created sad audiences everywhere by touring *The Student Prince* season after season until the late 1940s, long after the Twenty-First Amendment allowed those audiences to once again drown their sorrows and drink, drink, drink.

SWEENEY TODD

THE DEMON BARBER OF FLEET STREET

BY STEPHEN SONDHEIM AND HUGH WHEELER

By 1979, Stephen Sondheim's name had become synonymous with a certain level of erudition and wry wit. His Kabuki-inflected *Pacific Overtures* had offered glimpses of a broader sensibility three years earlier, but few theatergoers were prepared for the melodic sweep and grisly daring of *Sweeney Todd*. From its chorus repeatedly lingering on the "ee" sounds in Sweeney's first name (perhaps the shrillest vowel in English, and one that composers typically shy away from on extended notes) to the gallows humor with which Sweeney and Lovett parse the relative flavors of human corpses according to occupation ("And we have some shepherd's pie peppered / With actual shepherd on top"), *Sweeney Todd* upended any rules of what constituted a Broadway musical, and then wrote some new ones.

Sweeney Todd may have first appeared in a Victorian penny dreadful serial, but director Harold

DATES:

March 1, 1979–June 29, 1980 at the Uris Theater (557 performances)

SYNOPSIS:

After being unjustly imprisoned for fifteen years, Benjamin Barker returns to 1840s London and reestablishes himself as the titular barber. His lust for blood pairs up nicely with the ambitions of one Mrs. Lovett, whose pie shop begins to do great business right around the time Sweeney begins manufacturing corpses by the dozens.

AWARDS:

8 Tony Awards

NOTED REVIVALS AND ADAPTATIONS:

Broadway revivals in 1989 and 2005; movie version in 2007

ORIGINAL STARS:

Len Cariou, Angela Lansbury

ABOVE: Angela Lansbury with Ken Jennings, who played Tobias Ragg, the assistant to pompous barber Adolfo Pirelli (Joaquin Romaguera) in the original cast.

OPPOSITE PAGE: Mrs. Lovett (Lansbury) and Sweeney Todd (Len Cariou) stand before Lovett's lucrative pie shop in the original Broadway production of *Sweeney Todd*.

Prince painted this penny dreadful on a staggeringly large scale, heightening the Brechtian sensibility by engulfing the performers in a hulking, clanking set made from a real-life nineteenth-century foundry. The score includes some of Sondheim's most hummable melodies ("Pretty Women," "Not While I'm Around"), as well as songs that are murderously hard to sing in the lobby or anywhere else. Angela Lansbury, who had already won three Tony Awards by the time she created the role of Mrs. Lovett, remembers practicing "The Worst Pies in London" for weeks on end, with and without a daily clump of fresh dough from a nearby bakery.

The two subsequent Broadway revivals went a far more modest route than Prince had, at least in terms of budget, with the 1989 Circle in the Square revival earning the nickname "Teeny Todd." John Doyle's intriguing revival of 2005, which featured Michael Cerveris, Patti LuPone, and the rest of the cast members doubling up as the orchestra, made up for in ingenuity what it sacrificed in narrative clarity.

Sweeney Todd, with its exquisite mad scene ("Epiphany") and its nearly two dozen leitmotifs, is one of those rare musicals that exists equally comfortably in a Broadway house and an opera house. Many have questioned which one it is—an opera or a musical—though not Sondheim himself, who has referred to it as a "black operetta." Perversely enough, *Todd* has even become a staple in high schools, albeit with a few cuts. Wherever it is done, this much can be said: if this book were arranged in order of preference as opposed to alphabetically, *Sweeney Todd* would be much, much closer to the front.

THE TIME OF YOUR LIFE

BY WILLIAM SAROYAN

William Saroyan, a prickly Armenian American author who, as a child, had spent years in an orphanage despite not being an orphan, was an unlikely—and temporary— member of Manhattan's smart set. The esteemed Boston critic George Jean Nathan had taken a shine to Saroyan's first produced play, *My Heart's in the Highlands*, which led to an invite to the even more esteemed Algonquin Round Table in 1939. It was there that director/producer/actor Eddie Dowling said to Saroyan, "Any play you write, I'll buy sight unseen." The writer took Dowling at his word and, two days later, sat down to pen *The Time of Your Life*. Six days after that, he was done.

ABOVE: Center, from left, Julie Haydon (seated, as prostitute Kitty Duval) and Gene Kelly (aspiring dancer Harry) in the original Broadway production, set in Nick's Pacific Street Saloon, Restaurant, and Entertainment Palace in San Francisco.

OPPOSITE PAGE: William Saroyan in 1940. Saroyan's other major works include the novel *The Human Comedy*. *Photograph by Al Aumuller, Library of Congress*

That's the version Saroyan told, at least. Saroyan told lots of stories, barely pausing to take a breath, and he typically left out the part about Harold Clurman turning down *The Time of Your Life* before Dowling (who would eventually star as the enigmatic Joe) said yes. But Saroyan did write the play in less than a week, and then became the first playwright to win both the Pulitzer Prize and the New York Drama Critics Circle Award. He turned down the Pulitzer, however, on the grounds that businessmen had no business judging art.

Saroyan, who fired the play's director during the New Haven tryout and put himself and Dowling in charge, assembled a swell cast. Among the twenty-five actors were a twenty-seven-year-old Gene Kelly and a strong-chinned stunner named Julie Haydon, who would later originate the role of Laura in *The Glass Menagerie*, once again starring alongside Dowling. (Haydon brought *The Time of Your Life* full circle—and gave hope to theater critics everywhere—by marrying George Jean Nathan in 1955.)

DATES:
October 25, 1939–April 6, 1940 at the Booth Theater (185 performances)

SYNOPSIS:
As a dockworker strike percolates outside of a San Francisco waterfront dive, a wealthy cipher named Joe keeps a whimsical eye on a rogue's gallery of hoofers, hookers, swells, and flatfoots.

AWARDS:
Pulitzer Prize

NOTED REVIVALS AND ADAPTATIONS:
Broadway revivals in 1969 and 1975; movie version in 1948; TV version in 1958

ORIGINAL STARS:
Eddie Dowling, Gene Kelly, Julie Haydon, Edward Andrews

Shaggy, good-natured, unapologetically odd, and more optimistic than any play written at the height of the Great Depression had a right to be, *The Time of Your Life* flooded the stage with what the *New York Times*' Brooks Atkinson called "some of the most flavorsome characters we have had in the theater." Their arguably even odder creator could have given them a run for their money on that score.

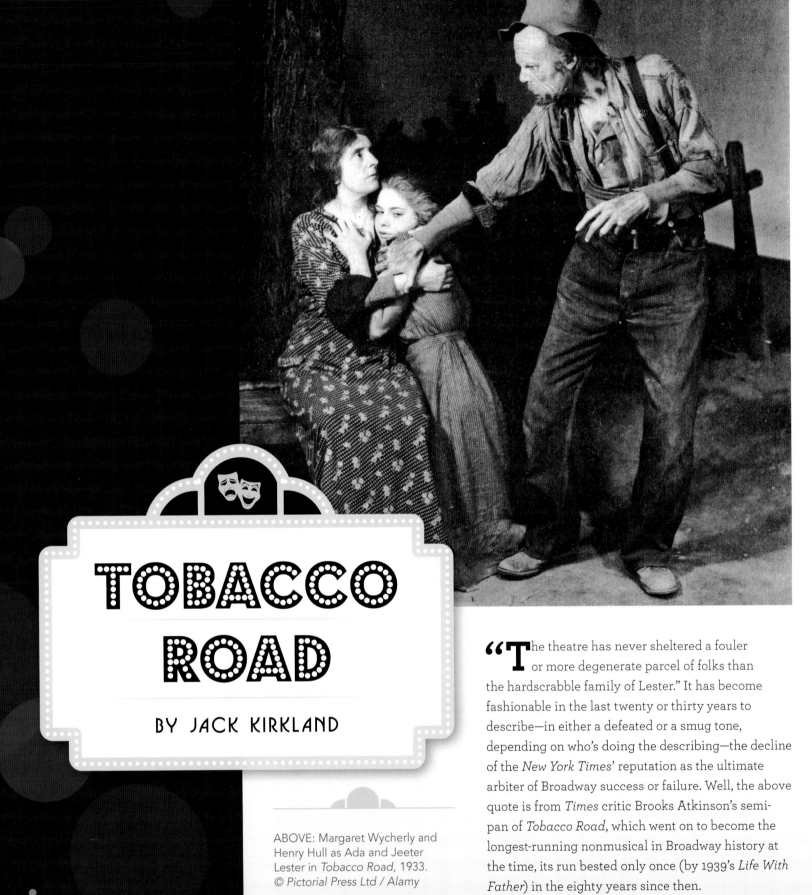

TOBACCO ROAD

BY JACK KIRKLAND

"The theatre has never sheltered a fouler or more degenerate parcel of folks than the hardscrabble family of Lester." It has become fashionable in the last twenty or thirty years to describe—in either a defeated or a smug tone, depending on who's doing the describing—the decline of the *New York Times*' reputation as the ultimate arbiter of Broadway success or failure. Well, the above quote is from *Times* critic Brooks Atkinson's semi-pan of *Tobacco Road*, which went on to become the longest-running nonmusical in Broadway history at the time, its run bested only once (by 1939's *Life With Father*) in the eighty years since then.

What was the secret of *Road*'s success? Topicality was certainly on its side: in a time when Depression-scarred audiences were flocking to escapist Hollywood fare like *King Kong* and tuning in to radio shows like *The Lone Ranger*, Jack Kirkland's adaptation of the 1932 Erskine Caldwell novel offered a relatively realistic portrait of life in the dirt-poor

South, including a protagonist whose main goal seemed to be being buried deep enough to keep the rats away from his corpse. (John Steinbeck's *Of Mice and Men* wouldn't appear until 1939.) The producers' decision to slash ticket prices from $3.30 to $1.10 presumably didn't hurt. And then there's the kind of publicity that you can't buy, the kind that only furious politicians and preachers can supply. *Tobacco Road* was banned on grounds of immorality in cities like Chicago and Detroit, which prompted all the expected headlines, sermons, lawsuits, and lines at the box office.

Caldwell routinely spoke on behalf of the play during these dust-ups, but he hadn't had high hopes for the stage adaptation originally. The first few months were rocky for the play, which received indifferent reviews (not all of them as bad as Atkinson's) and cycled through two theaters before settling into the Forrest in September 1934, where it would remain for nearly seven years.

The show's longevity is all the more impressive in light of the far shorter runs of the time, when an eight-*month* engagement was considered extremely successful. Case in point: Henry Hull, who starred as the rat-fearing Jeeter Lester, had appeared in a staggering twenty-six different Broadway plays in the twenty years prior to *Tobacco Road*. For the first time in a long while, Hull and his costars had what roughly a quarter of their fellow Americans desperately wanted: a steady job.

DATES:
December 4, 1933–May 31, 1941 at the Theater Masque, the 48th Street Theater, and the Forrest Theater (3,182 performances)

SYNOPSIS:
The Jeeter family had seventeen children; all but two of them are either dead or gone. Such is the miserable life of these tenant farmers in desolate Georgia, where bad soil and worse luck lead to thieving, cheating, sexual depravity, and worse.

AWARDS:
None

NOTED REVIVALS AND ADAPTATIONS:
Broadway revivals in 1942, 1943, and 1950; movie version in 1941

ORIGINAL STARS:
Henry Hull, Ruth Hunter, Margaret Wycherly

TORCH SONG TRILOGY

BY HARVEY FIERSTEIN

ABOVE: Harvey Fierstein, front, as Arnold Beckoff, with Susan Edwards (Lady Blues). Fierstein won two Tonys for *Torch Song Trilogy*, for Best Play and Best Actor in a Play. His subsequent Tonys have been for *Hairspray* and *La Cage aux Folles*, and he wrote the book for 2013's Best Musical, *Kinky Boots*.

OPPOSITE PAGE: From left, Court Miller, Diane Tarleton, Paul Joynt, and Harvey Fierstein in the original Broadway production.

"Eighty percent of what is now considered the American theater originated at La MaMa."

Harvey Fierstein is prone to provocative statements like the one above; they're part of the reason he is one of theater's most dependable librettists and raconteurs, with credits like *La Cage aux Folles* and *Hairspray* to his name. (His outer-borough bullfrog of a voice makes those claims sound even more daring.) While 80 percent might be a bit high, the Lower East Side's La MaMa Experimental Theater Club was indeed a creative oasis for the likes of Fierstein, Sam Shepard, and Lanford Wilson in the 1960s and 1970s.

Off-Broadway has been well-established as a theatrical incubator for decades now. Of the twenty Tony Award races for Best Play and Best Musical in the first decade of the twenty-first century, nineteen had at least one off-Broadway transfer among the nominees. The influence of off-off-Broadway (a blanket definition for theaters with fewer than one hundred seats) is subtler, yet commercial theater has been feasting on the thorny, campy, often confusing, and deeply satisfying fruits cultivated in those trenches for almost sixty years. Fierstein's *Torch Song Trilogy*, which got its start at La MaMa, is perhaps the most potent example.

In the 1970s, gay themes were handled gingerly, if at all, on the mainstream stage. Mart Crowley's 1968 play *The Boys in the Band* had trafficked in stereotypes and degrees of self-loathing that earned it the enmity of many, but it did expand the parameters of what gay and straight audiences alike were willing to watch. The three plays that Fierstein smashed into his four-hour *Trilogy* had their share of catty wit—"I'm aging about as well as a Beach Party movie," moans Arnold Beckoff, the brassy size-twenty drag queen at its center—but they also approached bisexuality and even gay parenthood in a way that was genuinely groundbreaking.

So was the speech given by producer John Glines at that year's Tony Awards, when he thanked his lover. *Torch Song*

DATES:
June 10, 1982–May 19, 1985 at the Little Theater (1,222 performances)

SYNOPSIS:
Arnold Beckoff, "a kvetch of great wit and want," juggles life as a drag queen with a bewildering set of relationships: with a bisexual man, with that man's new girlfriend, with a male model, with Arnold's strident mother, and with the troubled teenager he wants to adopt.

AWARDS:
2 Tony Awards

NOTED REVIVALS AND ADAPTATIONS:
Movie version in 1988

ORIGINAL STARS:
Harvey Fierstein, Estelle Getty, Fisher Stevens

was a surprise winner over *Plenty* and the Pulitzer Prize–winning *'Night, Mother*.

The theater community has long been out in front on gay issues, and Harvey Fierstein—who appeared in Andy Warhol's only play at, of course, La MaMa—has been at, or very near, the front of that front. The battle plans in the fight weren't drafted on Broadway. These three torch songs got their start in a basement on East Fourth Street; New York City has many, many other such basements.

Torch Song Trilogy (1982-1985 Broadway)
Play by Harvey Fierstein. Directed by Peter Pope.

289

A TRIP TO CHINATOWN

BY CHARLES H. HOYT
AND PERCY GAUNT

DATES:
November 9, 1891–August 7, 1893 at the Madison Square Theater (657 performances)

SYNOPSIS:
All that stands between four youngsters and a grand night on the town is the young men's guardian, Uncle Ben. A ruse involving a lady chaperone results in the young couples and Uncle Ben all ending up at the same restaurant. And Uncle Ben has forgotten his wallet!

AWARDS:
None

NOTED REVIVALS AND ADAPTATIONS:
Movie version in 1926

ORIGINAL STARS:
Harry Conor, George A. Beane Jr., Anna Boyd

Charles H. Hoyt may no longer have the name recognition of his fellow farceurs Harrigan and Hart, let alone George M. Cohan. But in the dwindling years of the nineteenth century, nobody churned out farces as dependably or successfully as Hoyt: he wrote roughly one a year for two decades, many of which played in a theater named for him.

Hoyt started out as a newspaperman, and it is said that his experience writing the *Boston Post*'s semi-humorous front-page column, "All Sorts," gave him a lifetime's worth of the juicy tales and recognizably all-American characters with which he filled his farces. His ability to pull from here and there, to slam together "all sorts" of pithy sayings, actual news events, and witty asides, would serve as a template for his extremely malleable theatrical texts.

To be fair, the bones of *A Trip to Chinatown* were solid: like Thornton Wilder (*The Matchmaker*), Jerry Herman (*Hello, Dolly!*), and Tom Stoppard (*On the Razzle*) after him, Hoyt had adapted the 1830s play *A Day Well Spent*. He also contributed the lyrics to a few decent songs in *Chinatown*, including "On the Bowery" (which had absolutely nothing to do with the San Francisco setting, but so be it) and "Reuben, Reuben, I've Been Thinking." But it took an enterprising composer named Charles K. Harris to help turn *Chinatown* into Broadway's longest-running musical for almost thirty years.

The show toured extensively, with a touring company landing in New York even as the original production was still playing. Hoyt had his own theater to manage and a breakneck writing pace to maintain, so he didn't always keep tabs on every stop of every tour. As a result, Harris managed to convince a company manager in Milwaukee to slide his new waltz into a matinee performance without telling Hoyt. "After the Ball" brought the house down. Hoyt wasn't too proud to see the song—which sold more than two million copies of sheet music in 1892 alone—become part of each and every subsequent *Chinatown* company.

It also became part of *Show Boat*, which used "After the Ball" as an example of the quintessential 1890s tune. Hoyt died at the age of forty-one in 1900, long before *Show Boat* opened. It's hard to imagine he would have minded the interpolation too much. After all, it takes all sorts.

"Glove contests brought up to date," as promised in a *Trip to Chinatown* poster, bespoke the physical comedy audiences could look forward to. *Library of Congress*

UNCLE TOM'S CABIN

BY GEORGE AIKEN

DATES:
Approximately July 18, 1853–May 13, 1854 at Purdy's National Theater (325 performances)

SYNOPSIS:
Kindly slave Uncle Tom is scheduled to be sold by an indebted Kentucky farmer, along with the young son of Eliza, the family maid. Eliza escapes slave traders by crossing the icy Ohio River with her young son in her arms, but Uncle Tom is not so lucky. That is the end of Act I. There are six acts.

AWARDS:
None

NOTED REVIVALS AND ADAPTATIONS:
Several Broadway revivals, the last in 1933; at least nine movie versions between 1909 and 1927

ORIGINAL STARS:
Cordelia Howard, Caroline Fox Howard, George Howard, G. C. Germon

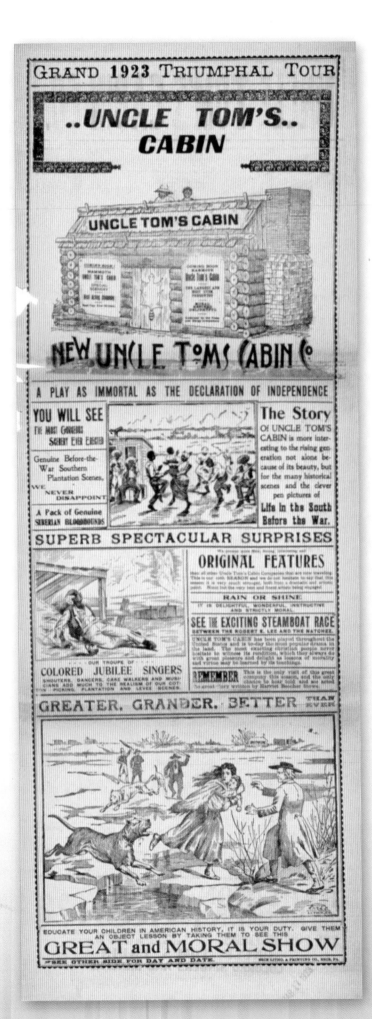

Although *Uncle Tom's Cabin* was rivaled only by the Bible among the reading public in nineteenth-century America, far more people at the time encountered it on the stage than on the page due to literacy rates at the time.

Before the entirety of Harriet Beecher Stowe's iconic anti-slavery novel had even been published (it began as a forty-part serial in an abolitionist periodical), producers had already begun adapting unsanctioned versions of *Uncle Tom's Cabin*, which became known as "Tom shows." Stowe was approached about writing or even authorizing an official version, but she was wary of the stage. Many, many others filled the void; most employed the loathsome tropes of minstrelsy, validating Stowe's skepticism. Some Southern theaters even presented pro-slavery variants, with titles like *Uncle Tom's Cabin As It Is*.

Dozens of Tom shows soon crisscrossed the North and South, often featuring such Stephen Foster standards as "My Old Kentucky Home," though choirs of "jubilee singers" would later insert more authentic spirituals. But the reigning commercial and artistic success was the one that dime novelist George Aiken wrote for his cousin, George Howard (whose four-year-old daughter, Cordelia, played saintly little Eva). Aiken's original version included a spectacular dramatization of Eliza escaping across the Ohio River ("Courage, my child!—we will be free—or perish!") and ended with Eva's death. The production opened in Troy, New York, and ran for one hundred performances, at which point Aiken added a sequel to complete the narrative.

It was that expanded, six-act *Uncle Tom's Cabin* that came to Purdy's National Theater, which a year earlier had presented a one-hour Tom show, complete with a happy ending for the title character. Never before Aiken's version, it is believed, had one story commanded a Broadway stage single-handedly, without an afterplay or a curtain raiser or any other bit of supplementary entertainment.

Even Harriet Beecher Stowe was won over by Aiken's production, while preachers took a break from inveighing

ABOVE: The bridge scene in a 1901 production of *Uncle Tom's Cabin*. *Library of Congress*

LEFT: Poster of Topsy, c. 1894. The character of Topsy is a young slave who famously replies "S'pect I grow'd" when asked who made her (a phrase that took on its own life as a way to explain the unplanned). *Library of Congress*

against the wicked stage and encouraged worshippers to attend "the great moral drama," a frequent tagline in *Uncle Tom's Cabin* advertisements.

It is not an exaggeration to say that the show, which toured more or less constantly until 1930, did more to change public opinion than any theatrical production before or since—about slavery in general but also about the humanity of the men and women being represented. Purdy's National Theater was very near the Bowery theaters featuring minstrel shows at the time, and the sight of a blackfaced G. C. Germon entering the stage as Uncle Tom was enough to rouse audiences into anticipatory giggles. Then Germon spoke with, as the *New York Times* review described it, "a broad and guttural negro accent, but the voice deep and earnest—so earnest, that the first laugh at his nigger words, from the pit, died away into deep stillness."

OPPOSITE PAGE: A 1923 tour of *Uncle Tom's Cabin* promised a "play as immortal as the Declaration of Independence" and advised parents to "educate your children in American history. It is your duty." *Library of Congress*

VERY GOOD EDDIE

BY JEROME KERN, SCHUYLER GREEN, PHILIP BARTHOLOMAE, AND GUY BOLTON

Ernest Truex (as the diminutive Eddie Kettle, center) and the cast of *Very Good Eddie*, 1915. *Eddie* premiered at the Princess Theater, then moved to two other theaters before completing its run back at the Princess.

After working on more than three dozen Broadway musicals during the previous decade, Jerome Kern was tired of propping up imported operettas and flimsy musical comedy tropes for the likes of the Shubert brothers. Producer Elizabeth Marbury came to the rescue by pairing the veteran composer (albeit a thirty-year-old veteran composer) with newbie bookwriter Guy Bolton, and then offering them the relatively intimate Princess Theater. Now Kern could mold his semiclassical compositional style to contemporary American stories instead of concocted kingdoms, outlandish plots, and old vaudeville bits pulled out of mothballs.

Kern and Bolton (along with nearly a half-dozen other folks credited with "additional material") were determined to succeed or fail on the simple yet honest characterizations of their mismatched lovers. Costars Ernest Truex and Alice Dovey were not transplanted vaudevillians; they were actors who could create comic

DATES:
December 23, 1915–October 14, 1916 at the Princess Theater, Casino Theater, and 39th Street Theater (341 performances)

SYNOPSIS:
Meek little Eddie Kettle is honeymooning with his statuesque, pants-wearing bride. As they cruise up the Hudson River, hijinks ensue when they cross paths with another pair of incompatible newlyweds.

AWARDS:
None

NOTED REVIVALS AND ADAPTATIONS:
Broadway revival in 1975

ORIGINAL STARS:
Ernest Truex, Alice Dovey, Helen Raymond, John Willard

Nicholas Wyman, Virginia Seidel, Charles Repole (as Eddie), and Spring Fairbank in the 1975 revival at the Booth Theater, which ran for 304 performances after transferring from Connecticut's Goodspeed Opera House.

The miniaturization of Broadway productions, and even the beginnings of off-Broadway, can be traced to *Eddie*'s success and to the intimacy of the Princess shows. (*See also entry on* Oh, Boy!) With a mere 299 seats, the theater could not support the expenditures attached to the usual throng of chorines. The *Eddie* chorus numbered twelve instead of ninety; the orchestra pit contained eleven rather than forty musicians. The limited backstage area made only one set change possible (from a ship to a honeymoon hotel, in this case)—and that had to happen during intermission.

A few grumbling critics who were accustomed to more flamboyant fare labeled *Eddie* a "kitchenette production," but the majority of scribes found that less was more. (They weren't alone: a teenage Richard Rodgers saw the show at least a dozen times.) While *Eddie* is not exactly an integrated musical, it laid the groundwork for the more coherent musical comedy storytelling to come.

roles. Bolton, whose snappy dialogue would make him the go-to librettist of the 1920s, took the novel step of giving each ensemble member an actual name—albeit goofy ones like Dyer Thirst, Chrystal Poole, and Always Innit. The show's title comes from the curtain line, uttered by a hotel clerk when—spoiler alert—our timorous protagonist finally finds the moxie to order his wife to sit down!

WAITING FOR GODOT

BY SAMUEL BECKETT

It has become conventional wisdom among a certain, rather superior set that Florida's reputation as a hotbed of experimental theater was forever put to rest on January 3, 1956. That was the night when Samuel Beckett's *Waiting for Godot* made its US premiere at the Coconut Grove Playhouse, fresh from a controversial opening in London the year before. ("I haven't really the foggiest idea what some of it means," the London director, Peter Hall, had sheepishly told his cast during rehearsals.) The response was, shall we say, muted. Or rather, it grew increasingly muted as more than half of the opening-night audience left before intermission.

Perhaps the blame might be better laid at the feet of the Coconut Grove's marketing department. If you were promised, as that first audience was, "the laugh sensation of two continents," featuring the Cowardly Lion himself (Bert Lahr) and the guy who ogled Marilyn Monroe on that subway grate (Tom Ewell), wouldn't you have a certain set of expectations? Ones that might not have correlated with the sight of two hobos wrestling—possibly for eternity—with the most existentially profound questions ever put on a stage?

DATES:
April 19–June 9, 1956 at the John Golden Theater (60 performances)

SYNOPSIS:
Vladimir and Estragon meet near a tree. They wait for Godot. And wait.

AWARDS:
None, unless you count topping the Royal National Theater's list of the most significant English-language plays of the twentieth century

NOTED REVIVALS AND ADAPTATIONS:
Broadway revivals in 1957, 2009, and 2013; TV versions in 1961, 1977, and 2001

ORIGINAL STARS:
Bert Lahr, E. G. Marshall, Alvin Epstein, Kurt Kasznar

LEFT: Robin Williams (Estragon) and Steve Martin (Vladimir) starred in a 1988 revival at the Mitzi E. Newhouse Theater at Lincoln Center, directed by Mike Nichols.

OPPOSITE PAGE: Bert Lahr (left, as Estragon) and E. G. Marshall (Vladimir) in the original Broadway production, 1956. Herbert Berghof (founder of New York's preeminent acting school the HB Studio) directed.

Whatever the case, the response was better when Lahr brought *Godot* to Broadway three months later with a new costar (E. G. Marshall), a new director, and a new tagline: "Wanted: 70,000 Playgoing Intellectuals."

Book upon book has been written about virtually every aspect of *Waiting for Godot*, though not by Beckett, who memorably said, "Why people have to complicate a thing so simple I can't make out." But complicate it they do, with vigorous discussions about everything from theological underpinnings to Jungian archetypes to the pronunciation of the unseen title character (GOD-oh or Gu-DOH). What you won't find is much on the various revolutionary stagings of the play—because there haven't been many. Beckett kept productions on an extremely tight leash in terms of casting and modifications to the text, and his estate has followed suit. (He banned all productions of his works in the Netherlands after the courts there permitted an all-female *Godot*.)

Nonetheless, "habit is a great deadener," as Vladimir puts it near the end of the play, and directors keep finding their own ways into this gloriously austere work. One of the highlights of my theatergoing lifetime was a Classical Theater of Harlem production of *Godot*, in which Vladimir and Estragon found themselves on a New Orleans rooftop, surrounded on all sides by the flood waters of Hurricane Katrina. "GODOT" had been scribbled in desperately large letters on the roof, in case he might come by helicopter. Not one word of the text was modified. It didn't need to be.

WAITING FOR LEFTY

BY CLIFFORD ODETS

ABOVE: Clifford Odets directed the Broadway production of his play alongside acting titan Sanford Meisner. Elia Kazan, with arms raised, starred as Agate Keller, a man who encourages those around him to "make a new world." Russell Collins, second from right, played union leader Harry Fatt.

OPPOSITE PAGE: Ruth Nelson as Edna in the original Broadway production.

Don't be fooled by that "None" to the right, where the Broadway revivals and Hollywood adaptations of *Waiting for Lefty* would be. Clifford Odets' game-changing piece of agitprop found a fast—and, for Odets and the crusading Group Theatre, thoroughly satisfying—afterlife within hours of its premiere.

That debut, part of a benefit for the leftist *New Theatre* magazine, inspired dozens of audience members to request permission to stage their own productions; it wasn't long before more than three hundred individuals would make similar requests. The cabdrivers' strike being debated, denounced, and finally demanded on the stage (and by the chanting audience) would have looked very familiar at the time: nearly two thousand strikes had broken out nationwide in the previous year alone.

One person who was not terribly familiar with the actual New York cabdrivers' strike of 1934, however, was Clifford Odets. "It is just something I kind of made up," he later said during a House Un-American Activities Committee hearing, as he denied that he had based his play on that strike.

"I have never been near a strike in my life." Other pieces of political theater at the time, including those being produced by the Group Theatre, addressed events and conditions taking place at that exact second. But while the general conditions and disparities described so scathingly in *Waiting for Lefty* remained pertinent, that particular strike was long since over. (It didn't end well for the cabdrivers.)

Judging from the tumultuous opening-night response—critic Harold Clurman described a scene in which "deep laughter, hot assent, a kind of joyous fervor seemed to sweep the audience toward the stage"—the play hardly seemed like old news. Audiences at a series of benefit matinees spurred a move uptown to Broadway, where *Waiting for Lefty* soon played in repertory with Odets' *Awake and Sing!*

Lefty Costello, Odets' would-be union leader, is part of a rich history of title characters who never appear in their own plays. There is always the hope, however slim, that Godot might show up one day; Harvey, the genial invisible rabbit, is presumably there if you just knew how to see him; Edward Albee's feuding academics merely sing about whether Virginia Woolf is fearsome. But Lefty's fate is much

DATES:
March 25–July 1935 at the Longacre Theater (144 performances)

SYNOPSIS:
To strike or not to strike? That is the question mulled by a half-dozen New York cabdrivers, with various agitators and naysayers weighing in.

AWARDS:
None

NOTED REVIVALS AND ADAPTATIONS:
None

ORIGINAL STARS:
Elia Kazan, Lewis Leverett, Russell Collins, Ruth Nelson, Clifford Odets

clearer. We learn at the end of the play that he has been found "behind the car barns with a bullet in his head." Any further waiting would be in vain.

A new form of action was required, in other words. And Odets' audiences—along with the dozens and hundreds that sprouted up in their wake—were ready.

WATCH YOUR STEP

BY IRVING BERLIN AND HARRY B. SMITH

ABOVE: Irving Berlin was born in Russia in 1888 and moved to New York in his youth. He would go on to write "White Christmas," "There's No Business Like Show Business," and many other American classics. *Library of Congress*

OPPOSITE PAGE: Irene and Vernon Castle in *Watch Your Step*. Berlin wrote the musical with the Castles, the most popular dance duo of the time, in mind. © *Bettman/Corbis*

DATES:
December 8, 1914–May 8, 1915 at the New Amsterdam Theater (175 performances)

SYNOPSIS:
A $2 million family inheritance awaits any relative who has never been in love, let alone married. Will the chemistry between two youngsters get the better of them?

AWARDS:
None

NOTED REVIVALS AND ADAPTATIONS:
None

ORIGINAL STARS:
Irene and Vernon Castle, Frank Tinney

Book writers are the perennial second-class citizens of the Broadway musical. They get pretty much all of the blame when something doesn't work and, unless they're P. G. Wodehouse or Larry Gelbart, none of the praise when it does. If they do a really great job of describing or developing a character through a speech, that monologue will often find its way into the score as a lyric.

Some productions have made light of this status, as when David Merrick initially credited a trio of book writers with mere "Lead Ins and Crossovers" when they adapted the tap-happy film *42nd Street* for the stage. That was in 1980, more than sixty-five years after the shockingly prolific Harry B. Smith—with more than three hundred credits to his name—received the following billing on *Watch Your Step*: "Plot (if any) by Harry B. Smith."

By all accounts, any plot at all had been too much for Irving Berlin, who loved the stylistic and melodic versatility of the revues that were in vogue in the early twentieth century. He dismissively called book musicals "situation shows" and had to be dragged kicking and screaming to the form, which was just beginning to pick up steam in 1914. (The Princess Theater shows, which heralded a new level of integration, would follow a year later.)

Watch Your Step was Berlin's first situation show, and to be honest, its extensive vaudeville-style turns might as well have been part of a revue. (One of those turns got a little too extensive during the out-of-town tryout in Syracuse, where comedian W. C. Fields was fired for getting more applause than headliners Irene and Vernon Castle.) Still, Berlin took great pleasure in the fact that the show marked what he called "the first time Tin Pan Alley got into the legitimate theater."

The self-taught Berlin liked the idea of composing an opera, and *Watch Your Step*'s spoofs of opera were the next best thing. "Ragtime Opera Medley" overlaid several familiar arias with the enormously popular syncopations of ragtime. Ragtime also inspired the show's best-known tune, "Play a Simple Melody." Or, rather, its best-known tunes: "Simple Melody" was the first of the counterpoint songs that Berlin made famous, in which a basic tune is followed by a second, more syncopated one; both are then played simultaneously, with surprisingly non-cacophonous results. Shows like *The Music Man* and *A Chorus Line* would follow suit with this audience-pleasing ploy, but Irving Berlin did it first and arguably best.

Harry B. Smith didn't need to write too much plot. Berlin had contributed enough words—and music—for the both of them.

WEST SIDE STORY

BY LEONARD BERNSTEIN, STEPHEN SONDHEIM, AND ARTHUR LAURENTS

The Act I "Dance at the Gym" showcased Jerome Robbins' choreography. Members of the Jets and Sharks face off as Tony and Maria fall in love. *Hank Walker, The LIFE Picture Collection, Getty Images*

By now, William Shakespeare seems like a no-brainer as a source for musical theater adaptations, with everyone from Cole Porter (*Kiss Me, Kate*) to Rodgers and Hart (*The Boys from Syracuse*) to Elton John (*The Lion King*, with its close parallels to *Hamlet*) setting the Bard—or at least his plots—to music. Two years after Stephen Sondheim saw his *Follies* lose the Tony for Best Musical to Galt MacDermot and John Guare's sprightly 1971 take on *The Two Gentlemen of Verona*, he converted a *Cymbeline* monologue into the song "Fear No More" in *The Frogs*—the only time Sondheim has set another person's words to music in one of his shows.

While modern pieces like *The Bomb-itty of Errors* have adapted Shakespeare to a wide variety of musical styles, Sondheim's fingerprints are also on what remains the most radical and revelatory musical reboot of Shakespeare: *West Side Story*. His lyrics and Arthur Laurents' book created a street-smart vernacular for the Jets and Sharks that put them a million miles away from sixteenth-century Italy, where the Montagues and Capulets squared off in *Romeo and Juliet*. (Though the authors didn't stray quite as far as they had wanted. That final line in "Gee, Officer Krupke"? "Krup you!"? Let's just say that was a compromise.)

DATES:

September 26, 1957–June 27, 1959 at the
Winter Garden Theater and Broadway Theater
(732 performances)

SYNOPSIS:

Intense hatred between two New York street gangs,
the Jets and the Sharks, doesn't prevent Tony, the
lead Jet, from meeting and falling in love with his
counterpart's little sister, Maria. As someone wrote
hundreds of years ago, "These violent delights have
violent ends."

AWARDS:

2 Tony Awards

NOTED REVIVALS
AND ADAPTATIONS:

Broadway revivals in 1960, 1980, and 2009; movie
version in 1961

ORIGINAL STARS:

Larry Kert, Carol Lawrence, Chita Rivera, Mickey
Calin, Ken Le Roy

ABOVE RIGHT: Tony (Larry Kert) and Maria (Carol Lawrence) were a
modern-day Romeo and Juliet, with a fire escape for a balcony.

BELOW RIGHT: The Jets, led by Riff (Mickey Calin), perform
"Cool." The song's tension was heightened by Leonard Bernstein's
use of fugues and major-minor combinations. *Fred Fehl, Museum
of the City of New York, Getty Images*

Leonard Bernstein toyed with writing the lyrics himself,
then approached Betty Comden and Adolph Green. He
ultimately contented himself with writing maybe the
single greatest Broadway score.

Choreographer and "conceiver" Jerome Robbins
supplied plenty of animosity on the stage. Some of it was
intentional, as when he segregated the actors playing Jets
and those playing Sharks during rehearsals, while some of
it stemmed from his personality. (None of the rest of the
creative team would speak to him by opening night.) But a
lot can be forgiven in light of Robbins' choreography, which
has become so entrenched in the pantheon of Broadway
dance that it's easy to forget just how ill-conceived the idea
of ballet-dancing gang members sounds on paper. The
extent to which he pulled it off is evident in Walter Kerr's

opening night review for the *New York Herald Tribune*:
"The radioactive fallout from *West Side Story* must still be
descending on Broadway this morning." Its half-life has
been very long indeed.

WHO'S AFRAID OF VIRGINIA WOOLF?

BY EDWARD ALBEE

Martha (Uta Hagen) doing what she and her husband, George, do best. Hagen was awarded three Tony Awards in her life (including a Lifetime Achievement Tony in 1999) and was a highly influential acting teacher.

During the 2005 Broadway revival of *Who's Afraid of Virginia Woolf?*, I received a curious assignment from the *New York Times*. As I watched a performance of the show, I kept track not of Edward Albee's withering putdowns but of the amount of alcohol each character imbibed. I then amassed both clinical and anecdotal evidence (basically, I talked to a liver specialist and a bartender) about what shape the warring spouses George and Martha and their houseguests/prey, Nick and Honey, would be in by the end of the play.

If Albee's shattering drama were to be judged by its toxicological accuracy, *Virginia Woolf* would be a complete failure: all but of one of the characters would likely be comatose or worse well before the play's three acts are over. (I lost count at twenty-seven drinks, which doesn't include the bottle Honey takes to the bathroom with her.) But when it comes to other forms of toxicity—the plausible and illicitly pleasurable wielding of savage truths—Albee has yet to be matched.

This take-no-prisoners gamesmanship was a bit too much for the actors—a second cast had to be hired for the matinees, one that soon included Elaine Stritch as Martha—and far too much for some of the easily offended old guard. When the Pulitzer Prize judges selected *Virginia Woolf* for the 1963 award, the Pulitzer board rejected the nomination; two judges resigned in protest. Four years later, no such turmoil took place when Albee won for *A Delicate Balance*, prompting this memorable telegram from Mike Nichols: "Well you can't lose them all."

A side note on Nichols, who directed the scorching black-and-white film version of *Virginia Woolf*, starring Richard Burton and Elizabeth Taylor: while this book focuses almost exclusively on Broadway productions—as opposed to not only off-Broadway but also the hundreds of regional theaters doing superb work year in and year out—I would be particularly negligent not to mention a 1980 revival of *Virginia Woolf* at the Long Wharf Theater in New Haven, Connecticut, featuring Nichols and his beloved comic counterpart, Elaine May. Let that particularly juicy example fill in for literally thousands of other productions of 150 shows in this book, which happen to have been produced outside of Midtown Manhattan.

Albee, for what it's worth, had a rich career as an off-Broadway playwright by 1962, with such probing works as *The Zoo Story* and *The American Dream* preparing actors, audiences, and even himself for the glorious *Virginia Woolf*. The lights are bright on Broadway, but they would be far dimmer—and possibly snuffed out altogether—without the energy, innovation, and talent that off-Broadway and regional theaters provide.

DATES:

October 13, 1962–May 16, 1964 at the Billy Rose Theater (664 performances)

SYNOPSIS:

The nightly sparring match between George, a college history professor, and his wife Martha, the daughter of the college president, assumes a particularly lacerating form with the arrival of a younger faculty couple, Nick and Honey.

AWARDS:

5 Tony Awards

NOTED REVIVALS AND ADAPTATIONS:

Broadway revivals in 1976, 2005, and 2012; movie version in 1966

ORIGINAL STARS:

Uta Hagen, Arthur Hill, George Grizzard, Melinda Dillon

Arthur Hill (George), Ben Piazza (George Grizzard's replacement as Nick), Rochelle Oliver (Melinda Dillon's replacement as Honey), and Hagen. Director Alan Schneider directed more than one hundred productions, including the US premieres of *Waiting for Godot* and Pinter's *The Birthday Party*.

WICKED

BY STEPHEN SCHWARTZ AND WINNIE HOLZMAN

ABOVE: Kristin Chenoweth and Idina Menzel have become beloved stage and screen actresses since originating the roles of Glinda and Elphaba, respectively.
© Joan Marcus

OPPOSITE PAGE: © Joan Marcus

DATES:
Opened October 30, 2003 at the Gershwin Theater (4,690 performances as of February 1, 2015)

SYNOPSIS:
Elphaba, the green-skinned future Wicked Witch of the West, and Glinda, the popular future Good Witch of the North, become unlikely friends at Shiz University.

AWARDS:
3 Tony Awards

NOTED REVIVALS AND ADAPTATIONS:
None

ORIGINAL STARS:
Idina Menzel, Kristin Chenoweth, Norbert Leo Butz, Joel Grey

Before we get into *The Wizard of Oz*'s backstory, let's take a quick look at Stephen Schwartz'. In the 1970s, Schwartz was seemingly incapable of writing anything that wasn't a massive hit. The off-Broadway success of his *Godspell* prompted him to dust off a college musical about Charlemagne's kid; the heavily modified result, *Pippin*, ran for five years. So did his next musical, a vehicle for the mustachioed magician Doug Henning (!) called *The Magic Show*. *Godspell* had since moved to Broadway, giving him three shows on Broadway simultaneously—and *The Baker's Wife* nearly made it four.

But that show closed out of town, with producer David Merrick personally going into the orchestra pit during one performance and removing the sheet music of the one song anyone today knows from it, "Meadowlark." *Working*, *Rags*, and *Children of Eden* all landed with similar thuds. For more than twenty years, Broadway was no place for Schwartz, who licked his wounds with a series of Disney soundtracks and won three Academy Awards in the process.

He finally finagled a Broadway comeback when he persuaded Gregory Maguire to give him the rights to *Wicked: The Life and Times of the Wicked Witch of the West*, Maguire's revisionist take on the events leading up to *The Wizard of Oz*. Librettist Winnie Holzman knew a few things about writing for young women, having created the

beloved TV series *My So-Called Life*. The two developed the project over several years—and then, crucially, over another three unsparing months after a pre-Broadway tryout in San Francisco received favorable, but hardly knockout, reviews.

To be honest, the reviews weren't that much better when *Wicked* reached New York. But it made no difference: tween girls flocked to the show at a rate more than double that of the typical Broadway audience, and Broadway producers began aggressively targeting this demographic with musicals like *Legally Blonde* and *Bring It On*. Kristin Chenoweth and especially Idina Menzel became icons. Productions have since been comparably popular everywhere from Sweden to South Korea, including in many countries where *The Wizard of Oz* has nowhere near the cultural currency it does in America.

It was such a smash that Broadway insiders were shocked when it lost several major Tony Awards, including what would have been Schwartz' first. The David to its Goliath was *Avenue Q*, whose co-composer, Robert Lopez, clearly learned from *Wicked*: when he and his wife got their own Disney film project, they found themselves writing another girl-power-ballad-heavy literary reimagining for Menzel. The result, *Frozen*, is the fifth-highest-grossing film of all time. Let's hope Lopez' return to Broadway isn't nearly as protracted as his predecessor's.

YIP YIP YAPHANK

BY IRVING BERLIN, WITH ADDITIONAL MUSIC AND LYRICS BY H. P. DANKS AND EBEN REXFORD

Certain cities get a reputation for hosting Broadway-bound musicals while they work out the kinks: New Haven, Boston, Philadelphia. In 1918, Yaphank, New York—a small town near the south shore of Long Island—joined that list, thanks to a US Army sergeant named Israel Isidore Baline, better known as Irving Berlin. While Sergeant Berlin was stationed at Camp Upton in Yaphank, he was asked to put together an all-soldier revue to raise money for a community building on the base. The result included all of the ingredients listed on the following page, plus Berlin's own rendition of his memorably lethargic "Oh! How I Hate to Get Up in the Morning" and a minstrel-show section that introduced the standard "Mandy." (Both would make their way into versions of the *Ziegfeld Follies*.)

Yip Yip Yaphank: A Military "Mess" Cooked Up by the Boys of Camp Upton did make at least one substantial change on its way to Broadway, cutting a patriotic final number that Berlin felt did not fit in the

DATES:

August 19–September 14, 1918 at the Century Theater and Lexington Theater (32 performances)

SYNOPSIS:

A little bit of everything, including World War I skits, soldiers dressed up as Ziegfeld girls, jugglers, choreographed military drills, and even a demonstration from the lightweight boxing champion Benny Leonard.

AWARDS:

None

NOTED REVIVALS AND ADAPTATIONS:

Were there ever! Keep reading.

ORIGINAL STARS:

Danny Healy, Sammy Lee, Irving Berlin

uptempo revue. It would be another twenty years before audiences heard "God Bless America." In its place was "We're on Our Way to France." The song itself may not hold a candle to the one it replaced, but its staging was sublime: some three hundred soldiers marched off the stage, up the aisles, and ostensibly off to war. In real life, the performing soldiers typically marched directly to the armory where they were bunking, but there was one notable exception. Their last performance at the Lexington Theater ended with the cast, led by Sergeant Berlin himself, marching out of the theater and onto a waiting troop carrier. They were, indeed, on their way to France.

That's a hard act to top, but Berlin returned to *Yip Yip Yaphank* in 1941, after visiting Camp Upton in the hectic months before Pearl Harbor. The idea of retooling the show for the soldiers was introduced; the result was *This Is the Army*, which ran at the Broadway Theater in the summer of 1942 and became a movie in 1943, both times using the original staging of *Yip Yip Yaphank* as a plot point. (Berlin, ever the pragmatist, was ready to call the show *This Is the Navy* or *This Is the Air Force* if the Army objected to the

"Oh! How I Hate to Get Up in the Morning" sheet music, 1918. "Someday I'm going to murder the bugler / Someday they're going to find him dead," Berlin's lyrics bemoan. *Sheet music*

name.) Franklin D. Roosevelt attended a performance in Washington, D.C., and the show went on to military bases around the world, with Berlin traveling with it—and singing "Oh! How I Hate to Get Up in the Morning"—most of the way. He would later refer to the two years he spent on tour as the most thrilling time of his life.

YOU CAN'T TAKE IT WITH YOU

BY MOSS HART AND GEORGE S. KAUFMAN

The third time was the charm for collaborators Moss Hart and George S. Kaufman. But then again, so were the first and second times . . . and several times after that.

Readers learned about the painstaking methods of this monumental team in 1959, with the release of Hart's wonderful memoir, *Act One*. The long passage describing how he and Kaufman fine-tuned their first collaboration, *Once in a Lifetime*, one line at a time offered an invaluable lesson in just how much work it is to be funny.

They streamlined the process for *You Can't Take It With You* by securing a theater and even casting the show before they had written it. And so characters were created in the likenesses of specific actors with whom Kaufman had worked in the past. The role of the iceman/fireworks manufacturer Mr. De Pinna, for instance, was plumped up to play to rubber-faced Frank Conlan's strengths.

Finding the right title took some doing. Among the discarded ones along the way were *Foxy Grandpa*, *Grandpa's Other Snake*, and *The King Is Naked*. A bigger issue arose when Kaufman had to go into hiding to dodge a subpoena involving him, the *Maltese Falcon* actress Mary Astor, a child custody suit, and an extremely racy diary. (The two added a thinly veiled allusion to that diary to *You Can't Take It With You*. Kaufman and Hart's—but especially Kaufman's—real-life goings-on can read like something out of a Kaufman and Hart play.)

Notwithstanding the behind-the-scenes turmoil, Depression-era audiences devoured the play's mix of familial uplift and oddball tenderness. Its delightfully daft group of characters

ABOVE: From left, Mitzi Hajos (as well-oiled actress Gay Wellington), George Heller, Paula Trueman, Oscar Polk, Frank Wilcox, Henry Travers, and Josephine Hull.

OPPOSITE PAGE: From left, George Tobias, Trueman, Heller, Travers, Frank Conlan, Virginia Hammond, William J. Kelly, Jess Barker, and Hull in *You Can't Take It With You*, directed by coauthor George S. Kaufman, 1936.

is led by the irrepressible Grandpa Martin Vanderhof, who hasn't paid income tax for twenty-four years on the grounds that the government wouldn't really know what to do with the money. ("Well, I might pay about seventy-five dollars, but that's all it's worth.") To this day, *You Can't Take It With You* remains the only farce to ever receive the Pulitzer Prize—an honor that most likely would not have been awarded to anything called *Grandpa's Other Snake*.

DATES:
December 14, 1936–December 3, 1938 at the Ambassador Theater, Booth Theater, and Imperial Theater (838 performances)

SYNOPSIS:
Xylophone players, fireworks makers, and snake-collecting tax dodgers: what kind of family are the Vanderhofs, anyway? Daughter Alice hopes her new boyfriend doesn't find out when he comes over to meet them—along with a Russian ballet instructor and a batch of federal agents.

AWARDS:
Pulitzer Prize

NOTED REVIVALS AND ADAPTATIONS:
Broadway revivals in 1965, 1983, and 2014; movie version in 1938; TV versions in 1979 and 1984

ORIGINAL STARS:
Henry Travers, Josephine Hull, George Tobias, Frank Conlan, Oscar Polk

ZIEGFELD FOLLIES OF 1919

BY IRVING BERLIN, VICTOR HERBERT, AND MORE THAN A DOZEN OTHERS

ABOVE: The *Ziegfeld Follies of 1919*. © *Bettmann, Corbis*

OPPOSITE PAGE: Before "There She Is, Miss America" became the Miss America theme song, "A Pretty Girl Is Like a Melody" was the pageant's frequent anthem. John Steel performed the song in the 1919 production of the *Follies*; a recording of him singing it was made that year by Victor Records. *Sheet music*

DATES:

June 16–December 6, 1919 at the New Amsterdam Theater (171 performances)

SYNOPSIS:

Well, there was a scene with a harem and another with an osteopath. And Prohibition came in for a drubbing with the song "You Cannot Make Your Shimmy Shake on Tea."

AWARDS:

None

NOTED REVIVALS
AND ADAPTATIONS:

None

ORIGINAL STARS:

Eddie Cantor, Bert Williams, Marilyn Miller, John Steel

So many headliners, so many stunning Art Deco designs, so many chorines (including Barbara Stanwyck, Paulette Goddard, and Louise Brooks). How to choose just one edition of the annual *Ziegfeld Follies*, which ran for almost two decades?

It's actually not that hard of a choice. Other years may have included as many as seventy-eight "Ziegfeld girls" and career-defining numbers by the likes of Fanny Brice and Eddie Cantor, while audiences in 1918 ventured back out in droves after a devastating influenza epidemic to see W. C. Fields and Will Rogers. (Any stage door Johnnies who could wangle a visit to rehearsals that year also would have seen a young fellow by the name of George Gershwin accompanying the performers on piano.)

But by nearly all accounts, the finest example of Florenz Ziegfeld's absurdly lavish revues, with their sumptuous sets, beautiful women, and freewheeling comics, came the following year. The 1919 roster wasn't Ziegfeld's glossiest—Cantor, Marilyn Miller, and Bert Williams had all done previous *Follies*, and they shared the stage this time with the likes of the "pennant-winning battery of songland" known as Van and Schenk. Yet the 1919 *Follies* did represent a coming-out party of sorts for Irving Berlin, who had contributed songs to five earlier iterations. While a decent chunk of the score was the usual mishmash of bits, tunes, and sketches from seemingly every composer on Tin Pan Alley, Berlin contributed eleven songs (two of them retreads from his *Yip Yip Yaphank*, including the minstrel-style "Mandy"), making this easily the most musically consistent of the *Follies* thus far. One of those tunes, "A Pretty Girl Is Like a Melody," became virtually synonymous with Ziegfeld's leggy showgirls, who were often displayed in stage designer Ben Ali Haggin's tableaux vivants.

None of this came cheap, nor did Joseph Urban's jaw-dropping sets. The budget for the *Ziegfeld Follies of 1919* topped a then-unheard-of $100,000. It did, however, become the longest-running *Follies* to date—and would have logged even more performances if an Actors' Equity strike hadn't shut down the production in August.

Later editions would cost more, run longer, and rely more heavily on Berlin. But this was as good as the *Follies* got.

ACKNOWLEDGMENTS

Warm thanks to Ken Bloom, Gerald Bordman, Linda Buchwald, Garrett Eisler, Elizabeth Harre, John Kenrick, Robert Kimball, Ken Mandelbaum, Eric Rayman, Steven Suskin, Frank Vlastnik, and especially John Pike, whose knowledge and insight proved invaluable several steps along the way.

BIBLIOGRAPHY

Aiken, George L. *Uncle Tom's Cabin, or, Life Among the Lowly: A Domestic Drama in Six Acts.* Woodstock: Dramatic Publishing, 1911, p. 18.

Apple, R. W. "Gallery in London Presents an Exhibition for All Seasons." *New York Times*, December 4, 1977.

Atkinson, Brooks. "Christmas Night Adds *Pal Joey* and *Meet the People* to the Musical Stage." *New York Times*, December 26, 1940. http://timesmachine.nytimes.com/timesmachine/1940/12/26/91598201.html?pageNumber=22.

———. "The Play: Henry Hull in *Tobacco Road*, Based on the Novel by Erskine Caldwell." *New York Times*, December 5, 1933. http://timesmachine.nytimes.com/timesmachine/1933/12/05/105825790.html?pageNumber=31.

Barnes, Clive. "Stage: Shaffer's *Sleuth.*" *New York Times*, November 13, 1970. http://timesmachine.nytimes.com/timesmachine/1970/11/13/76791648.html?pageNumber=24.

Bentley, Eric. *From the American Drama, Volume 4.* New York: Doubleday Anchor, 1956, p. 361.

———. *What Is Theatre?: A Query in Chronicle Form.* New York: Atheneum, 1968, p. 261.

Berkvist, Robert. "Kim Stanley, Reluctant but Gripping Hollywood Actress, Dies at 76." *New York Times*, August 21, 2001. http://www.nytimes.com/2001/08/21/arts/kim-stanley-reluctant-but-gripping-broadway-and-hollywood-actress-dies-at-76.html.

Bikel, Theodore. *Theo: An Autobiography.* Madison: University of Wisconsin Press, 2002, p. 210.

Bloom, Ken, and Frank Vlastnik. *Broadway Musicals: The 101 Greatest Shows of All Time.* New York: Black Dog and Leventhal Publishers, 2004.

Bock, Jerry, Joseph Stein, Sheldon Harnick and Sholem Aleichem. *Fiddler on the Roof.* Milwaukee: Hal Leonard, 1965, p. 135.

Bordman, Gerald. *American Musical Theater: A Chronicle.* Oxford: Oxford University Press, 1986.

———. *The Concise Oxford Companion to American Theater.* Oxford: Oxford University Press, 1990.

Brantley, Ben. "*The Iceman Cometh*: Bottoms Up to Illusions." *New York Times*, April 9, 1999. http://partners.nytimes.com/library/theater/040999iceman-theater-review.html.

The Cambridge Companion to Eugene O'Neill. Cambridge: Cambridge University Press, 1998.

Chase, Mary. *Harvey: A Play in Three Acts.* New York: Dramatists Play Service, 1944.

Citron, Stephen. *Noel & Cole: The Sophisticates.* Milwaukee: Hal Leonard, 2005, p. 123.

Clurman, Harold. *The Collected Works of Harold Clurman.* Milwaukee: Hal Leonard, 1999, p. 134.

Cohen, Patricia. "In Search of Sexual Healing, Circa 1891." *New York Times*, November 19, 2006. http://www.nytimes.com/2006/11/19/theater/19cohe.html.

Coward, Noël. *The Letters of Noël Coward.* New York: Knopf Doubleday, 2008, p. 243.

———. *Private Lives.* Reissue ed. London: A&C Black.

Davis, Lee. "Musical Mutiny." *New York Times*, December 20, 1987. http://www.nytimes.com/1987/12/20/arts/l-musical-mutiny-399687.html.

Dickstein, Morris. *Dancing in the Dark: A Cultural History of the Great Depression.* New York: W. W. Norton and Company, 2009, p. 290.

Ebert, Roger. "*Yankee Doodle Dandy.*" Rogerebert.com, July 5, 1998. http://www.rogerebert.com/reviews/great-movie-yankee-doodle-dandy-1942.

Fierstein, Harvey. *Torch Song Trilogy.* New York: Samuel French, 1979.

Finn, William, and James Lapine. *Falsettos.* New York: Samuel French, 1995, p. 55.

Fitch, Clyde. *Captain Jinks of the Horse Marines: A Fantastic Comedy in Three Acts.* New York: Doubleday, Page and Company, 1902, p. 5.

Forbes, Camille F. *Introducing Bert Williams: Burnt Cork, Broadway, and the Story of America's First Black Star.* New York: Basic Books, 2008, p. 298.

Frank, Anne. *The Diary of a Young Girl: The Definitive Edition.* New York: Random House, 2011.

French, Sean. *Patrick Hamilton: A Life.* London: Faber and Faber, 1993, p. 48.

Fugard, Athol. *"Master Harold"… and the boys.* New York: Knopf, 1982.

Gaelic American. "Irishmen Will Stamp Out the *Playboy.*" October 14, 1911.

Gale, Steven H. *Sharp Cut: Harold Pinter's Screenplays and the Artistic Process.* Lexington: University Press of Kentucky, 2015.

Gershwin, Ira. *Lyrics on Several Occasions.* Milwaukee: Hal Leonard, 1997, p. 205.

Gilliatt, Penelope. *Unholy Fools: Wits, Comics, Disturbers of the Peace: Film and Theater.* New York: Viking Press, 1973, p. 112.

Goldman, William. *The Season: A Candid Look at Broadway.* Milwaukee: Hal Leonard, 1969.

Green, Adam. "The Heart of Things." *Vogue*, April 26, 2010. http://www.vogue.com/874138/vd-theater-the-heart-of-things/.

Green, Jesse. "Let Her Entertain You. Please!" *New York Times*, July 8, 2007. http://www.nytimes.com/2007/07/08/theater/08gree.html?ref=pattilupone&pagewanted=all.

Green, Stanley. *The World of Musical Comedy.* Boston: Da Capo Press, 1980, p. 267.

Grode, Eric. Hair: *The Story of the Show That Defined a Generation.* Philadelphia: Running Press, 2010.

Grode, Eric. "A View From the Pit." *Show Music*, July 1998.

———. "Who's Afraid of Liver Failure?" *New York Times*, April 10, 2005. http://www.nytimes.com/2005/04/10/theater/newsandfeatures/10grod.html.

Gussow, Mel. *Edward Albee: A Singular Journey.* Milwaukee: Hal Leonard, 2001.

———. "The Knives Got Lost." *The Guardian*, March 12, 2003. http://www.theguardian.com/stage/2003/mar/13/theatre.artsfeatures.

———. "With Sleuth, Another Shaffer Catches Public Eye." *New York Times*, November 18, 1970. http://timesmachine.nytimes.com/timesmachine/1970/11/18/78820598.html?pageNumber=38.

———, and Bruce Weber. "Ellen Stewart, Off Off Broadway Pioneer, Dies at 91." *New York Times*, January 13, 2011. http://www.nytimes.com/2011/01/14/theater/14stewart.html?pagewanted=all.

Hagy, Jessica. "Poor Things." Thisisindexed.com, November 5, 2010. http://thisisindexed.com/2010/11/poor-things-2/.

Hamilton, Patrick. *Angel Street: A Victorian Thriller in Three Acts.* Reissue ed. New York: Samuel French, 1966.

Hansberry, Lorraine. *To Be Young, Gifted and Black: A Portrait of Lorraine Hansberry in Her Own Words.* New York: Samuel French, 1999, p. 14.

Hart, Moss. *Act One: An Autobiography.* New York: Random House, 1959.

Hart, Moss, and George S. Kaufman. *You Can't Take It With You: A Comedy in Three Acts.* Reissue ed. New York: Dramatists Play Service, 1964, p. 21.

Hayes, Helen. *On Reflection: An Autobiography.* Reissue ed. Lanham: Rowman and Littlefield, 2014, p. 166.

Healy, Patrick. "Race an Issue in Wilson Play, and in Its Production." *New York Times*, April 22, 2009. http://www.nytimes.com/2009/04/23/theater/23wils.html.

Hermann, Dorothy. *With Malice Toward All.* New York: G. P. Putnam and Sons, 1982, p. 41.

Herzberg, Max John. *The Reader's Encyclopedia of American Literature.* Crowell, 1962, p. 1,230.

Hischak, Thomas S. *Boy Loses Girl: Broadway's Librettists.* Lanham: Scarecrow Press, 2002, p. 104.

Ibsen, Henrik. *A Doll's House: A Play in Three Acts.* Translated by William Archer. Boston: Walter H. Baker & Co., 1890, p. 93.

Ilson, Carol. *Harold Prince: A Director's Journey.* Milwaukee: Hal Leonard, 1989.

Kaufman, George S., and Edna Ferber. *Three Comedies: The Royal Family, Dinner at Eight, Stage Door.* Milwaukee: Hal Leonard, 1999, p. 219.

Kellow, Brian. *Ethel Merman: A Life.* New York: Penguin, 2007, p. 30.

Kelly, George. *The Show-Off: A Transcript of Life in Three Acts.* New York: Samuel French, 1924, p. 25.

Kenrick, John. *Musical Theater: A History.* New York: Bloomsbury Publishing USA, 2010.

Kerr, Walter. "Its Pleasures Last." *New York Times,* December 7, 1969. http://timesmachine.nytimes.com/timesmachine/1969/12/07/89390047.html?pageNumber=261.

———. "Theater: *West Side Story.*" New York Herald Tribune, September 27, 1957.

Kimball, Robert, and Linda Emmet. *The Complete Lyrics of Irving Berlin.* New York: Applause Theatre & Cinema Books, 2001, p. 170.

Kissel, Howard. *David Merrick, the Abominable Showman: The Unauthorized Biography.* Milwaukee: Hal Leonard, 1993.

Klein, Julia M. "*Falsettos*: A Musical That's a Family Show With a Difference." *Philadelphia Inquirer,* December 26, 1993. http://articles.philly.com/1993-12-26/entertainment/25942243_1_room-bitching-falsettos-william-finn.

Knowlson, James. *Damned to Fame: The Life of Samuel Beckett.* New York: Simon and Schuster, 1996.

Kobler, John. *Damned in Paradise: The Life of John Barrymore.* New York: Atheneum, 1977, p. 82.

Kushner, Tony. *Angels in America: A Gay Fantasia on National Themes.* London: Royal National Theater, 1994, p. 210.

Lahr, John. "Master of Revels." *New Yorker,* May 3, 2010. http://www.newyorker.com/magazine/2010/05/03/master-of-revels.

———. *Prick Up Your Ears: The Biography of Joe Orton.* New York: Penguin, 1987, p. 229.

———. *Tennessee Williams: Mad Pilgrimage of the Flesh.* New York: W. W. Norton and Company, 2014, p. 53.

Lawrence, Greg. *Dance with Demons: The Life of Jerome Robbins.* New York: Penguin, 2001.

Lawrence, Jerome, and Robert Edwin Lee. *Inherit the Wind.* New York: Random House, 1955.

Lindsay, Howard, and Russel Crouse. *Life With Father.* Reissue ed. New York: Dramatists Play Service, 1948.

Loesser, Frank. *The Complete Lyrics of Frank Loesser.* New York: Knopf, 2003.

———. *The Most Happy Fella.* Milwaukee: Hal Leonard, 1983.

Lott, Eric. *Love and Theft: Blackface Minstrelsy and the American Working Class.* Oxford: Oxford University Press, 2013, p. 224.

Mandelbaum, Ken. A Chorus Line *and the Musicals of Michael Bennett.* New York: St. Martin's Press, 1989.

Mamet, David. *Glengarry Glen Ross.* New York: Grove Press, 1984.

Maslon, Laurence. *Broadway: The American Musical.* New York: Bulfinch, 2004.

Matlaw, Myron, ed. *Nineteenth Century American Plays: Seven Plays Including* The Black Crook. New York: Applause, 2001, p. 332.

Mencken, H. L. "Et-Dukkehjemiana." *Theatre Magazine,* volumes 11–12, 1910, p. 42.

Mercado, Mario R. "*Lady in the Dark* on Broadway." Masterworks Broadway CD reissue, 1997.

Merman, Ethel, and Pete Martin. *Who Could Ask for Anything More.* New York: Doubleday, 1955, p. 78.

Meyerson, Harold, and Ernie Harburg. *Who Put the Rainbow in* The Wizard of Oz?: *Yip Harburg, Lyricist.* Ann Arbor: University of Michigan Press, 1995, p. 261.

Miller, Arthur. *The Crucible: A Play in Four Acts.* Reissue ed. New York: Penguin, 1968.

———. *Death of a Salesman.* New York: Viking Press, 1949.

Miller, Scott. "Inside *Man of La Mancha.*" New Line Theatre. http://www.newlinetheatre.com/lamanchachapter.html.

Mordden, Ethan. *Beautiful Mornin': The Broadway Musical in the 1940s.* Oxford: Oxford University Press, 1999, p. 87.

———. *Better Foot Forward: The History of American Musical Theatre.* New York: Grossman Publishers, 1976, p. 49.

Most, Andrea. "'You've Got to Be Carefully Taught': The Politics of Race in Rodgers and Hammerstein's *South Pacific.*" *Theatre Journal* 52, No. 3 (October 2000), p. 306.

New York Times. "Comstock Won't See Bernard Shaw's Play." October 26, 1905. http://timesmachine.nytimes.com/timesmachine/1905/10/26/101369862.html?pageNumber=9.

———. "The Court Approves Bernard Shaw's Play." July 7, 1906. http://timesmachine.nytimes.com/timesmachine/1906/07/07/101786756.html?pageNumber=7.

———. "The Grand Duke Theatre: A Once Noted Place of Amusement Makes Room for a Tenement." July 28, 1887. http://query.nytimes.com/gst/abstract.html?res=9503E7DA1430E633A2575BC2A9619C94669FD7CF.

———. "Sondheim Takes Issue With Plan for Revamped *Porgy and Bess.*" August 10, 2011. http://artsbeat.blogs.nytimes.com/2011/08/10/stephen-sondheim-takes-issue-with-plan-for-revamped-porgy-and-bess/?_r=0.

New York Tribune. "Frohman Calm; Not Concerned About Death, Welcomed It as Beautiful Adventure, He Told Friends at End." May 11, 1915.

O'Casey, Sean. *Three Dublin Plays.* Reissue ed. London: Faber and Faber, 1998, p. 105.

Odets, Clifford. *Waiting for Lefty and Other Plays.* Reissue ed. New York: Grove Press, 1994.

Oja, Carol A. *Bernstein Meets Broadway: Collaborative Art in a Time of War.* Oxford: Oxford University Press, 2014.

O'Neill, Eugene. *A Moon for the Misbegotten.* Reissue ed. New Haven: Yale University Press, 2006, p. 106.

Orton, Joe. *Loot.* Reissue ed. London: A&C Black, 1994, p. 62.

Parker, Trey; Robert Lopez and Matt Stone. *The Book of Mormon.* New York: HarperCollins, 2012.

Piepenburg, Erik. "Fantasy Casting Calls, Imagined by Insiders." *New York Times,* February 24, 2008. http://www.nytimes.com/2008/02/24/theater/24revivals.html.

Pinter, Harold. *The Caretaker.* New York: Dramatists Play Service, 1963, p. 43.

Porter, Cole. *Kiss Me, Kate.* Milwaukee: Hal Leonard, 1981.

Porter, Cole, and Robert Kimball. *The Complete Lyrics of Cole Porter.* Boston: Da Capo Press, 1983, p. 172.

Red Channels: The Report of Communist Influence in Radio and Television. New York: Counterattack, 1950.

Rice, Elmer. *Minority Report: An Autobiography.* New York: Simon and Schuster, 1963, p. 236.

Rich, Frank. *Hot Seat: Theater Criticism for the New York Times, 1980–1993.* New York: Random House, 1998.

Robertson, Nan. "Dramatist Against Odds." *New York Times,* March 8, 1959. http://timesmachine.nytimes.com/timesmachine/1959/03/08/89157714.html?pageNumber=448

Rodgers, Richard, and Oscar Hammerstein II. *6 Plays by Rodgers and Hammerstein.* New York: Random House, 1955, p. 127.

Saroyan, William. *The Time of Your Life.* Reissue ed. London: A&C Black, 2009.

Sater, Steven. *A Purple Summer: Notes on the Lyrics of* Spring Awakening. New York: Applause Theatre and Cinema Books, 2012.

Saturday Night Live, "On Broadway." Aired February 28, 1987.

S.D., Trav. *No Applause, Just Throw Money: The Book That Made Vaudeville Famous.* New York: Faber and Faber, Inc., 2005, p. 233.

Secrest, Meryle. *Somewhere for Me: A Biography of Richard Rodgers.* Milwaukee: Hal Leonard, 2001, p. 212.

———. *Stephen Sondheim: A Life.* Reissue ed. New York: Vintage, 2011, p. 388.

Shaffer, Peter. *Peter Shaffer's Amadeus.* New York: Signet, 1989.

Shellard, Dominic. *Kenneth Tynan: A Life.* New Haven: Yale University Press, 2003, p. 162.

Simon, Neil. *The Odd Couple: A Comedy in Three Acts.* New York: Samuel French, 1966, p. 9.

The Simpsons, "Krusty Gets Kancelled." Aired May 13, 1993.

Sinnott, Susan. *Lorraine Hansberry: Award-Winning Playwright and Civil Rights Activist.* Newburyport: Conari Press, 1999.

Sondheim, Stephen. *Finishing the Hat: Collected Lyrics (1954–1981).* New York: Knopf, 2010.

Sondheim, Stephen, and Anthony Shaffer. "Theater: Of Mystery, Murder and Other Delights." *New York Times,* March 10, 1996. http://www.nytimes.com/books/98/07/19/specials/sondheim-shaffer.html.

Steppenwolf Theatre website. "Race, Pulitzers and Punchlines." 2011–2012, Volume 1. http://www.steppenwolf.org/watchlisten/program-articles/detail.aspx?id=260.

Stirling, Richard. *Julie Andrews: An Intimate Biography.* London: Macmillan, 2008.

Stoppard, Tom. *Arcadia.* New York: Samuel French, 1993, p. 75.

———. *Rosencrantz and Guildenstern Are Dead.* Reissue ed. London: Faber and Faber, 2013.

Sullivan, Dan. "Young British Playwright Here for Rehearsal of *Rosencrantz.*" *New York Times,* August 29, 1967. http://timesmachine.nytimes.com/timesmachine/1967/08/29/90398365.html?pageNumber=27.

Suskin, Steven. *Opening Night on Broadway.* New York: Schirmer Books, 1990, p. 274.

———. *Show Tunes: The Songs, Shows, and Careers of Broadway's Major Composers.* Oxford: Oxford University Press, 2010.

Synge, John Millington. *Synge: Complete Plays*. Reissue ed. London: Bloomsbury Publishing, 2014.

Tallmer, Jerry. "'Heart-Stopping' Broadway Documentary." *Downtown Express*, June 4, 2004.

Taubman, Howard. "Theatre: Modern Parable of Scorn and Sorrow." *New York Times*, October 5, 1961. http://www.nytimes.com/interactive/2012/05/07/theater/20120507-caretaker.html?ref=reviews.

———. "Theater: *Hello, Dolly!* Has Its Premiere." *New York Times*, January 17, 1964. http://www.nytimes.com/1964/01/17/theater-hello-dolly-has-premiere.html?_r=0.

Tommasini, Anthony. "Theather; The Seven-Year Odyssey That Led to Rent." *New York Times*, March 17, 1996. http://www.nytimes.com/1996/03/17/theater/theather-the-seven-year-odyssey-that-led-to-rent.html?pagewanted=all.

United States Courts. *Decisions of the United States Courts Involving Copyright*. Washington, DC: US Government Printing Office, 1936, p. 881.

Vaill, Amanda. *Somewhere: The Life of Jerome Robbins*. New York: Crown/Archetype, 2008, p. 110.

Wadler, Joyce. "Public Lives: A Cat Now and for 17 Years (Nearly Forever)." *New York Times*, February 25, 2000. http://www.nytimes.com/2000/02/25/nyregion/public-lives-a-cat-now-and-for-17-years-nearly-forever.html.

Wasson, Sam. *Fosse*. Boston: Houghton Mifflin Harcourt, 2013, p. 411.

Weales, Gerald Clifford. *Odets, the Playwright*. London: Methuen, 1971, p. 42.

Weill, Kurt, and Ira Gershwin. *Lady in the Dark*. Milwaukee: Hal Leonard, 1981.

Weintraub, Stanley. *Journey to Heartbreak: The Crucible Years of Bernard Shaw, 1914–1918*. New York: Weybright and Talley, 1971, p. 21.

Weiss, Peter. *The Persecution and Assassination of Jean-Paul Marat as Performed by the Inmates of the Asylum of Charenton Under the Direction of the Marquis de Sade*. Woodstock: Dramatic Publishing, 1964, p. 37.

Wheeler, Hugh, and Stephen Sondheim. *Sweeney Todd, the Demon Barber of Fleet Street*. Reissue ed. Milwaukee: Hal Leonard, 1981, p. 111.

Wilde, Oscar. *The Importance of Being Earnest*. London: Leonard Smithers and Company, 1899.

Wilder, Thornton. *Our Town: A Play in Three Acts*. Reissue ed. New York: Harper and Row, 1960.

———. *The Skin of Our Teeth: A Play in Three Acts*. Reissue ed. New York: Samuel French, 1972, p. 13.

Williams, Tennessee. *The Glass Menagerie*. Reissue ed. New York: New Directions Publishing, 2011, p. 51.

———. *The Selected Letters of Tennessee Williams*: 1920–1945. New York: New Directions Publishing, 2002, p. 184.

———. *A Streetcar Named Desire*. Reissue ed. New York: New Directions Publishing, 2014, p. 145.

Wilson, August. *Fences*. Reissue ed. New York: Plume, 1986.

———. *Joe Turner's Come and Gone*. Reissue ed. New York: Samuel French, 1990.

Wood, Mrs. Henry. *East Lynne*. Leipzig: Tauchnitz, 1861.

Zadan, Craig. *Sondheim & Co*. Reissue ed. Boston: Da Capo Press, 1994.

Zimmerman, Mary. *Metamorphoses: A Play*. Chicago: Northwestern University Press, 2002, p. 83.

INDEX

Page numbers in italics indicate an item in a photograph or caption.

ABOUT THE AUTHOR

Eric Grode has written about theater and film for the *New York Times* since 2010. He previously served as the head theater critic for the *New York Sun*, and his articles and reviews have also appeared in the *Village Voice*, *New York* magazine, the *Wall Street Journal*, and more than a dozen other publications. He is the author of *Hair: The Story of the Show That Defined a Generation*, the authorized history of the Broadway musical. He teaches writing at Syracuse University in the Goldring Arts Journalism Program, where he sits on the advisory board.